Conflicting Objectives in Democracy Promotion

The agenda of external actors often includes a number of objectives that do not necessarily go together. Fostering security and stability in semi-authoritarian regimes collides with policies aimed at the support of processes of democratization prone to provoke conflict and destabilization. Meanwhile, the promotion of national self-determination and political empowerment might lead to forms of democracy, partially incompatible with liberal understandings. These conflicting objectives are often problematized as challenges to the effectiveness of international democracy promotion.

This book presents systematic research about the emergence and effects of conflicting objective in democracy promotion. The contributing authors investigate (post-) conflict societies, developing countries, and authoritarian regimes in Southeast Europe, Latin America, Africa, and Asia. They identify the socio-economic and political conditions in the recipient country, the interaction between international and local actors, and the capacity of international and local actors as relevant for explaining the emergence of conflicting objectives. And they empirically show that faced with conflicting objectives donors either use a 'wait and see'-approach (i.e. not to act to overcome such conflicts), or they prioritize security, state-building and development over democracy, or they compromise democracy promotion with other goals. However, convincing strategies for dealing with such conflicts still need to be devised.

This book was published as a special issue of *Democratization*.

Julia Leininger is Senior Researcher at the German Development Institute / Deutsches Institut für Entwicklungspolitik (DIE) in Bonn. She has previously published a handbook on international organizations ('Handbuch internationaler Organisationen' with Dr Katja Freistein) and developed an approach to study international democracy promotion. For more information refer to http://tinyurl.com/bek65ed.

Sonja Grimm is Senior Researcher and Lecturer on International and Comparative Politics at the University of Konstanz. She specializes in studies of transition to democracy in postconflict societies and has previously edited (with Prof. Dr Wolfgang Merkel) *War and Democratization: Legality, Legitimacy, and Effectiveness*, a *Democratization* special issue (2008, Vol. 15, No. 3). For more information refer to http://www.sonja-grimm.eu.

Tina Freyburg is post-doctoral researcher at ETH Zurich, Switzerland and Leverhulme Trust Visiting Fellow at the University of Warwick, United Kingdom. Her current research projects explore new avenues in the study of the international dimension of democratization, in particular the democratizing potential of transgovernmental networks. For more information refer to [http://www.tina-freyburg.eu].

Democratization Special Issues

Series editors:
Jeffrey Haynes, London Metropolitan University, UK
Aurel Croissant, University of Heidelberg, Germany

Conflicting Objectives in Democracy Promotion
Do All Good Things Go Together?
Edited by Julia Leininger, Sonja Grimm and Tina Freyburg

Political Opposition in Sub-Saharan Africa
Edited by Elliott Green, Johanna Söderström and Emil Uddhammar

PREVIOUSLY PUBLISHED BOOKS FROM DEMOCRATIZATION

Coloured Revolutions and Authoritarian Reactions
Edited by Evgeny Finkel and Yitzhak M. Brudny

Ethnic Party Bans in Africa
Edited by Matthijs Bogaards, Matthias Basedau and Christof Hartmann

Democracy Promotion in the EU's Neighbourhood
From Leverage to Governance?
Edited by Sandra Lavenex and Frank Schimmelfennig

Democratization in Africa: Challenges and Prospects
Edited by Gordon Crawford and Gabrielle Lynch

Democracy Promotion and the 'Colour Revolutions'
Edited by Susan Stewart

Promoting Party Politics in Emerging Democracies
Edited by Peter Burnell and Andre W. M. Gerrits

Religion, Democracy and Democratization
Edited by John Anderson

Democracy and Violence
Global Debates and Local Challenges
Edited by John Schwarzmantel and Hendrik Jan Kraetzschmar

Religion and Democratizations
Edited by Jeffrey Haynes

The European Union's Democratization Agenda in the Mediterranean
Edited by Michelle Pace and Peter Seeberg

War and Democratization
Legality, Legitimacy and Effectiveness
Edited by Wolfgang Merkel and Sonja Grimm

Democratization in the Muslim World
Changing Patterns of Authority and Power
Edited by Francesco Volpi and Francesco Cavatorta

On the State of Democracy
Edited by Julio Faundez

Conflicting Objectives in Democracy Promotion
Do All Good Things Go Together?

Edited by
Julia Leininger, Sonja Grimm and Tina Freyburg

LONDON AND NEW YORK

First published 2014 by Routledge

2 Park Square, Milton Park, Abingdon, Oxfordshire OX14 4RN
711 Third Avenue, New York, NY 10017

Routledge is an imprint of the Taylor & Francis Group, an informa business

First issued in paperback 2018

Copyright © 2014 Taylor & Francis

This book is a reproduction of *Democratization*, vol. 19, issue 3. The Publisher requests to those authors who may be citing this book to state, also, the bibliographical details of the special issue on which the book was based.

All rights reserved. No part of this book may be reprinted or reproduced or utilised in any form or by any electronic, mechanical, or other means, now known or hereafter invented, including photocopying and recording, or in any information storage or retrieval system, without permission in writing from the publishers.

Notice:
Product or corporate names may be trademarks or registered trademarks, and are used only for identification and explanation without intent to infringe.

British Library Cataloguing in Publication Data
A catalogue record for this book is available from the British Library

ISBN13: 978-0-415-82590-0 (hbk)
ISBN13: 978-1-138-38327-2 (pbk)

Typeset in Times New Roman
by Taylor & Francis

Publisher's Note
The publisher would like to make readers aware that the chapters in this book may be referred to as articles as they are identical to the articles published in the special issue. The publisher accepts responsibility for any inconsistencies that may have arisen in the course of preparing this volume for print.

Contents

Citation Information   x

Foreword
Thomas Carothers   1

1. Not all good things go together: conflicting objectives in democracy promotion
Sonja Grimm and *Julia Leininger*   3

2. Democracy promotion, empowerment, and self-determination: conflicting objectives in US and German policies towards Bolivia
Jonas Wolff   27

3. Financing poverty alleviation vs. promoting democracy? Multi-Donor Budget Support in Zambia
Jörg Faust, Stefan Leiderer and *Johannes Schmitt*   50

4. Coerced transitions in Timor-Leste and Kosovo: managing competing objectives of institution-building and local empowerment
Nicolas Lemay-Hébert   77

5. Power-sharing and democracy promotion in post-civil war peace-building
Jai Kwan Jung   98

6. Two at one blow? The EU and its quest for security and democracy by political conditionality in the Western Balkans
Solveig Richter   119

7. Inconsistent interventionism in Palestine: objectives, narratives, and domestic policy-making
Sandra Pogodda   147

8. Peace-building and democracy promotion in Afghanistan: the Afghanistan Peace and Reintegration Programme and reconciliation with the Taliban
Marissa Quie   165

9. The two sides of functional cooperation with authoritarian regimes: a multi-level perspective on the conflict of objectives between political stability and democratic change
   Tina Freyburg 187

Index 214

Citation Information

The chapters in this book were originally published in *Democratization*, volume 19, issue 3 (June 2012). When citing this material, please use the original page numbering for each article, as follows:

Foreword
Thomas Carothers
Democratization, volume 19, issue 3 (June 2012) pp. 389-390

Chapter 1
Not all good things go together: conflicting objectives in democracy promotion
Sonja Grimm and Julia Leininger
Democratization, volume 19, issue 3 (June 2012) pp. 391-414

Chapter 2
Democracy promotion, empowerment, and self-determination: conflicting objectives in US and German policies towards Bolivia
Jonas Wolff
Democratization, volume 19, issue 3 (June 2012) pp. 415-437

Chapter 3
Financing poverty alleviation vs. promoting democracy? Multi-Donor Budget Support in Zambia
Jörg Faust, Stefan Leiderer and Johannes Schmitt
Democratization, volume 19, issue 3 (June 2012) pp. 438-464

Chapter 4
Coerced transitions in Timor-Leste and Kosovo: managing competing objectives of institution-building and local empowerment
Nicolas Lemay-Hébert
Democratization, volume 19, issue 3 (June 2012) pp. 465-485

CITATION INFORMATION

Chapter 5
Power-sharing and democracy promotion in post-civil war peace-building
Jai Kwan Jung
Democratization, volume 19, issue 3 (June 2012) pp. 486-506

Chapter 6
Two at one blow? The EU and its quest for security and democracy by political conditionality in the Western Balkans
Solveig Richter
Democratization, volume 19, issue 3 (June 2012) pp. 507-534

Chapter 7
Inconsistent interventionism in Palestine: objectives, narratives, and domestic policy-making
Sandra Pogodda
Democratization, volume 19, issue 3 (June 2012) pp. 535-552

Chapter 8
Peace-building and democracy promotion in Afghanistan: the Afghanistan Peace and Reintegration Programme and reconciliation with the Taliban
Marissa Quie
Democratization, volume 19, issue 3 (June 2012) pp. 553-574

Chapter 9
The two sides of functional cooperation with authoritarian regimes: a multi-level perspective on the conflict of objectives between political stability and democratic change
Tina Freyburg
Democratization, volume 19, issue 3 (June 2012) pp. 575-601

Foreword

In his classic 1968 book *Political Order in Changing Societies*, Samuel Huntington criticized Americans for believing that 'all good things go together' in Third World societies attempting modernization. Huntington was referring to a defining belief among US policy-makers and aid practitioners in the 1960s: namely, the idea that the different parts of the modernization package that they were seeking to advance in those countries – political, economic, and social development – would mutually reinforce each other and, in so doing, also advance American security objectives. The shattering of this optimistic idea on the harsh shoals of experience in the second half of the 1960s and first half of the 1970s – when democracy, development, and security often worked at violent cross-purposes to each other – was a painful experience for an entire generation of Western politicians and scholars.

The idea gained new life in the wake of the Cold War. Freed from the pressures of superpower rivalries and conflicting ideologies, a new generation of Western actors saw the exciting potential for democracy and development to move ahead hand in hand and to reinforce core security goals, above all maintaining peace, in the process. The intervening 20 years, however, have not been especially kind to these post-Cold War hopes. No outright shattering of the proposition has occurred, but significant doubts and questions have accumulated. For example, sceptics of international democracy support point to evidence that elections may actually increase the odds of violent civil conflict. They also note that authoritarian developmental states seem to be better at producing prosperity for their citizens than fractious democratic states are.

Although debates over the proper relationship between democracy support and other policy objectives have multiplied, careful and systematic analysis of the issue has not kept pace. Happily, a few capable young scholars, representatives of an encouragingly vital new generation of democracy researchers, took notice of this gap and set about to fill it. They have assembled a set of articles that tackle the issue from multiple perspectives and have provided an overarching conceptual framework for the collection. Their goal is not to bury the 'all good things…' theory once and for all, but rather to illuminate how complex the international policy landscape has become with regard to these issues. Common political, economic, and security goals are now widely shared, much more so than in the divided world of the 1960s, yet still refuse to march in a simple line.

Thomas Carothers
Carnegie Endowment for International Peace, Washington, DC, USA

Reference

Huntington, Samuel. *Political Order in Changing Societies*. New Haven: Yale University Press, 1968.

Not all good things go together: conflicting objectives in democracy promotion

Sonja Grimm[a]* and Julia Leininger[b]

[a]*Department of Politics and Public Administration, University of Konstanz, Konstanz, Germany;* [b]*German Development Institute/Deutsches Institut für Entwicklungspolitik (DIE), Bonn, Germany*

> Conflicting objectives are often problematized as challenges to the effectiveness of international democracy promotion. However, systematic research about their emergence and effects is still missing. This special issue addresses this research gap and seeks to provide conceptual and empirical answers in the field of conflicting objectives in international democracy promotion. The authors represented in this special issue investigate (post-) conflict societies, developing countries, and authoritarian regimes, attempting to identify the patterns of conflicting objectives in democracy promotion, the reasons for their emergence, and their consequences. This introduction presents a conceptual framework that pursues four aims: first, it differentiates between two types of conflicting objectives (intrinsic and extrinsic); second, it offers an approach for identification of their phases of emergence; third, it proposes reasons for their emergence; and fourth, it discusses how political actors deal with these conflicting objectives. The empirical findings of the contributions to this special issue illustrate and substantiate the theoretical and conceptual reflections.

Introduction

This special issue of *Democratization* studies the emergence and consequences of conflicting objectives in democracy promotion. It pursues two aims: (1) to systematize significant conflicts of objectives in democracy promotion (conceptual dimension), and (2) to analyse these conflicts of objectives in order to explore their origins and their consequences for the effectiveness of democracy promotion (empirical dimension). To this end, the authors in this special issue have investigated selected

African, Asian, Middle Eastern, and Latin American processes of political change, seeking to clarify the patterns and consequences of democracy promotion policies. They focus their analyses on possible *intrinsic* trade-offs between various factors in democracy promotion, as well as on *extrinsic* trade-offs between democracy promotion and other relevant areas of external support, such as peace-building, state-building, stabilization, security, and capacity-building.[1]

Conflicting objectives are inherent in any kind of policy-making and cooperation between two or more actors. Scholars and practitioners widely acknowledge that conflicting objectives challenge the effectiveness of democracy promotion.[2] Any target country of democracy promotion will find itself facing a multitude of international actors pursuing divergent interests and goals. Consequently, the objective of democratization is likely to compete with alternative objectives of foreign policy of the various international actors. At times, the same actor can simultaneously attempt to pursue competing objectives. The individual nature of the paths that democratization can follow aggravates this complex situation further. In general, democratization does not follow a universal pattern that could serve as a guideline for facilitation of external support. Accordingly, there is no blueprint for successful democracy promotion. In each individual case, democracy promoters must rethink how, when, and by what means democratization can be supported.

Faced with such complex realities, since the end of the Cold War international actors have often pursued democratization from the point of view that 'all good things go together'.[3] They have integrated into their democracy promotion portfolio a mixture of objectives including peace, stability, freedom, prosperity, good governance, and the rule of law – objectives that, in their perspectives, could all be conducive to democratization. In other cases, international actors have indirectly assumed that policies such as economic assistance or peace- and security-building will positively complement measures to support democratization. Over time, international actors and scholars of democratization and international relations have become increasingly aware of the fact that 'not all good things do necessarily go together', learning from experience that 'good things go together only under certain favourable conditions'.[4] In order to promote democracy effectively, the conditions and time spans in which good things such as peace, security, and development do indeed go together must be investigated in a detailed and systematic fashion. This special issue seeks to explore this topic and to enrich the empirical foundations of the current debate on the challenges of democracy promotion.

The contributions to this special issue cover a representative range of conflicting objectives, in particular trade-offs between security, stability, peace, and democratization, as well as between the diverging norms, concepts, and instruments applied in democracy promotion. The authors study nine countries and a variety of international actors; the latter range from international and regional organizations (such as the European Union (EU), the United Nations (UN), and the North Atlantic Treaty Organization (NATO)) to multilateral peace missions like

United Nations Mission in Kosovo (UNMIK) in Kosovo or United Nations Transitional Administration in East Timor (UNTAET) in Timor-Leste, to actors exerting influence in bilateral development cooperation (such as the governments of the United States of America (USA) and Germany). Authors describe typical country contexts in which conflicting objectives are likely to emerge: unstable environments and post-conflict settings are the most vulnerable to divergent objectives. One of the countries examined is currently embroiled in a war situation (Afghanistan), another one trapped in a violent conflict (Palestine), and five of the cases are post-conflict countries (Bosnia and Herzegovina, the Former Yugoslav Republic of Macedonia, Kosovo under UN Security Council Resolution 1244, and Timor-Leste). The case studies of Bolivia, Morocco, and Zambia illustrate that trade-offs in democracy promotion can also arise in generally peaceful, stable settings.

In this introduction, we establish a conceptual framework for the analysis of conflicting objectives in democracy promotion; we substantiate our theory-driven concepts using evidence from the contributions included in this special issue. Accordingly, each section in this introduction starts with a conceptual outline, followed by empirical findings. In the first section, we briefly review the literature. Given the lack of previous theoretical contributions on conflicting objectives in foreign policy-making we focus on identifying research gaps. In view of these gaps, we formulate four guiding research questions that will be addressed by the contributions to this special issue. In the second section, we present our concept of conflicts of objectives and highlight which are covered in the following contributions. In the third section, we argue that conflicts may equally evolve during the norm-building, strategy-building, and implementation phases of democracy promotion. In the same section, we explore the conditions under which conflicts of objectives may evolve and identify which of these are addressed in this special issue. In the fourth section, we propose a scheme for how the actors involved could theoretically deal with conflicts of objectives and illustrate how domestic and international actors have handled trade-offs in real-world situations. In the fifth section, we theoretically explore the effects of conflicting objectives on democratization and present whether the empirical findings of this issue confirm this correlation. We conclude by summarizing the main challenges of democracy promotion derived from the special issue's contributions.

Setting the stage: what are the most pressing questions, in light of existing research gaps?

Until now, two branches of research have addressed the question of whether 'all good things go together' in a more or less explicit fashion. The 'older' branch focuses on the relationship between democracy and development, asking whether socio-economic development is best suited for democratization, and vice versa. The 'newer' branch is founded in peace and security studies and researchers ask to what extent and under what conditions processes of democratization complement, support, or undermine stabilization and peace in a post-conflict society. Both research strands have also served to inform policy-makers in international democracy promotion. In what follows, we briefly summarize the two extant research fields and identify research gaps.

S.M. Lipset (1960) was one of the first to argue that democracy is related to a country's socio-economic development or level of modernization. With a quantitative large-N study measuring wealth, extent of industrialization, degree of urbanization, and level of education in selected countries using various indicators, Lipset found that the more democratic countries consistently had higher levels of socio-economic development than the more authoritarian countries.[5] His concise conclusion – 'the more well-to-do a nation, the greater the chances that it will sustain democracy'[6] – inspired the international development community by presenting the prospect of the uncomplicated democratization of developing countries by socio-economic modernization.[7] However, Lipset did not reflect about possible conflicting objectives for international support to democratization.

Since the early 1990s, in reflecting on the scholarly debate on the causes of democratization, the member states of the Organisation for Economic Co-operation (OECD) have begun to consider democratic rule not as a logical outcome of development, but as a necessary requisite for it.[8] In consequence, strengthening socio-economic development has evolved into an important objective of democracy promotion. However, democracy promotion and support of socio-economic development have historically belonged to two parallel worlds that have rarely intersected. Only recently have donor countries like the USA and Germany begun to conceptualize programmes that pursue both objectives, seeking to mainstream sectoral programmes and to ensure that they are supportive of democratic governance.[9] However, to date there has been little evidence that democratization and consequently democracy promotion actually work as a motor of socio-economic development.[10] Given the limited resources of development cooperation, new policy choices are likely to be made at the expense of democracy support.[11]

Meanwhile, in search of strategies to handle the challenging post-war and post-conflict regime changes in south-eastern Europe, the Caucasus, and sub-Saharan Africa, peace-builders seem to have resurrected the idea that 'all good things shall go together' from the development debate.[12] For the sake of stability- and peace-building, they aspire to support domestic actors in removing the root causes of violent conflict and create a pacific atmosphere (1) by reforming the security sector in order to secure public life and provide legitimate means to control the use of force, (2) by developing the rule of law in order to reduce human rights violations, (3) by investing in a market economy free from corruption in order to discourage individuals from believing that the surest path to fortune is by capturing the state, and – last but not least – (4) by supporting democracy in order to reduce the tendency toward arbitrary power and give a voice to all segments of society.[13] Their conflict-management tools are intended to support the replacement of a culture of war and violent conflict with a culture of tolerance and respect. However, seldom do peace-builders achieve this comprehensive aim successfully.[14]

In fact, the expectations of supporters of development policies, peace-builders, and democracy promoters that the implementation of democratic institutions and practices necessarily strengthens positive characteristics such as peace, stability, prosperity, freedom, good governance, and the rule of law, and vice versa, have not been met in the last two decades.[15] International actors and researchers in the field have acknowledged the potential tension between these objectives in several official concept documents.[16] However, the assessment of their activities leads to the conclusion that conflicting objectives remain inadequately addressed in democracy support.[17]

It remains an open question in the literature whether these 'conflicting objectives' or in other words 'challenges', 'tensions', 'dilemmas', or 'paradoxes' influence the effectiveness of democracy promotion.[18] Some authors argue that divergent goals are always 'conflicting'; others suggest that diverging objectives might be complementary and are therefore a strength, not a weakness of democracy promotion.[19] However, neither side has systematically investigated the underlying factors that can lead to or prevent conflicts between objectives, or examined how these conflicting objectives may under certain conditions hinder or support effective democracy promotion. Although individual research results are of importance in the understanding and explanation of the effectiveness of democracy promotion policy, no major efforts have hitherto been made to investigate conflicting objectives as an interdisciplinary topic or to draw conclusions on the broader basis of comparative case studies. There is still an overwhelming lack of conceptualization based on theoretical reasoning and systematic empirical research that clarifies the relationship between democratization processes and conflicting objectives in international democracy support.[20]

In examination of the state-of-the-art, the following research gaps become apparent. First, there is a need for fine-tuning and expansion of the understanding of how other objectives (for instance, stability, security, and socio-economic development) work together with the aim of promoting democracy. Moreover, we need to understand to what extent locally-driven political processes, and externally-driven democracy promotion can come into conflict. Second, we still lack empirically-based evidence of whether objectives actually 'go together' in democracy promotion and, if they do, under what conditions which specific objectives can go together. Thus far, research has provided only limited systematic evidence regarding the interplay between different elements of democracy support in certain political contexts. Third, there is a need to learn more about how international actors deal with conflicting objectives, especially the extent to which diverging goals become compromised and what kinds of solutions would be suitable for the resolution of conflicts of objectives. Finally, given the lack of research on conflicting objectives, we still have much to learn about their effects on processes of democratization.

Acknowledging the accomplishments of previous research, we now take the gaps in research as the starting point for our special issue. Accordingly, we recognize the need to identify conflicting objectives and to capture the characteristics of this phenomenon on a conceptual level; such a conceptualization can then be used for empirical analysis. Our intended aim is to contribute a conceptualization of conflicting objectives to current democracy promotion research that will facilitate the understanding and explanation of the output side of democracy promotion – in other words, its effectiveness. Furthermore, we seek to enrich the 'Do all good things go together?' debate with systematic empirical evidence drawn from carefully selected case studies. Specifically, we will answer the following questions:

(1) What are the conflicting objectives in democracy promotion?
(2) When and under what conditions do they emerge?
(3) How do internal and external actors deal with these conflicting objectives?
(4) What are the effects of conflicting objectives on democratization?

The following sections address the conceptual and theoretical dimensions of these research questions and seek to provide answers based on the empirical findings of this special issue.

Constructing concepts and facing realities: what are the 'conflicting objectives' in democracy promotion?

If we want to get an idea of the possible conflicting objectives in democracy promotion, we must first clarify what we mean by the terms 'democracy', 'democracy promotion', and 'conflicting objectives'. Following Dahl's lean 'polyarchy' concept, we define *democracy* as a political regime in which representatives are periodically selected in free and fair elections and in which political actors regularly participate in peaceful public contestation for voter support.[21] To ensure political competition and participation, a democratic system should guarantee a catalogue of political rights and civil liberties, as well as institutional checks and balances for horizontal and vertical accountability. As a result, democracy is closely connected to the rule of law.[22] *Democratization* means the transition from 'no' or 'less' to 'more' democracy, or, in other words, from autocratic to democratic rule.[23]

Democracy promotion entails activities by external actors that seek to support democratization; that is, to enable internal actors to establish and develop democratic institutions that play according to democratic rules. We differentiate between direct and indirect democracy promotion. Direct democracy promotion targets the development of democratic core institutions and the capacity-building of political and social actors; indirect democracy promotion seeks to improve basic conditions to create a favourable context for the transition to and the survival of democracy. Indirect democracy support might also entail measures integrated into forms of technical and financial cooperation.

In practice, democracy promoters do not often base their work on such clear-cut definitions as we have proposed above; on the contrary, some practitioners avoid the term 'democracy promotion', preferring to refer to 'good governance' (for example, World Bank), while others have a broader agenda in mind (for example, European Union); for example, they might include what we would call socio-economic development under the umbrella of 'democracy promotion'. Since the definition of democratization and other policy goals determines whether one can identify conflicting objectives or not, we prefer to use parsimonious concepts. This facilitates the careful identification of conflicts of objectives, the discovery of their origins, and the determination of how actors deal with them; in addition, it simplifies the analysis of their consequences. Equally, not all scholars do follow Dahl's lean concept. Where authors of the special issue use a different understanding of what democracy is this is clearly indicated in their texts.

Neither in political science nor in democracy promotion research, is there a common definition of the term *conflicting objectives*.[24] Thus, to develop a definition, we borrow the concept of conflicting objectives from macroeconomics. Scholars in this discipline agree on the fact that not all macroeconomic objectives – what they would call 'goals' – can be simultaneously achieved by an actor. Take, for example, the macroeconomic goal of a low inflation rate and the goal of a high employment rate. In theory, these two objectives have an inverse relationship. If a government tries to reduce unemployment through reflationary measures such as lower interest rates or increased public spending, the resulting reduction in unemployment will push wages and consequently prices higher. On the other hand, when the government tries to control high inflation with higher interest rates and reduced spending, the resultant reduction in consumer spending and lower investment will create job losses. This conflict of objectives thus has undesired consequences, whichever decision the government takes. Among the different schools of economic theory, it is an unresolved question whether unemployment is a price worth paying for achieving lower inflation.[25]

In accordance with this idea, we define *conflicting objectives* as the clash of two competing goals, whereby the achievement of one goal is impaired by the achievement of the other goal. In the case of democracy promotion, for example, the goal to support the selection of certain political leaders by free and fair elections may clash with the goal of integrating all relevant groups into an all-inclusive government, which would require a negotiated agreement that would trump democratic elections. In a broader sense, the support of democratization may clash with alternative policy goals, such as security, stability, peace, or socio-economic development.

Following Spanger and Wolff,[26] we identify two types of conflicting objectives in democracy promotion (see also Table 1):

(1) *Intrinsic* conflicting objectives emerge when different elements of democracy promotion clash;
(2) *Extrinsic* conflicting objectives emerge when the goal of democracy promotion – that is, democratization – interferes with other objectives of foreign policies and development cooperation.

Table 1. Intrinsic and extrinsic conflicting objectives in democracy promotion.

Conflict	Intrinsic conflicts of objectives	Extrinsic conflicts of objectives
Definition	Conflict of objectives that are inherent in democracy promotion	Conflicts of objectives of democracy promotion with other relevant policy goals
Examples	Free and fair elections vs. negotiated power-sharing	Democratization vs. peace-building (security, monopoly of force)
	Institution-building vs. empowerment	Democratization vs. state-building (state authority, administrative capacity)
	Inclusion vs. exclusion	Democratization vs. regime stability
	Ownership vs. donor control	Democratization vs. socio-economic development

Source: Based on Spanger and Wolff, 'Universales Ziel – partikulare Wege?', and adapted by the authors.

Intrinsic conflicting objectives emerge foremost if direct democracy promotion is used; extrinsic conflicting objectives rather appear if indirect democracy promotion comes into play.

Table 1 presents examples of the intrinsic and extrinsic conflicts of objectives discussed in this special issue. We list typical objectives that the authors of this special issue have found in their empirical research. *Intrinsic* conflicts of objectives in democracy promotion emerge when different dimensions or sub-goals of democracy promotion come into conflict with one another. As Jung's analysis of the peace-building intervention in Bosnia and Herzegovina shows (in this issue),[27] free and fair elections can conflict with negotiated power-sharing mechanisms. As defined above, free and fair elections are the institutional core of a democracy and therefore a priority in democracy promotion. In post-conflict societies, however, it is often impossible to have free and fair elections immediately following hostilities, as elections might under-represent already-threatened minorities and return to power those political elites who had plunged the country into civil unrest. Here, power-sharing instruments trump pure democratic selection by the establishment of consensually pre-arranged representation of conflict parties in the government. This allows for short-term stability, but may in the long run also entrench pre-war conflicts in the political system.[28] Even in the core definition of democracy, there is a conflict between the concepts of 'institution-building and the empowerment' of actors. As outlined in the case studies of Bolivia (Wolff), Kosovo and Timor-Leste (Lemay-Hébert), empowerment of local actors in some circumstances is achieved at the expense of Western-style democratic institution-building. As actors become more empowered to follow democratic rules, they may become less content with the institutions supported by international democracy promoters. The 'inclusion vs. exclusion' conflict deals with the problem of whom to include or exclude in the transition process. In the case of Afghanistan, it has become clear that the exclusion of relevant actors in the early stages of democratization may create spoilers for democratization in the long run, although inclusion in the early stages could have hindered the initiation of the democratization process (Quie). Finally, the 'ownership vs. donor control' conflict refers to the problem of who is in the driver's seat of democratization: the actors in the recipient country of democracy promotion or the democracy promoters themselves. 'Ownership' has recently been highlighted as a basic principle of development cooperation in the 2005 Paris Declaration on Aid Effectiveness. The Paris agenda prescribes that recipient countries should be in charge of defining development plans and policies. Their norms, strategies, and priorities, however, might not coincide with those of international actors, which could, in turn, provoke a conflict of objectives. As the analysis of multi-donor budget support in Zambia reveals, conflicts between domestic and international actors' norms, strategies, and priorities can easily undermine democracy promotion (Faust et al.).[29]

Extrinsic conflicting objectives emerge when the goal of achieving democratization interferes with other objectives of foreign policy and development cooperation. In all transitional settings, one very important objective is security, understood as the development of a legitimate monopoly on the use of force. Richter addresses this trade-off in her research on the EU's goals in the Western Balkans, in which the Union prioritized security issues over democratization. Although this strategy turned out to be successful in avoiding a further escalation of the conflict in the short and middle term, it came at a high cost for democratic consolidation in the long term. Especially in post-conflict societies, an additional goal is peace-building; like the majority of the literature since the 1992 UN 'Agenda for Peace', we define peace-building as those post-conflict activities that seek to avoid a 'relapse into conflict' (see also Lemay-Hébert and Jung).[30] According to Call, the policy objective of state-building is 'to establish, reform, or strengthen the institutions of the state and their relation to society'.[31] This includes institutions that provide the monopoly of power and the legitimacy and administrative capacity to govern. All these activities may contribute to the stabilization of a political regime, whether it is democratic or authoritarian. This becomes evident in the case of Morocco, where capacity-building in the water sector might contribute to democratization on the local level and stabilization of the autocratic regime on the macro-level at the same time (Freyburg). Jung, Lemay-Hébert, and Pogodda analyse the conflict between building a state and aiding democracy in the cases of Bosnia and Herzegovina, Kosovo, Timor-Leste, and Palestine, showing that delaying either state-building or democratization has negative effects on each other goal. Finally, socio-economic development focuses on economic and human progress, which includes the access of individuals and groups to certain rights and basic services.[32] A conflict with the support of democratization can emerge if this access is not open to everybody, but only to privileged groups and elites, as Wolff shows in his case study on Bolivia.

These conflicts seldom emerge alone. We assume that external actors who support democracy face not one, but several conflicts between objectives. Accordingly, this special issue presents empirical research that traces not only individual conflicts of objectives in democracy promotion, but that also highlights the co-existence of and interconnections between several conflicts of objectives in the process of democracy promotion (see especially Faust et al., Quie, and Wolff). The empirical investigations demonstrate that at times the emergence of extrinsic and intrinsic conflicts of objectives goes hand-in-hand; it is unlikely that one of these intertwined conflicts could be solved completely independently of the others. As Quie notes, in the Afghan peace process that began after the 2001 external military intervention, the extrinsic conflict between democratization and peace-building was closely connected with the intrinsic conflict over the inclusion or exclusion of Taliban combatants in the demobilization and reintegration programme. The extrinsic conflict hindered effective democracy promotion as long as the intrinsic conflict remained unsolved. Wolff's analysis of democracy promotion in Bolivia reveals that the empowerment of the populace during democratization has two conflicting dimensions. As an intrinsic conflict, this empowerment endangers the survival of existing democratic institutions; as an extrinsic conflict, it interferes with the maintenance of intra-state peace. These two conflicts are affiliated in the course of democratization and thereby present a challenge to the effectiveness of democracy promotion.

Identifying phases and causes: when and under what conditions do conflicting objectives emerge?

Although the existence of conflicting objectives is known, we lack systematic understanding of their origins. As an initial step, we propose an analytical systematization that individuates the phases of the policy process and the conditions that foster the emergence of conflicting objectives.

Phases of emergence of conflicting objectives

As in any other policy process, conflicting objectives emerge at different stages and at different times in the course of democracy promotion. Thus, our conceptualization of conflicts between objectives is process-oriented. We base our process-understanding on a policy cycle that is divided into three phases: During the *normative* phase, norm- and value-building takes place; during the *strategic* phase, actors decide upon their goals and select the adequate instruments to achieve them; and during the *operative* phase, policies are implemented.[33] In each of these phases, conflicts of objectives may emerge as a consequence of pre-existing concepts, as a consequence of decisions that have been taken during the preceding phase, or as a consequence of a widening of the available concepts and strategies (for example, because new actors have entered the scene).

Concerning the *normative* phase, there may be intrinsic conflicts between various norms in democracy promotion. Different democracy promoters may rely upon different and frequently incompatible democracy concepts – for example, liberal individualistic approaches would be at odds with collective approaches, ideas about individual rights would clash with group rights, and the goal of majority rule could threaten minority protection. Different norms may result in different priorities and interests for strategies and instruments, thus leading to inconsistent strategy-building and implementation. The same is true for the emergence of extrinsic conflicts between the goal of democratization and other relevant policy goals (see also Table 1 above).

In the *strategic* phase, intrinsic and extrinsic conflicts of appropriate timing, sequencing, and systemic interdependencies may occur. There is also a risk of unintended side-effects, as well as the need to consider the effects of policies in other areas (security, development, etc.) and to devise coherent democracy promotion policies accordingly.[34] Furthermore, the interaction between international and national actors may bear conflict potential if the two groups diverge on adequate reform strategies.

With regard to the *operative* phase, once again intrinsic and extrinsic conflicts can occur during the implementation of democracy promotion. During this phase, the interactions between the different agencies of one donor, between agencies of different donors, and particularly between donors and recipients can result in conflicts. For example, donors and recipients may disagree over priorities for the implementation of policy goals. Variations in prioritization will subsequently influence the results of democracy promotion (for an overview, see Figure 1).

As Jung describes in his case study, in the normative phase (here, the creation of the peace agreement in Dayton that was designed to end the civil war in Bosnia and Herzegovina in 1995), the three conflict fractions (Bosniaks, Croats, and Serbs) could not accept anything other than a strict system of institutionalized power-sharing. However, during the implementation phase, this system – combining a weak central state with strong entities, reserved seats in the parliament encouraging voting along strict ethnic lines, strong veto rights that are almost impossible to override, and a lack of incentives for cooperation across ethnic borders – has created immense challenges for both peace-building and democratization. The initial agreement on norms was undermined by its lack of effectiveness during implementation. War-time cleavages were enshrined in the institutional setting; today, the governmental system in Bosnia and Herzegovina can only very loosely be regarded as democratic.

It is important to note that the phases of the democracy promotion process are not isolated from one another. In fact, it is possible for a trickle-down effect to occur: the decision to pursue diverging norms might trigger conflicts in strategy-building, for example. The Afghan case mentioned above sheds light on this interdependence between norms and strategies. Once international actors had decided that they would seek to build peace and democracy simultaneously (in the normative phase), they then had to determine whether to exclude the Taliban from the process for the sake of stability or include them to guarantee democratic procedures (part of the strategic phase).

Conditions for the emergence of conflicting objectives

Scholars addressing the challenges of democracy promotion point to three interacting types of factors that might create tension between policy goals in general and in democracy promotion in particular.[35] These are:

Phase in policy process	Conflict	Intrinsic dimension of conflicting objectives	Extrinsic dimension of conflicting objectives
NORMATIVE	Conflicts of norms	Proposal of different, often irreconcilable democracy concepts; different norms result in different strategies, interests, and instruments	Democracy promotion may clash with establishing security, peace-building, state-building, socio-economic development
STRATEGIC	Conflicts of strategies	Disagreement over the most successful democracy promotion approach: endogenous vs exogenous democratization; external interference vs self-administration and local ownership	Extrinsic conflicts of objectives imply conflicts over means to achieve them
OPERATIVE	Conflicts of priorities	Conflict over prioritization of goals during democratization; different prioritizations influence the output/outcome of democracy promotion	Conflict over prioritization of different policy goals; democracy promotion may be compromised

Figure 1. The emergence of conflicting objectives in the policy process.

(1) the socio-economic and political conditions in the recipient country (in particular, the level of conflict, the level of development, and the type of political regime);
(2) the interaction between international and local actors; and
(3) the capacity of international and local actors (for example, human and institutional resources and management skills).

In the following, we will define these factors that have all been investigated by the authors of this special issue in greater detail and present our findings on their role.

With regard to factor (1) specific socio-economic and political conditions in the recipient country are presumed to increase the likelihood of the emergence of conflicting objectives. The authors of the special issue attribute explanatory power to three particular factors in the recipient country:

(a) Level of conflict (for example, ongoing conflict, post-conflict). Democracy promotion is particularly difficult in the context of an ongoing conflict (as in Afghanistan, Palestine, and the Democratic Republic of the Congo (DRC)) and in post-conflict settings (as in Kosovo and Timor-Leste). The legacies of war and violent conflict, including security dilemmas (Jung, Richter, Quie) and state failure (Lemay-Hébert, Quie) contribute to the emergence of extrinsic and intrinsic conflicts of objectives. We assume that international actors and recipients are overwhelmed by the number of tasks that must be accomplished to organize conflict management and post-conflict recovery, including state-building and advancements in democratization.

(b) Level of development (for example, developing, least developed). In societies with low levels of socio-economic and human development, existential problems such as hunger, disease, and unemployment require urgent political answers. Under such conditions, international actors face the challenge of balancing the fulfilment of humanitarian and social needs with democracy support. Although supporting efficient and effective governance to facilitate access to basic services and public goods has become a mainstay of international development cooperation, socio-economic development is likely to outrank democracy support in these contexts. For instance, Wolff found evidence that defining the fight against socio-economic inequalities as one attribute of democracy, has contributed to the emergence of conflicting objectives in Bolivia. In addition, well-developed countries which attract economic interests of OECD states might also cause conflicting objectives in foreign policies. For instance, the United States' trade relations might undermine their efforts to protect human rights and promote democracy in the Arab world.

(c) Type of political regime (for example, democratic, non-democratic). Conflicting objectives are more likely to emerge when international actors target authoritarian regimes or regimes in which authoritarian elements prevail. Although the aim of democracy promoters is regime change, at the same time they seek security and stability through development cooperation. In doing so, they foster regime survival and might actually undermine change. Freyburg's analysis of Morocco shows that the EU fosters the authoritarian regime on the macro-level but attempts democracy support on the micro-level.

Regarding factor (2), the mode of interaction between international and domestic actors can also determine the emergence of conflicting objectives in democracy promotion.[36] Various constellations of international actors and recipients can be placed on an inclusion-exclusion continuum, where one pole represents the inclusion of recipients in democracy promotion policies and the other pole, their exclusion. Dialogue and cooperation-oriented democracy promotion policies can be found near the inclusion pole; in such cases, recipients are in the driver's seat of democratization and international actors support ongoing democratization with caution, leaving the outcomes of democratization open (Wolff on Bolivia). Highly intrusive forms of democracy promotion can be found near the exclusion pole of the continuum; here, international trusteeship administrations plan in detail democratic institutions, determining which political fractions will be represented at the regime level (Jung on Bosnia and Herzegovina, Lemay-Hébert on Kosovo and Timor-Leste). In between the two poles, varying forms of temporary inclusion and exclusion of actors in the process of democratization can be found (for example, Quie on Afghanistan and Pogodda on Palestine). The more intrusive democracy promotion policies are, the higher the risk that conflicts of objectives will emerge as a consequence of diverging interests between donors and recipients.

Intra-organizational disputes can also cause conflicting objectives. External actors (such as the EU or the USA) that pursue a multitude of diverse interests are more likely to 'produce' conflicting objectives than more unified actors who have limited interests and follow a narrowly defined democracy promotion agenda (Richter, Wolff).[37] Multilateral coalitions and organizations are also vulnerable to conflicting objectives, as their norms and strategies are very often the result of negotiated policies and compromises between their member states, or they reflect the interests of the most powerful members of the group. For instance, the case of Zambia in this special issue reveals that a high fragmentation of the donor organizations in small developing countries can instigate the emergence of conflicting objectives if the recipient countries lack the capacity to coordinate different donor interests or if donors fail to harmonize their incentive systems (see Faust et al.).[38] It is also possible, of course, that actors within recipient countries could have conflicting ideas about what their country's priorities should be. Mixed signals to donors caused by unresolved internal conflict can further contribute to the emergence of conflicting objectives.

Against the backdrop of the empirical findings of this special issue, we find the following factors in the relationship between actors particularly significant in explaining conflicting objectives in democracy promotion:[39] (a) a clash between (security, political, commercial, or cultural) interests, norms, and values; (b) a mismatch of incentives; (c) a lack of ownership; and (d) a lack of coordination between international and domestic actors or between international donors.

As stated in factor (3) above, the lack of capacity of international and local actors can create conflicting objectives in democracy promotion. Resource scarcity, time pressure, and the lack of information on the actual needs of the populace and on the consequences of decisions can all limit an actor's capacity. Developing countries very often lack the human and institutional resources and management skills to negotiate their own agendas of political change and to respond to donor demands (Faust et al.). If external actors do not adequately manage resources and foreign aid and are not willing or able to overcome such problems, the emergence of conflicting objectives becomes more likely (Jung, Lemay-Hébert, Pogodda, Quie, and Richter).

In summary, the analyses in this special issue especially highlight (post-) conflict settings with a generally low level of socio-economic development, diverging interests between donors and recipients, and capacity deficits on both sides as factors that explain the formation of conflicts between objectives in democracy promotion.

Facing conflicting objectives: how do internal and external actors deal with conflicting objectives?

Under certain conditions, conflicts between foreign policy goals may be inseparably intertwined with democratization, but not affect democracy promotion. However, we presume that the contradictions and hindering effects of conflicting objectives outweigh any consequences that are conducive to democracy.[40] Thus, if local and international actors fail to address these conflicts constructively, they are likely to hinder the effectiveness of democracy promotion in transitional, post-war, and developmental contexts. If a conflict of objectives emerges and the actors involved – international and local – perceive it to be a conflict that might impact on the effectiveness of democracy promotion, theoretically, they have four options for dealing with it (see Figure 2).

The first option is 'no action'; that is, actors simply ignore the conflict and continue policy-making without making any changes at the norm-building, the strategy-building, or the implementation phase. In a best-case scenario, the conflict will simply disappear over time; however, in most cases, a policy of resolution by inaction seems unlikely to succeed.

The second option is 'prioritization', which refers to the individual objectives within in a policy. In this case, actors give one goal precedence over another. In the extreme case, a goal that is seen as less relevant could be completely abandoned.

The third option is 'sequencing', whereby actors first prioritize goals and subsequently rank these goals in a successive order.[41] One objective will be addressed, before focus turns to another. This order should be based on a functional logic of preconditions. For instance, the rule of law should be established or stability guaranteed before elections can take place.

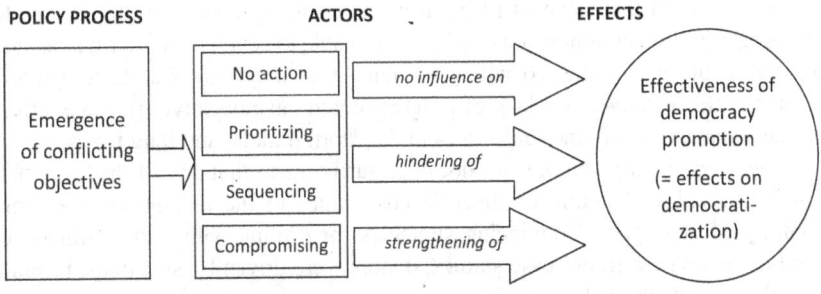

Figure 2. Impact of conflicting objectives on the effectiveness of democracy promotion.

The fourth option is 'compromise'. Here, actors balance two or more objectives and combine them in their policy. Compromise can be the result of decision-making processes within the organization of one actor or a consequence of negations between two or more actors. In either case, the expectations of what can be achieved are often reduced due to limited resources or other context restrictions.

The authors featured in this issue have found evidence in their case studies and case comparisons of the use of three of these four options for dealing with the emergence of conflicting objectives. In some cases, donors are aware of conflicts of objectives, but they prefer not to engage actively in addressing them in a sustainable fashion (*no action*). Either the actors sit the problems out using a 'wait-and-see' approach (for example, Wolff's description of US actions in the first phase after government change in Bolivia) or they engage in emergency dialogue, but without the creation of a consistent fall-back scenario (as donors did in the Zambian case, see Faust et al.).

In other cases, donors prioritized their goals (*prioritization*). They put security (Richter, Jung), state-building (Lemay-Hébert), or development (Wolff) first; in none of these cases was democracy promotion prioritized right from the beginning (for example, in the form of actively supporting empowerment or by local participation and consultation). A shift towards giving higher priority to democracy promotion has taken place only when it has become apparent that improvements in democracy were necessary to serve other objectives.

Interesting examples of *compromise* can be found in the cases of Kosovo and Timor-Leste, where local consultation and participation has only recently been considered to be constructive for post-conflict recovery (Lemay-Hébert), and in the case of Bolivia, where donors adapted their policies only after they had grudgingly accepted the changed political situation (Wolff). Where donors have started by negotiating compromises among donors collectively or with recipients, they have for the most part failed due to the complexity of the conditions, as seen in the case of diverging interests between donors and recipients in Afghanistan on the question of inclusion vs. exclusion of Taliban combatants (Quie).

None of the authors found evidence of a clear-cut *sequencing* strategy. No donor included in our investigations made a strategic decision before policy implementation to delay the promotion of one objective until a prioritized objective had been completely achieved. At this stage of research we can only speculate on the reasons for this behaviour. Either donors are unwilling or unable to develop long-term strategies, or, due to the interconnected nature of objectives, they may fear to temporarily abandon one objective, as a lack of progress could have negative spill-over effects on the achievement of other objectives in the short, middle, and long terms.

These empirical examples do not necessarily mean that any of the aforementioned strategies of action or inaction contributes to the resolution of existing conflicts of objectives. Convincing strategies for dealing with such conflicts still need to be devised. In our case studies, donors were driven by situations, meaning that they were obliged to react, but appeared to not pro-actively strategize or manage conflicts between objectives in a controlled fashion.

Observing the consequences: what are the effects of conflicting objectives on democratization?

In democracy promotion research, conflicting objectives are of special interest because their existence, emergence, and how actors deal with them might be explanatory factors for the effectiveness or lack of effectiveness of democracy promotion. We hypothesize that the management of conflicting objectives could influence the effectiveness of democracy promotion in three main ways (see Figure 2).

Conflicting objectives may have *no impact at all* on the effectiveness of democracy promotion and thereby on democratization. For instance, in a post-conflict society, an actor could support civil society participation and at the same time foster state-building without interference between goals. Although democratization is likely to hinder stabilization, the two goals do not necessarily contradict each other in the practice of democracy promotion.

Conflicting objectives may have *a negative impact* on the effectiveness of democracy promotion. In the worst case, they will hinder democratization in a recipient country instead of fostering it. For instance, if a donor seeks to stabilize a post-conflict society but at the same time supports the transformation of power structures, stabilization can be endangered. Should violent conflict break out, democratization would be at risk.

Conflicting objectives can *strengthen* the effectiveness of democracy promotion if a democracy promoter openly considers the conflict in the decision-making process. Resources can be allocated in a prioritized, sequenced, or balanced manner, leading to a positive trade-off or complementarity between various policy goals. For instance, investment in the rule of law in the short run can also support stabilization and thereby democratization in the long run.

Evidence for the second (negative) hindering mechanism outweighed the other options in most of the case studies in this special issue. Inadequate methods of dealing with conflicting objectives has contributed to a lack of progress in democratization (Faust et al., Quie, Jung, Pogodda) and to the entrenchment of semi-democratic institutions (Lemay-Hébert). Richter even found evidence of the enforcement of a few forms of inner-ethnic conflict. In all these cases, the external actors have failed to exert a consistent democratizing pressure or to set the right incentives for domestic actors to continue democratic reform.

Only in the case of the EU's functional cooperation with Morocco was it shown that the conflict of objectives between regime stabilization and democracy promotion turned out to be less crucial than originally expected (Freyburg). Although the cooperation supported regime stability on the macro-level, the awareness and acceptance of democratic participation was raised, at least on the micro- and meso-levels. However, it remains difficult to predict how effects on the micro- and meso-levels will contribute to regime change on the macro-level in the medium or long term.

Thus, depending on what actors do in a certain context, they can either constructively address conflicting objectives and might thereby strengthen the effectiveness of democracy promotion, or they could fail to find an adequate strategy to treat conflicting objectives, thus hindering the effectiveness of democracy promotion. The analysis of conflicting objectives can help actors to identify conflicts of interests and preferences, misperceptions, and undesirable developments, opening a window of opportunity for changes in norms, priorities, and/or objectives. Once conflicting objectives have been acknowledged, actors can assess whether they are complementary in the short and long terms, either in terms of content or in the order they should be pursued. It is therefore important to learn more about the factors that influence the different origins and effects of conflicting objectives in democracy promotion in cases beyond those presented in this issue.

Conclusions: coming to terms with conflicts of objectives in democracy promotion

At the beginning of our research, we set out to investigate whether conflicting objectives matter in democracy promotion. Although their importance is commonly acknowledged in the literature, almost no systematic research has been done on this topic. We therefore sought to conceptualize and systematize conflicting objectives in order to learn more about their origins, how international actors deal with them, and how conflicting objectives influence democratization. Our empirical findings provide evidence that conflicting objectives impact the effectiveness of democracy promotion.

For the success of democracy support, it makes a difference whether actors openly address conflicting objectives or ignore them. In our case studies, however, we have primarily observed 'wait and see' approaches and uncoordinated activism instead of the systematic integration of conflicting objectives into the formulation of norms and strategies in democracy promotion. In particular, post-conflict settings in which international actors have a comprehensive mandate are prone to mismanagement of conflicting objectives. The studies of military and civil interventions in Afghanistan, Bosnia and Herzegovina, Kosovo, and Timor-Leste in this special issue demonstrate that democracy promoters and peacebuilders generally set overly broad agendas at the beginning of a mission. Although different goals may seem compatible during norm-building and strategy formulation, they often clash during implementation. As a result of 'learning by doing' in the implementation process, most actors then narrow their agendas, prioritizing certain goals over others. When the divergent foreign-policy goals of donors interfere with the objective of promoting democracy, the former is likely to be prioritized at the expense of the latter (Faust et al., Pogodda, Quie).

We recommend that practitioners seeking to improve their democracy promotion policies acknowledge the relevance of conflicting objectives and consider how intrinsic and extrinsic conflicts could develop as a part of their strategy-building. Our empirical investigations demonstrate the overall lack of strategies for addressing intrinsic conflicts and also for embedding democracy promotion efficiently in the framework of other foreign policies, such as development policies (Faust et al., Freyburg) or post-conflict state-building (Lemay-Hébert, Pogodda).

It is not only practitioners who should be occupied with conflicting objectives in democracy promotion. There is also a great deal to be done in research. If reliable patterns for the origins of conflicting objectives and for their explanatory factors are to be identified, further research is required in three directions: the scope of conditions, the conceptual framework, and methods to effectively deal with conflicting objectives. With regard to the scope of conditions in the recipient countries, the case studies in this special issue focus primarily on (post-)conflict settings in developing countries and political regimes with democratic features. To obtain systematic data on the emergence of conflicts, further research on this topic should focus not only on these settings, but should also include more cases of stable developing countries and of authoritarian regimes. We suspect that other conflicts may emerge in these situations that will need careful treatment in order to render democracy promotion more effective.

With regard to the conceptual framework, we suggest further investigation tracing the emergence of conflicting objectives and their consequences, not only in the three phases of the democracy promotion process (norm-building, strategy-building, and implementation) but also on the different levels of political regimes (the macro-, meso-, and micro-levels). As Freyburg has illustrated in this issue, there may be substantial differences regarding the importance of conflicting objectives on these three levels. If this is true, the logical conclusion would be that different strategies for the management of conflicting objectives would be required at the different levels. Such an empirical analysis would shed further light on how conflicting objectives can affect the success or failure of democratization.

Finally, it would be intriguing to identify those patterns of inaction, prioritization, sequencing, and compromise in democracy promotion that lead to a positive trade-off and complementarity between different policy goals. Our sample of cases leads us to conclude that conflicting objectives primarily negatively affect democratization, whatever actions actors take. However, we doubt that this is the case in all circumstances. To allow for substantive theory-building on the influence of conflicting objectives in democracy promotion on transition outcomes, further systematic and comparative examination of additional cases and expansion of the time period under investigation would be worthwhile. Perhaps, in the long run, it might turn out that at least some good things do indeed go together, even when that appears not to be the case at individual snapshot points in time.

In this special issue, we provide a conceptual framework for researching conflicting objectives, and we illustrate how one can address this issue in comparative empirical research. We hope that the reader will find this fruitful and take it as a starting point for further research on this topic along the proposed lines.

Acknowledgements

This special issue is a product of the Research Network 'External Democratization Policies' (EDP) which is funded by the German Science Foundation (DFG). For activities, publications and members of the EDP please go to http://www.external-democracy-promotion.eu. We especially wish to thank Peter Burnell, Thomas Carothers, Anna Jarstad, Carry Manning, Wolfgang Merkel, and Brigitte Weiffen for their helpful comments on an earlier version of this introduction. We also would like to thank all our authors for contributing to this issue, both for their empirical investigations and for their participation in the SGIR conference in Stockholm in September 2010 and at the authors' meeting in Zurich in March 2011 that improved the conceptual design of this special issue. We thank twelve anonymous reviewers for their comments as well as Claire Bacher and Okka Lou Mathis for their careful language and layout editing of the special issue's manuscripts. We are very grateful to Jeff Haynes and Gordon Crawford for their constructive editorial support. Generous financial support of this project by the National Center of Competence in Research (NCCR) Democracy at the ETH Zurich and the University of Zurich, the Swiss National Fund, and the German Science Foundation is gratefully acknowledged.

Notes

1. We use the terms 'trade-off' and 'conflicting objectives' simultaneously. The differentiation between intrinsic and extrinsic conflicts of objectives and their respective definitions are adapted from Spanger and Wolff, 'Universales Ziel – partikulare Wege?', 267.
2. Burnell, 'The Elusive Quest'.
3. Robert Packenham in 1973 was to our knowledge the first to express the idea that 'all good things go together' in Liberal America: Packenham, *Liberal America in the Third World*. See also Paris, 'Saving Liberal Peace', 341.
4. See Grävingholt, Leininger, and von Haldenwang, 'Effective Statebuilding'.
5. Lipset, *Political Man*. Other authors who follow a similar line of argument are Lerner, *The Passing of Traditional Society*; Rostow, *The Stages of Economic Growth*.
6. Lipset, *Political Man*, 31.
7. Further methodological and theoretical advancements of this argument can be found in Przeworski and Limongi, 'Modernization'; Acemoglu et al., 'Reevaluating the Modernization Hypothesis'; Levitsky and Way, 'Competitive Authoritarianism'.
8. Przeworski et al., *Democracy and Development*.
9. Carothers, 'Democracy Support and Development Aid'.
10. Faust, 'Democracy's Dividend'.
11. This development has been reinforced by the role that China has recently been playing in global politics. Autocratic China's extraordinary economic growth offers a new and successful model for development that seems to be attractive for some governments in developing regions. Based on the Chinese model, authoritarian regimes stress the importance of stability – rather than uncertain democratization – as a precondition for successful economic development. See Bader, Grävingholt, and Kästner, 'Would Autocracies Promote Autocracy?'; Ramo, *The Beijing Consensus*.
12. See Call and Cook, 'On Democratization and Peacebuilding', 237, for a similar assessment.
13. Grimm, 'External Democratization after War'; Paris, *At War's End*; Paris, 'International Peacebuilding and the "Mission Civilisatrice"'; Wesley, 'The State of the Art on the Art of State Building'.
14. Barnett and Zürcher, The Peacebuilder's Contract', 2.
15. Given the experiences of unsuccessful democracy promotion in recent years, democracy promoters have come to recognize the problems that emerge from an 'all good things go together' approach. Nevertheless, this is rarely reflected in their policies.
16. Grävingholt, Leininger, and von Haldenwang, 'Effective Statebuilding', chapter 4.
17. OECD, *Monitoring the Principles for Good*.

18. Call and Cook, 'On Democratization and Peacebuilding'; Jarstad and Sisk, *From War to Democracy*; Rothchild and Roeder, 'Dilemmas of State-Building in Divided Societies'; Suhrke, 'Peacekeepers as Nation-builders'; Zaum, *The Sovereignty Paradox*.
19. Carothers, 'Democracy Assistance'.
20. A concept is the 'basic unit of thinking' which constructs the political phenomena that lead up to theory-building. In order to be a sharp and functional instrument of analysis, a concept should be parsimonious and built in an unambiguous way while adequately reflecting the level of complexity of the subject of inquiry. See Sartori, 'Guidelines for Concept Analysis', 17; Leininger, 'Bringing the Outside in', 66–7.
21. Dahl, *Polyarchy*, 6.
22. Merkel, 'Defective Democracies'.
23. O'Donnell and Schmitter, *Transitions from Authoritarian Rule*.
24. In accordance with the mainstream literature, we use the terms 'dilemma' and 'conflicting objectives' synonymously.
25. Abel, Bernanke, and Croushore, *Macroeconomics*; Mankiw, *Principles of Economics*, 783–90.
26. Spanger and Wolff, 'Universales Ziel – partikulare Wege?', 267.
27. References in the text and in parentheses always refer to contributions in this special issue.
28. Höglund, Jarstad, and Söderberg Kovacs, 'Predicament of Elections'; Jarstad and Nilsson, 'From Words to Deeds'.
29. High Level Forum, *Paris Declaration*.
30. Call and Cook, 'On Democratization and Peacebuilding', 235; United Nations, *Agenda for Peace*, para. 55.
31. Call, 'Ending Wars', 5.
32. Sen, *Development as Freedom*.
33. We have adapted the policy cycle from David Easton's five-step cycle proposed in *A Framework for Political Analysis*. In our abbreviated model, norm-building corresponds to Easton's preference formation and interest aggregation, our strategy-building corresponds to Easton's agenda-setting and decision-making, and implementation remains the same.
34. Grävingholt, Leininger, and Schlumberger, *The Three Cs of Democracy Promotion Policy*.
35. There is no literature that refers systematically to the emergence of conflicting objectives in democracy promotion as such. The conflict and peace literature hints at individual factors that can create conflicting objectives in peace- and state-building. See, for example, Gleditsch and Ward, 'War and Peace'; Jarstad and Sisk, *From War to Democracy*; Ottaway, 'Rebuilding State Institutions'; Ottaway, *Democracy Promotion*. Moreover, recent analyses and evaluations of the structures and effectiveness of development cooperation have shed light on various factors that lead to conflicting objectives. We therefore trace our explaining factors for the emergence of conflicting objectives in democracy promotion from this branch of the literature. See, e.g., Faust and Messner, 'Organizational Challenges'; Riddell, *Does Foreign Aid Really Work*.
36. For a similar argument with regard to peace-building, see Barnett and Zürcher, 'The Peacebuilder's Contract'.
37. Carothers, 'Promoting Democracy'; Diamond, *Promoting Democracy*.
38. Fraser and Whitfield, 'Understanding Contemporary'; Gibson et al., *The Samaritan's Dilemma*.
39. Empirical evidence from the study of interactions in development cooperation supports the relevance of these explanatory factors. See, e.g., Whitfield, *The Politics of Aid*.

40. Compare the first section on the status quo of research.
41. 'Sequencing' goes one step further than 'prioritization' because it combines several elements and implies strategic thinking. There is no sequencing without prioritization, but priorities without sequencing are possible.

Notes on contributors

Sonja Grimm is Senior Researcher and Lecturer on International and Comparative Politics at the University of Konstanz. She specializes in studies of transition to democracy in post-conflict societies and has previously edited (with Prof. Dr Wolfgang Merkel) 'War and Democratization: Legality, Legitimacy, and Effectiveness', a *Democratization* special issue (2008, Vol. 15, No. 3). She obtained her PhD on 'Imposing Democracy: Political Re-organisation under External Oversight after Military Intervention' at Humboldt University Berlin.

Julia Leininger is Senior Researcher at the Deutsches Institut für Entwicklungspolitik/ German Development Institute (DIE) in Bonn. She has previously published a handbook on international organizations ('Handbuch international Organisationen' with Dr Katja Freistein) and developed an approach to study international democracy promotion. Her research focuses on (de-)democratization and international democracy promotion in developing countries and fragile states, and on religious actors, with particular emphasis on sub-Saharan Africa.

Bibliography

Abel, Andrew B., Ben S. Bernanke, and Dean Croushore. *Macroeconomics*. Boston, MA: Pearson Education Limited, 2011.

Acemoglu, Daron, James A. Robinson, Simon Johnson, and Pierre Yared. 'Reevaluating the Modernization Hypothesis'. *Journal of Monetary Economics* 56, no. 8 (2009): 1043–58.

Bader, Julia, Jörn Grävingholt, and Antje Kästner, 'Would Autocracies Promote Autocracy? A Political Economy Perspective on Regime-type Export in Regional Neighbourhoods'. *Contemporary Politics* 16, no. 1 (2010): 81–100.

Barnett, Michael, and Christoph Zürcher. 'The Peacebuilder's Contract: How External Statebuilding Reinforces Weak Statehood'. In *The Dilemmas of Statebuilding: Confronting the Contradictions of Postwar Peace Operations*, ed. Roland Paris and Timothy Sisk, 23–52. London: Routledge, 2009.

Burnell, Peter. 'Democracy Promotion: The Elusive Quest for Grand Strategy'. *Internationale Politik und Gesellschaft*, no. 3 (2004): 100–16.

Call, Charles T. 'Ending Wars, Building States'. In *Building States to Build Peace*, ed. Charles Call and Vanessa Wyeth, 1–24. Boulder, CO: Lynne Rienner, 2008.

Call, Charles T., and Susan E. Cook. 'On Democratization and Peacebuilding'. *Global Governance* 9, no. 2 (2003): 233–46.

Carothers, Thomas. 'Democracy Assistance: Political vs. Developmental?'. *Journal of Democracy* 20, no. 1 (2009): 5–19.

Carothers, Thomas. 'Democracy Support and Development Aid: The Elusive Synthesis'. *Journal of Democracy* 21, no. 4 (2010): 12–26.

Carothers, Thomas. 'Promoting Democracy and Fighting Terror'. *Foreign Affairs* 82, no. 1 (2003): 84–97.

Dahl, Robert A. *Polyarchy: Participation and Opposition*. New Haven, CT; London: Yale University Press, 1971.

Diamond, Larry. *Promoting Democracy in the 1990s: Actors, Instruments, Issues and Imperatives*. New York: Carnegie Commission on Preventing, 1995.

Easton, David. *A Framework for Political Analysis*. Englewood Cliffs, NJ: Prentice-Hall, 1965.
Faust, Jörg. 'Democracy's Dividend: Political Order and Economic Productivity'. *World Political Science Review* 3, no. 2 (2007), 1–26.
Faust, Jörg, and Dirk Messner. 'Organizational Challenges for an Effective Aid Architecture – Traditional Deficits, the Paris Agenda and Beyond'. Discussion Paper 20/2007. Bonn: German Development Institute 2007.
Fraser, Alistair, and Lindsay Whitfield. 'Understanding Contemporary Aid Relationships'. In *The Politics of Aid: African Strategies for Dealing with Donors*, ed. Lindsay Whitfield, 74–107. Oxford: Oxford University Press, 2009.
Gibson, Clark. C., Krister Andersson, Elinor Ostrom, and Sujai Shivakumar. *The Samaritan's Dilemma: The Political Economy of Development Aid*. Oxford: Oxford University Press, 2005.
Gleditsch, Kristian S., and Michael D. Ward. 'War and Peace in Space and Time: The Role of Democratization'. *International Studies Quarterly* 44, no. 1 (2000): 1–29.
Grävingholt, Jörn, Julia Leininger, and Oliver Schlumberger. *The Three Cs of Democracy Promotion Policy: Context, Consistency and Credibility*. Bonn: Deutsches Institut für Entwicklungspolitik, 2009.
Grävingholt, Jörn, Julia Leininger, and Christian von Haldenwang. 'Effective Statebuilding: A Review of Studies of and Evaluations of International Support for Statebuilding in Fragile Contexts'. Draft manuscript. Bonn: German Development Institute, 2012.
Grimm, Sonja. 'External Democratization after War: Success and Failure'. *Democratization* 15 (2008): 525–49.
High Level Forum. *Paris Declaration on Aid Effectiveness: Ownership, Harmonisation, Alignment, Results and Mutual Accountability*. Paris: OECD, 2005.
Höglund, Kristine, Anna Jarstad, and Mimmi Söderberg Kovacs. 'The Predicament of Elections in War-torn Societies'. *Democratization* 16, no. 3 (2009): 530–57.
Jarstad, Anna, and Desiree Nilsson. 'From Words to Deeds: The Implementation of Power-sharing Pacts in Peace Accords'. *Conflict Management and Peace Science* 25, no. 3 (2008): 206–23.
Jarstad, Anna, and Timothy D. Sisk. *From War to Democracy: Dilemmas of Peace-building*. Cambridge: Cambridge University Press, 2008.
Leininger, Julia. 'Bringing the Outside in': Illustrations from Haiti and Mali for the Re-conceptualization of Democracy Promotion'. *Contemporary Politics* 16, no. 1 (2009): 65–81.
Lerner, Daniel. *The Passing of Traditional Society: Modernizing the Middle East*. Glencoe: Free Press of Glencoe, 1958.
Levitsky, Steven, and Lucan A. Way. 'The Rise of Competitive Authoritarianism'. *Journal of Democracy* 13, no. 2 (2002): 51–65.
Lipset, Seymour Martin. *Political Man: The Social Bases of Politics*. Baltimore, MD: Johns Hopkins University Press, 1960.
Mankiw, Nicholas G. *Principles of Economics*. Mason, OH: South-Western Cengage Learning, 2008.
Merkel, Wolfgang. 'Embedded and Defective Democracies'. *Democratization* 11, no. 5 (2004): 33–58.
O'Donnell, Guillermo, and Philippe C. Schmitter, eds. *Transitions from Authoritarian Rule: Tentative Conclusions about Uncertain Democracies*. Baltimore, MD: Johns Hopkins University Press, 1989.
OECD. *Monitoring the Principles for Good International Engagement in Fragile States and Situations Fragile States Principles Monitoring Survey: Global Report*. Paris: Organisation for Economic Cooperation and Development, 2010.

Ottaway, Marina. *Democracy Promotion in the Middle East: Restoring Credibility*. Washington, DC: Carnegie Endowment for International Peace, 2008.

Ottaway, Marina. 'Rebuilding State Institutions in Collapsed States'. *Development and Change* 33, no. 5 (2002): 1001–23.

Packenham, Robert. *Liberal America in the Third World*. Princeton, NJ: Princeton University Press, 1973.

Paris, Roland. *At War's End: Building Peace After Civil Conflict*. Cambridge: Cambridge University Press, 2004.

Paris, Roland: 'International Peacebuilding and the "Mission Civilisatrice"'. *Review of International Studies* 28, no. 4 (2002): 637–56.

Paris, Roland. 'Saving Liberal Peace'. *Review of International Studies* 36, no. 2 (2010): 337–65.

Przeworski, Adam, Michael E. Alvarez, Jose Antonio Cheibub, and Fernando Limongi. *Democracy and Development: Political Institutions and Well-Being in the World, 1950–1990*. Cambridge: Cambridge University Press, 2000.

Przeworski, Adam, and Fernando Limongi. 'Modernization. Theories and Facts'. *World Politics* 49, no. 2 (1997): 155–83.

Ramo, Joshua C. *The Beijing Consensus*. London: Foreign Policy Centre, 2004.

Riddell, Roger C. *Does Foreign Aid Really Work?* Oxford: Oxford University Press, 2007.

Rostow, Walt W. *The Stages of Economic Growth: A Non-Communist Manifesto*. Cambridge: Cambridge University Press, 1959.

Rothchild, Donald, and Phillip G. Roeder. 'Dilemmas of State-building in Divided Societies'. In *Sustainable Peace: Power and Democracy After Civil Wars*, ed. Phillip G. Roeder and Donald Rothchild, 1–26. Ithaca, NY: Cornell University Press, 2005.

Sartori, Giovanni. 'Guidelines for Concept Analysis'. In *Social Science Concepts: A Systematic Analysis*, ed. by Giovanni Sartory, 15–85, Beverly Hills, CA: Sage, 1984.

Sen, Amartya. *Development as Freedom*. Oxford: Oxford University Press, 1999.

Spanger, Hans-Joachim, and Jonas Wolff. 'Universales Ziel – partikulare Wege? Externe Demokratieförderung zwischen einheitlicher Rhetorik und vielfältiger Praxis'. In *Schattenseiten des Demokratischen Friedens. Zur Kritik einer Theorie liberaler Außen- und Sicherheitspolitik*, ed. Anna Geis, Harald Müller, and Wolfgang Wagner, 261–84. Frankfurt; New York: Campus, 2007.

Suhrke, Astri. 'Peacekeepers as Nation-builders. Dilemmas of the UN in East Timor'. *International Peacekeeping* 8, no. 4 (2001): 1–20.

United Nations. *An Agenda for Peace*. New York: United Nations, 1992.

Wesley, Michael. 'The State of the Art on the Art of State Building'. *Global Governance* 14, no. 3 (2008): 369–85.

Whitfield, Lindsay, ed. *The Politics of Aid. African Strategies for Dealing with Donors*. Oxford: Oxford University Press, 2009.

Zaum, Dominik. *The Sovereignty Paradox: The Norms and Politics of International Statebuilding*. Oxford: Oxford University Press, 2007.

Democracy promotion, empowerment, and self-determination: conflicting objectives in US and German policies towards Bolivia

Jonas Wolff

Peace Research Institute Frankfurt (PRIF), Frankfurt am Main, Germany

Promoting democracy implies fostering political empowerment and self-determination. Although this creates obvious problems for any external policy seeking to change authoritarian regimes, mainstream thinking on democratization in the case of post-transition countries would predict a somewhat easier task for potential democracy promoters: cooperation with the elected government strengthens the democratic regime, while democracy assistance that supports institutional capacities and civil society participation simultaneously contributes to the protection and deepening of democracy. This article argues that such a view is far too simple. In the broad range of 'normal' post-transition countries, democracy promotion can be confronted with a variety of conflicts of objectives associated with the fact that there is no democracy without some kind of self-determination and no process of democratization without some degree of political empowerment. The article presents a typology of these conflicts of objectives and applies it to the case of Bolivia. Subsequently, it offers an analysis of how two important democracy promoters in the country – namely, the US and Germany – reacted to Bolivia's 'democratic revolution' and handled their respective conflicting objectives.

Introduction

Democracy means self-determination of the people; democratization entails political empowerment. How, then, could these two processes possibly present a challenge to external democracy promotion? There is no question that in dealing with non-democratic regimes, the dual aim to support democratization as a process of regime change and democratic self-determination as a result is intrinsically contradictory: The former implies participation in the toppling of an existing regime, an activity clearly in opposition to the notion of self-determination. More specifically, it is commonly acknowledged that processes of political empowerment associated with the introduction of democratic institutions may increase the risk of violent conflict. Such processes can overburden the capacity of state institutions ill-prepared to handle broad-based political mobilization and participation, threaten entrenched authoritarian elites, or incite empowered majorities to turn against (for example, ethnic) minorities.[1]

Consequently, the idea that democracy promotion is the best way to foster peace both within countries and internationally is increasingly being called into question, especially in light of recent experiences with regime change in Iraq and Afghanistan.[2] However, this critical debate on the premises of external democracy promotion has focused on the prominent and particularly difficult cases of coerced regime change, the democratization of authoritarian regimes, and the implementation of democracy in post-conflict societies. This tends to create the illusion that these important but specific problems do not affect the day-to-day business of democracy promotion concerned with strengthening political institutions, supporting civil society, and dissolving 'democratic defects' and 'authoritarian legacies' in regimes that are, at least in a basic sense, already democratic. In such post-transition countries, the agenda for would-be democracy promoters is largely seen as straight-forward: Cooperation with the elected government strengthens the democratic regime, while democracy assistance that supports institutional capacities and civil society participation simultaneously contributes to the stabilization of democratic institutions (protection of democracy) and to improving the quality of the democratic regime (deepening of democracy). Certainly, there is a wide-ranging debate about the (limited) impact of democracy promotion and the best strategies and measures to be implemented under various circumstances.[3] However, this debate has focused on problem-solving within an unquestioned agenda of democracy promotion and largely avoids critical examination of the normative and conceptual premises behind this agenda.[4]

This article argues that also in the broad range of 'normal' post-transition countries, democracy promotion is regularly confronted with a variety of conflicts of objectives. The article examines the plausibility of this general argument with regard to democracy promotion in Bolivia, and namely US and German reactions to the ongoing transformation of Bolivian democracy. Two of the research questions outlined in the introduction to this special issue are addressed: (1) What are the conflicting objectives in democracy promotion? (2) How do democracy promoters deal with these conflicts?[5] Regarding the first question, the article presents a typology of conflicts of objectives associated with self-determination and empowerment in post-transition countries, and applies this typology to Bolivia's ongoing democratic transformation. The main empirical part of the article investigates the second question, analysing how two important democracy promoters in the country – the US and Germany – reacted to Bolivia's 'democratic revolution' and handled their respective conflicting objectives.

The case of Bolivia has been selected because it represents a fairly easy case for democracy promotion. Following a turbulent transition to democracy in the early 1980s, Bolivia has now experienced almost three decades of continuous democratic rule. In the 1990s, the country was regarded as a development model that successfully combined democratization, stabilization, and (neo-)liberal economic reform.[6] Identification of conflicts of objectives in the Bolivian case would therefore strongly support the claim that these are general phenomena and are not limited to very specific difficult circumstances. A comparison of US and German policies towards Bolivia is promising because of the diverging profiles of these two 'donors': The US has important tangible interests in Bolivia, especially concerning the so-called 'War on Drugs', and thus severe *extrinsic* conflicts of objectives (democracy promotion vs. donor interests) can be expected; for Germany, Bolivia is mainly relevant only as a recipient of German development aid, and thus the *intrinsic* side of the conflicts of objectives can be assessed without much 'noise' stemming from economic or security interests. The case studies trace US and German reactions to political change in Bolivia by drawing on secondary sources (including media reports), official documents (including data on foreign assistance), and interviews conducted in Bolivia, Germany, and the US.[7]

The article starts by presenting a typology of the conflicts of objectives that democracy promoters can be expected to face in post-transition countries (second section) and, then, applies it to the case of Bolivia (third section). Subsequent sections analyse how the US and Germany reacted to Bolivia's 'democratic revolution' (fourth section) and compare how they handled their respective conflicts of objectives (fifth section).

Self-determination and empowerment as challenges to democracy promotion

In a basic sense, the conflicts of objectives that are potentially relevant for post-transition countries correspond to those usually discussed in relation to the democratization of authoritarian regimes and post-conflict societies (see above and the introduction to this special issue). This is due to the fact that promoting democracy in countries that have established at least rudimentary democratic institutions also implies democratization, albeit a further democratization of the existing democracy. Of course, improving the quality of – or deepening – democracy can refer to any of the multiple dimensions of democracy, including the strength and capacity of democratic institutions and the rule of law. However, questions of political empowerment and national self-determination are obviously relevant here: Democracy as it exists in particular in developing countries (countries usually featuring sharp social inequalities and/or high poverty rates) is characterized by extreme asymmetries in de facto political participation, representation, and responsiveness; at the same time, asymmetric inter- and transnational interdependencies mean that national sovereignty as a condition for democratic self-determination is particularly constrained in the developing world. Promoting democracy under such circumstances should include actions to reduce these asymmetries by contributing to the political empowerment of disadvantaged social sectors and increasing the scope for national self-determination.

The very nature of democracy as self-determination and of democratization as political empowerment, however, gives rise to conflicts of objectives in post-transition countries.[8] I propose to distinguish four types of conflicting objectives (see Table 1).

The political empowerment of marginalized sectors of society, when successful, entails at least a partial change in political elites and should have an impact on a given country's official political preferences, if there is any real substance to democratic self-determination. Given the highly asymmetric distribution of economic welfare and political power in the contemporary world, such changing preferences (driven by formerly marginalized sectors in relatively disadvantaged countries) will often challenge the economic and political privileges of those 'North-Western' countries that usually engage in democracy promotion. Such deviance from donor preferences might concern not only tangible economic or security interests, but also divergence in terms of the concepts of what democracy and 'good' governance are.[9] In each case, the recipient country, based on its claim for national self-determination, will challenge donor preferences. For democracy promoters, the democratically driven divergence from donor interests – (1) in Table 1 – and universalist donor conceptions of 'good, democratic governance' – (2) in the table – raises the question of whether to tolerate deviance in the name of democratic self-determination or not.

The empowerment and inclusion of marginalized sectors of society requires the redistribution of political power. However, the democratic state (like any state) institutionalizes social power relations; post-transition democracies are regularly built on (institutionalized) pacts and social compromises, and, in general, democracy under conditions of structural social inequalities depends on systematic limits to democratic participation in order to prevent the elites from defecting from the democratic rules of the game.[10] Thus, empowerment in the sense of

Table 1. Conflicts of objectives.

Problem	Conflicting objectives
Self-determination (political deviance *of* recipient country)	(1) Self-determination vs. donor interests (*extrinsic*) (2) Self-determination vs. universalist donor conceptions (*intrinsic*)
Empowerment (political conflict *in* recipient country)	(3) Political empowerment vs. protection of democracy (*intrinsic*) (4) Political empowerment vs. intra-state peace (*extrinsic*)

Source: Own compilation

enhanced participation by marginalized sectors requires levelling the democratic playing field, which may include profound institutional and possibly constitutional change. The attempt to redistribute political power can therefore lead to a dismantling of the democratic institutions that are already in place. At the same time, the empowerment of marginalized sectors, regardless of whether they are accompanied by institutional change, may give rise to radical demands for the redistribution of economic resources and political power. If this is met with resistance from threatened elites (including privileged middle sectors), polarization can lead to an escalation of violent conflicts with the looming threat of civil war. In either case, empowerment in the recipient country clashes with the donors' aim to protect a stable and peaceful constitutional order. Rising tensions between the goal to increase the political participation of marginalized sectors of society, on the one hand, and to protect existing democratic institutions – (3) in Table 1 – and uphold intra-state peace – (4) in the table –, on the other, prompt questions of whether too much political empowerment could eventually threaten democracy.

The conflicts (1) and (2) in Table 1 refer to contradictions between donor and recipient preferences; the conflicts (3) and (4) emerge from contradictory developments within the recipient country that lead to conflicting objectives on the part of the donor. Following the distinction by Spanger and Wolff[11] adopted in the introduction to this special issue, types (2) and (3) refer to intrinsic conflicts of objectives where different sub-goals of democracy promotion clash, while types (1) and (4) concern extrinsic conflicts: here, the aim of democracy promotion clashes with other objectives (donor interests or intra-state peace).

The transformation of democracy in Bolivia

Between 2000 and 2005, Bolivia experienced a series of political crises. Massive social protests forced the resignation of both President Sánchez de Lozada in 2003 and his successor Carlos Mesa in 2005. In the course of these crises, Evo Morales, a union leader, coca grower, and the head of the Movement towards Socialism (MAS), established himself as the leading representative of the diverse protest movements. In December 2005, Morales was elected President of Bolivia by an absolute majority of the vote and became the country's first indigenous head of state. Following his election, Morales initiated a period of profound political change that included the convocation of a Constituent Assembly and the adoption of a new constitution (by referendum in January 2009), as well as a change in economic and social policies exemplified by the 'nationalization' of the hydrocarbon sector – Bolivia's most important export sector – and a series of social programmes. In December 2009, Morales was re-elected with 63% of the vote, and his MAS party won a two-thirds majority in the new parliament. This article examines the period of Morales's first term as president (2005–2009). With regard to democracy promotion, five characteristics of Bolivia's self-proclaimed 'democratic revolution' stand out.

First, the democratic legitimization of the government and the overall process of political change stands in contrast to the series of procedural irregularities and outright breaches of constitutional and administrative law that have occurred during the period between 2005–2009. While impressive electoral victories since 2005 have demonstrated that Morales and his MAS party can rely on solid support from a clear majority of the population, the process of constitutional reform has been accompanied by controversial acts. For example, in a highly disputed procedure, the draft for the new constitution was adopted by the Constituent Assembly by a two-thirds majority of the members of the Assembly *present* at the time of voting, while the most important opposition groups had boycotted the vote. Following nine months of political struggle, a two-thirds majority in Congress agreed to a detailed revision of the constitutional draft; this procedure lacked any legal basis, but was crucial for enabling the constitutional reform to be accepted even by a significant part of the opposition, thus preventing further escalation of the political conflict.[12]

Second, in terms of representation and participation, the quality of Bolivian democracy has improved, but there have been at least temporary declines in institutional controls and in transparent and rule-bound ('good') governance. Both the government and parliament are considerably more representative today than ever before, and political participation (measured by participation in elections, among other factors) has clearly grown. At the same time, the restructuring of political institutions has meant that respect for the established institutional order was low; during the process of constitutional reform, old institutional controls and procedural rules were gradually dismantled before new ones had been established. Disputes between the government and the highest branches of the judiciary escalated, with the latter gradually losing their authority due to a series of resignations that (until 2010) were not followed by new appointments.

Third, the profound restructuring of the political system has generally been in accordance with the usual standards of democracy and human rights, but includes significant deviations from more specific liberal-democratic (donor country) conceptions. The new constitution includes the classical set of political and civil rights, and the new political system is dominated by mechanisms and institutions of representative democracy. However, this basic liberal-democratic order has been amended and modified in non-trivial ways: indigenous (customary) law has been established as a second judicial system of equal status alongside the ordinary legal system; indigenous collective rights now permit self-government in autonomous indigenous territories in accordance with indigenous customs and practices; indigenous minority groups in rural areas elect their delegates to the national parliament through special electoral districts; mechanisms of direct democracy such as recall, referendums, and popular legislative initiatives have been established; the highest branches of the judiciary are now to be elected by popular vote; and 'organized civil society' has gained vaguely defined but potentially far-reaching rights to participate in the design of public policy and to control public administration. Furthermore, social and economic rights now clearly go beyond anything generally found in established liberal democracies, with possibilities for privatization (for example, of public services) constrained and property rights (for example, for land) delimited.[13]

Fourth, changes in economic and social policies promoted by the new government, while in line with a solid majority of the Bolivian population, differ significantly from both US and German conceptions of 'sound' development policies *and* from US and German economic interests. The most important example here is the policy of nationalization, particularly (but not exclusively) in the hydrocarbon sector. In general, international companies have been forced into new contractual relationships, the control by the state (and state companies) of the affected sectors has been strengthened, and fiscal participation (royalties and taxes) has increased. Another example of political deviance from donor interests – that specifically concerns the US – is connected to the policy of coca eradication: the Morales government has shifted from the US-style 'War on Drugs' (that had included the coerced eradication of coca plants) towards a combination of cooperative coca eradication and continuing counter-narcotics efforts against drug trafficking.

Fifth, the political inclusion of anti-systemic social movements contributing to political stabilization and a de-escalation of the conflict between the state and these movements has been accompanied by a political marginalization/alienation of the former political and economic elites, thereby reinforcing regional and ethnic divisions, political polarization and an escalation of this new kind of conflict. Following the toppling of President Sánchez de Lozada in 2003, it had become virtually impossible to govern the country against the will of the 'popular sectors', as represented by the social and indigenous movements. Thus it was expected that Morales's election would lead to political stabilization. Indeed, although social protests led by a diverse spectrum of popular-sector groups continued throughout Morales's first term in office, he initially brought relative stability to the country; however, in the context of the constitutional reform process in particular, serious political disputes and social conflicts resurfaced. The opposition now came from regional autonomy movements in the south-eastern lowland departments (the so-called *media luna*), led by the elected governors of these regional governments and 'civic committees'. In September 2008, protests in the opposition-dominated lowlands peaked; cities, streets, and gas pipelines were blocked, federal institutions were occupied, and violence escalated between oppositional and pro-government groups.

From the very beginning, the 'democratic revolution' initiated by Morales has represented a series of challenges to German and especially to US policies. The rejection of 'neo-liberal' economic policies and the US-driven 'War on Drugs' compromises the development strategies promoted by the US and Germany and directly affects their economic and security interests. In addition, the political transformation promoted by Morales deviates from the model of democratic governance to which the US and Germany adhere. In actual fact, this transformation meant replacing the democratic institutions that were established after the transition to democracy in the 1980s (with active support from both the US and Germany).

In this sense, the first three characteristics of Bolivia's process of political change – which refer to the contradictory nature of the transformation of democracy – lead to intrinsic conflicts of objectives on the part of external democracy promoters: the emphasis on self-determination, including related principles such as alignment and ownership, clashes with the donors' universalist notions of what good democratic governance means (self-determination vs. universalism) as well as with the aim to protect and strengthen existing democratic institutions, good governance standards, and the rule of law (empowerment vs. protection of democracy). The fourth and fifth characteristics – which point to the policy changes and the political polarization that have accompanied Bolivia's 'democratic revolution' – implicate extrinsic conflicts of objectives: here, democracy promotion becomes at odds with specific donor interests and potentially threatens intra-state peace.

US and German reactions to Evo Morales

Before the premature end of Sánchez de Lozada's second presidency in 2003, the US and German interactions with Bolivia were characterized by good bilateral relations. In the case of US foreign policy, close bilateral relations at the time generally included support of democratic governments and, in particular, of elected presidents in times of domestic political crises. US support to Bolivia primarily consisted of diplomatic approval, trade preferences, and financial and technical assistance, all heavily focused on cooperation with the US-driven 'War on Drugs' and involving a high degree of direct political involvement in Bolivian domestic affairs. Germany has been far less exposed and committed in Bolivia, but again, bilateral relations have traditionally been good and for the most part smooth. German support to Bolivia's elected governments has primarily consisted of development assistance; in general, German foreign policy towards Bolivia *is* mainly development policy. With regard to democracy assistance, US and German development aid to Bolivia has encompassed a range of projects explicitly intended to strengthen democratic institutions, processes, and actors (see below). The following analysis examines how the US and Germany reacted to Morales's election and administration and the resulting conflicts of objectives, in terms of both diplomatic relations and democracy assistance.

The United States
Diplomatic relations

Following Morales's election, the US took a wait-and-see approach. The official line was to 'congratulate the people of Bolivia on a successful election', but also to emphasize that 'the behavior of the new government' would determine the course of the bilateral relationship: 'It's important that the new government govern in a democratic way [...].'[14] Even prior to the election, the US government had taken a low-key attitude, a significant difference to the 2002 presidential election, during which then Ambassador Manuel Rocha openly threatened the possible withdrawal of US assistance if the Bolivian people dared to elect Morales. There were no negative repercussions, even when the newly-elected Morales called President George W. Bush a terrorist and appointed a cabinet that was widely perceived as friendly to the indigenous and social movements and critical of neo-liberal economics and the US 'War on Drugs'. The US Embassy in La Paz even signalled its willingness to shift the focus of its policies on coca eradication towards a fight against cocaine and 'surplus' coca only.[15]

Given the history of hostile relations between the US government and Morales, bilateral relations during the first two years of the Morales presidency were remarkably calm. Although both sides made critical statements, their impact on US policies and bilateral relations was fairly limited.[16] For example, in June 2006, the Assistant Administrator of the US Agency for International Development (USAID), Adolfo Franco, stated that the Bolivian government had 'on several occasions, demonstrated inclinations to consolidate executive power and promote potentially anti-democratic reforms through the Constituent Assembly and other means'.[17] In September 2006, President Bush expressed concern 'with the decline in Bolivian counternarcotics cooperation'.[18] The Director of National Intelligence at the time, John Negroponte, in 2007 stated that he viewed democracy as 'most at risk in Venezuela and Bolivia'. 'In both countries, the elected presidents, Chavez and Morales, are taking advantage of their popularity to undercut the opposition and eliminate checks on their authority.'[19] In return, the Bolivian government periodically rejected US 'impositions' and accused the Bush administration of using US assistance to support the opposition and destabilize Bolivia.[20]

In 2008, the situation changed dramatically from rhetorical tension to 'diplomatic breakdown'.[21] In June 2008, the *cocalero* movement and local mayors from Bolivia's largest coca growing region, Chapare, declared they would not sign any further agreements with USAID and de facto expelled USAID from the region, a decision endorsed by the Bolivian government. In September, amid a severe domestic political crisis provoked by the autonomy movements in the south eastern lowlands, Morales declared US Ambassador Philip Goldberg *'persona non grata'*, accusing him of supporting opposition forces. The US government retaliated by expelling Bolivia's ambassador to Washington. A few days later, President Bush declared that Bolivia had 'failed demonstrably' to adhere to its 'obligations under international counternarcotics agreements'. Bush avoided the automatic termination of US aid by declaring the bilateral programmes in Bolivia to be 'vital to the national interests of the United States'.[22] However, 'decertification' meant that Bolivia lost access to US trade preferences in the framework of the Andean Trade Promotion and Drug Eradication Act (ATPDEA). The Bolivian government responded by expelling the Drug Enforcement Administration (DEA) from the country.

In addition, Bolivia lost access to funding from the Millennium Challenge Account (MCA). In 2004, Bolivia had been selected as eligible for the MCA by meeting conditions concerning 'ruling justly', 'investing in people', and 'encouraging economic freedom'. In December 2008, however, the Board of Directors of the Millennium Challenge Corporation (MCC) decided not to reselect Bolivia. Although the country's scores on three governance indicators that are relevant for MCA eligibility had actually declined, comparisons with other MCC beneficiaries and interviews in Washington suggest that this gradual deterioration alone would not have triggered the suspension, had it not been in the context of the crisis in US-Bolivian relations.[23]

In order to rebuild bilateral relations with Bolivia, the incoming Obama administration launched a bilateral dialogue with the Bolivian government. The first meetings were held in May and October 2009. However, Obama refrained from reinstating Bolivia's trade preferences and, in September 2009, again 'decertified' Bolivia. Bolivian authorities responded by continuing to accuse the US of supporting opposition groups. In this context, neither side could agree upon a new framework for bilateral cooperation (in November 2011, however, a new framework agreement was signed).

Development cooperation and democracy assistance

The decline in US foreign aid to Bolivia preceded this deterioration in overall bilateral relations. It originates from Mesa's interim government (2004–2005) and continued throughout Morales's first presidency (2006–2009): the total US foreign assistance per year declined continuously from more than $150 million per year in 2002–2004 to less than $100 million in 2008 and 2009. US assistance remained significant, however, and the request for Fiscal Year (FY) 2010 even sought to increase the flow of aid, signalling an interest to remain engaged, albeit at a lower level than in the early 2000s.[24]

Officially, continued foreign assistance to Bolivia was justified by persistent local needs, especially with regard to narcotics control, poverty reduction, and democracy promotion,[25] but it was also to serve US political interests. Following the election 'of a government that campaigned on promises that included decriminalizing coca and nationalizing private property', the US felt the need to demonstrate 'flexibility to protect our core interests'; flexibility here meant trying 'to engage with the new government (as circumstances allow)', but also with 'the military and, particularly, the regional governments'.[26] Indeed, the new programme Strengthening of Democratic Institutions (*Fortalecimiento de Instituciones Democráticas*, or FIDEM) prioritized the departments, that is, the regional governments. This change was a direct reaction to the first elections of departmental governors in December 2005. While Morales and his MAS party obtained majorities at the national level in these elections, opposition candidates won in six of the nine departments. As a result, when FIDEM was launched in October 2006, USAID directly supported Morales's strongest opponents.

An additional instrument in the US' response was the USAID Office of Transition Initiatives (OTI). In reaction to the political crisis surrounding Sánchez de Lozada's resignation, OTI launched a programme in March 2004 'to help reduce tensions in areas prone to social conflict and to assist the country in preparing for key electoral events'. After the December 2005 elections, OTI re-targeted its programme towards 'building the capacity of prefect-led departmental governments'. Between March 2006 and June 2007, OTI approved more than 100 grants for a total of $4.5 million, which included technical support and training for prefecture staff 'to help departmental governments operate more strategically'.[27]

Reflecting this new focus, the outline of US foreign assistance for FY 2008 did not even mention the Bolivian central government as a partner. Continued US cooperation with the national government notwithstanding,[28] the document stated that 'partnerships will be developed with regional and local governments and non-governmental organizations (NGO), the private sector, and other non-executive branch entities to prevent further erosion of democracy, combat cocaine production and trafficking, improve healthcare, and increase educational opportunities'. Funding for democracy and governance assistance was to 'be used to strengthen the Congress as well as state and local governments, encourage moderate national leaders, support legislation that complies with international standards to combat corruption and money laundering, and expand public diplomacy to emphasize the positive correlation between democracy and development'. Assistance was also provided 'to support an active, credible civil society [...] and to strengthen political parties'.[29] In addition, the National Endowment for Democracy (NED) more than doubled its grants for activities in Bolivia from about $560,000 in 2007 to over $1.3 million per year since 2009, reinforcing the US shift toward the support of civil society.[30]

The emphasis on departmental governments – the bastion of the opposition – and 'civil society' aligned perfectly with a strategy explicitly outlined by USAID: to focus assistance on 'the support of counterweights to one-party control such as judicial and media independence, a strong civil society, and educated local and state level leaders'.[31] Given the highly sensitive Bolivian government (which had on several occasions denounced US support to the opposition), this decidedly political mission was framed and implemented 'in an apolitical, balanced manner'. As a result, support for regional and local authorities included assistance for jurisdictions led by representatives from both the opposition and the ruling party. US-funded programmes supporting political parties have been limited since late FY 2007 to 'multi-party training events so as to ensure a clear public perception of apolitical "balance"', putting on hold '[o]ne-on-one political party trainings and consultations, which were a key part of a political party strengthening program'.[32]

This last move has especially affected the local offices of the International Republican Institute (IRI) and the National Democratic Institute (NDI). Up until September 2007, IRI trained candidates for the Constituent Assembly and NDI organized debates between candidates from across the political spectrum. From October 2007 to July 2008, IRI and NDI supported political parties (including the governing MAS party), citizen groups, and indigenous peoples via multi-party activities such as events and workshops. Even before USAID decided to limit party support to multi-party activities (and before Morales's election), the US political party institutes had included MAS in their activities.[33] However, originally USAID's programme to strengthen political parties was explicitly intended to 'dovetail' with the (then-governing party) Movimiento Nacionalista Revolucionario (MNR) and to 'help build moderate, pro-democracy political parties that can serve as a counter-weight to the radical MAS'.[34]

The Congressional Budget Justification (CBJ) for FY 2010 signalled important adaptations to official Bolivian preferences. It reintroduced references to 'Bolivian government counterparts' and requested a significant increase in funding to support Integrated Justice Centres, a programme implemented in direct cooperation with the Bolivian Ministry of Justice. Most notably, a new 'priority program' to strengthen the performance of municipalities across Bolivia was announced.[35] This reflected a crucial adjustment to the US democracy assistance portfolio. USAID had supported local governments in Bolivia since 1996, but from 2006 onwards, the new programme FIDEM had prioritized the departmental level over the municipal level. However, US support for the departments was met with fierce criticism from the Bolivian government, culminating in the expulsion of the US Ambassador. With the phase-out of FIDEM in 2009, the US ended support for departmental governments and focused again on the municipal level, in line with the demands by the Bolivian government. This decision predates Obama's election, so this change cannot be explained by the new president's revised foreign policy approach. The desire to adjust US democracy promotion activities to better match official Bolivian preferences indicates a decision to adapt to a government that was likely to remain in power for some time, and signalled an interest by the US to remain engaged.[36]

Before a new USAID democracy programme could be launched, however, a new bilateral agreement was needed, which the two governments (until late 2011) were unable to successfully negotiate. In August 2009, the Bolivian government instructed USAID to halt its democracy promotion activities, but signalled its willingness to accept US support for municipal governments. Accordingly, in 2009, USAID terminated its democracy and governance programmes, 'with the exception of some municipal strengthening activities'.[37] NDI also halted its Bolivian programme in 2009, after the Bolivian authorities rejected its application for registration. Like NDI, IRI also lost USAID funding, but continued to support good governance at the municipal level through a NED grant.

Germany

Diplomatic relations

Bilateral relations between Germany and Bolivia, focused primarily on development assistance, have been far less affected by the election of Morales than US-Bolivian relations. Indeed, official German reactions to Morales's victory were decidedly positive. In February 2006, the Federal Minister for Economic Cooperation and Development, Wieczorek-Zeul, promised to continue supporting

Bolivia.[38] Two months later, she travelled to La Paz to 'signal that the Federal Republic [of Germany] is a reliable partner for Bolivia and that we support the new government's efforts especially regarding poverty reduction, nature conservation and the strengthening of the rights of the indigenous population'.[39] The German Foreign Office was reportedly not as enthusiastic as the Development Ministry, but did not take a public position. Nonetheless, the German Embassy in La Paz was fairly sympathetic to the new government, and officially Germany's position combined hope for political change with an offer to support it.[40]

On the issue of drug policy, Germany had traditionally been sceptical of coerced coca eradication, favouring a more cooperative stance. As a result, the German government was much less alarmed by the changes in this policy field, announced by the new Bolivian government, than the US was. It was primarily the nationalization of gas that was met with German scepticism. In fact, this was the only topic that provoked a public statement on Bolivia by the German Foreign Minister: In an interview, Frank-Walter Steinmeier expressed his 'great scepticism' about the decision 'to nationalize the Bolivian oil and gas industry'.[41] However, Wieczorek-Zeul directly responded to Steinmeier, stating that every country should 'have the sovereignty to decide how to organize its natural resources'. She argued that it would be 'wrong and counterproductive' to threaten Bolivia with a suspension of development cooperation over 'business disputes about the status of energy companies'.[42]

With regard to the one German company (Oiltanking) affected by the nationalization, the German Embassy continuously engaged the Bolivian government to reach a negotiated solution, and Chancellor Angela Merkel reportedly dedicated a good part of her conversation with Morales at the EU-Latin America/Caribbean Summit in Lima in May 2008 to this subject. The German government also suspended a climate change and energy project as a direct sanction, but in general this dispute had no discernible wider implications for bilateral relations.[43]

Development cooperation and democracy assistance

German development aid to Bolivia has been largely characterized by continuity. With Morales barely six months into his first term, the two governments agreed to continue German development cooperation in the three established priority areas, 'water supply/sanitation', 'sustainable agriculture', and 'modernization of state and democracy'. However, this continuity has been accompanied by some flexibility from Germany in response to the priorities set by the new Bolivian government. For example, in the area of democracy assistance, Berlin promised support to the Constituent Assembly.

In a new country strategy adopted in June 2007, Germany's Ministry for Economic Cooperation and Development stated that the Bolivian government's 'new orientation of economic and societal policies' and, in particular, its aim to include the marginalized indigenous majority offered 'new chances for development cooperation'. Although the document mentioned the risks of 'radicalizing political polarization' and raised 'doubts' regarding the consistent commitment to 'democratic rules' within the 'very heterogeneous MAS movement', the core problems highlighted were structural 'deficits', including socio-economic inequality, poverty, weak institutional and administrative capacities, corruption, and a 'deficient culture of conflict resolution'. All of these were problems the Morales government had inherited and thus required support to address.[44]

As mentioned above, democracy assistance continued to be among the priority areas of German development cooperation with Bolivia. The data on German Official Development Assistance (ODA) confirms this continuity in both the general amount of aid and the absolute size and relative weight of democracy assistance. Indeed, since 2006, Germany has, during intergovernmental negotiations, agreed to increase development assistance to Bolivia. In 2007, the German government promised a total of €52 million for the two years 2007 and 2008, and in 2009 it agreed to give €62 million for 2009 and 2010. In general, aid in the OECD category of 'Government & Civil Society' accounted for between one-fifth and one-third of German ODA to Bolivia. In 2008, new German ODA commitments to Bolivia went mainly (60.7%) to the subsector 'government administration', with 'legal and judicial development' and 'strengthening civil society' each accounting for 16.7%.[45]

The most important German aid programme in this area was 'Decentralized Governance and Poverty Reduction Support' (*Programa de Apoyo a la Gestión Pública Descentralizada y Lucha contra la Pobreza*, or PADEP). This programme was administered by the Deutsche Gesellschaft für Technische Zusammenarbeit (GTZ), the organization that implemented the bulk of official German technical assistance (until 2011, when it was merged into the newly-formed Deutsche Gesellschaft für Internationale Zusammenarbeit, or GIZ). PADEP began in 2002 with a thematic focus on poverty reduction, decentralization, and municipal development, and a regional focus on two particularly poor regions (Norte de Potosí and Chaco). The programme was subdivided into different (three to six) components that changed frequently. PADEP's first phase ended in 2005, so that the initiation of the second phase (2006–2009) coincided with the change in the Bolivian government. A third and final phase (2010–2011) started in 2010.

The adjustments made to PADEP clearly reflect an adaptation to new Bolivian priorities and to the new political setting in general: cooperation at the national level grew in relevance (relative to subnational entities), with much greater focus on structural political reforms than had been originally anticipated. Most notably, a new component was added to support the Constituent Assembly, the most important political initiative Morales promoted after taking office. This component supported the Bolivian government's coordinating agency representing the presidency (REPAC) that was established in March 2006 to organize the assembly and gave direct assistance to the assembly itself, including its directorate, technical unit, and commissions.[46] After the end of the Constituent Assembly, PADEP shifted its focus to support the constitutional transition process, the implementation of the new constitution, and the new parliament (the *Asamblea Legislativa*

Plurinacional). With regards to PADEP's decentralization component, the GTZ worked closely with the Bolivian Ministry of Autonomies to support the new process of creating autonomous governments at the subnational level. In addition, at the request of the Bolivian government, support for the national planning system was (temporarily) upgraded to an independent component of PADEP.[47]

Another adjustment in the German development cooperation concerns an enhanced emphasis on crisis prevention and conflict resolution.[48] One component of PADEP focused on 'Constructive Conflict Resolution and Culture of Peace', and since 2007, German aid has implemented instruments including 'Peace and Conflict Assessments' and 'Do No Harm'. Germany also planned to introduce a common procedure for all German development programmes and projects to identify and eventually avoid conflict-aggravating effects. The sensitivity in democracy promotion activities to potential political and conflict-enhancing ramifications of supposedly 'technical' cooperation seems to have grown. Consequently, PADEP's work with political institutions – national and subnational governments, Parliament, the Constituent Assembly – has at least in part shifted from offers of technical advice to efforts at promoting dialogue.[49]

A significant example of the latter is the unofficial role that German development cooperation has played in facilitating negotiations between the central government and regional opposition, which ultimately led to a congressional agreement on constitutional reform. Furthermore, in 2009, GTZ started a new programme (*Programa de Fortalecimiento a la Concertación y al Estado de Derecho*, or CONCED) funded by the German foreign ministry to support dialogue processes and improve the rule of law in the implementation of the new constitution. An additional project (*Proyecto de Apoyo al Desarrollo de un Ordenamiento Jurídico Intercultural en el Marco de un Estado de Derecho Democrático*, or PROJURIDE), funded by the Development Ministry, assists Bolivia's Ministry of Justice in establishing a new 'intercultural legal system' in which indigenous jurisdiction is to be given the same weight as formal law, as envisioned by the new constitution.

German democracy assistance as implemented by GTZ is largely aimed at the Bolivian government at various state levels and, in general, GTZ is eager to maintain 'an image of neutrality'.[50] In contrast, Germany's political foundations take explicit political stances. The Social-Democratic Friedrich Ebert Stiftung (FES), for example, has developed a relationship with the governing MAS party. This was not easy, given the foundation's previous engagement with former governments and Bolivia's 'traditional' parties. It also represented a clear departure from Germany's prior position, reportedly taken by the foreign ministry, to not cooperate with those opposition forces represented by Morales and the MAS, although it did directly follow the German government's decision to engage the Morales government. However, FES's approach has not involved explicit political support for the MAS party.[51] On the other side of the political spectrum, the Hanns Seidel Stiftung (HSS), which has close connections to Germany's Christian Social Union, has openly supported the main opposition party PODEMOS (through the Bolivian political foundation FUNDEMOS). Meanwhile, the Christian-Democratic Konrad Adenauer Stiftung (KAS), although very critical of Morales in public statements, has implemented relatively neutral activities.[52] From these different angles, all three German foundations present in Bolivia have contributed to the process of constitutional reforms. In fact, FES played an important role in preparing the groundwork for the congressional agreement on the draft constitution in October 2008.[53]

Notwithstanding the general support for Morales, German officials, like their US counterparts, have been concerned about what they see as deviance from standards of liberal democracy and the rule of law, although they almost always mention this only in private (for example, in interviews). Under certain circumstances, however, German aid activities have been suspended. When irregularities and conflicts in the Constituent Assembly peaked in December 2006 and again during the Assembly's final months in 2007, German support for the process was suspended (as part of a common European decision). As a reaction to the Assembly's controversial conclusion, Germany stepped back from its original plan to support the public dissemination of the draft constitution. Similarly, in 2008 when the opposition departments adopted their 'autonomy statutes' in referenda lacking any legal basis, GTZ/PADEP temporarily abstained from new cooperation initiatives with the departments, and made support to them dependent on approval from the Bolivian government, and limited support to areas that would not contribute to the process of regional autonomy. Interviews conducted with German organizations in Bolivia confirm that these German reactions were rooted in a conflict-related aim to 'do no harm'. Considerations of empirical legitimacy or factual approval – not formal legality or democratic correctness – led Germany to suspend or reconsider its cooperation.

Dealing with conflicting objectives: a comparative analysis

The four general conflicts of objectives identified at the beginning of this article were clearly relevant for both US and German democracy promotion policies towards Bolivia. Unsurprisingly, the varying characteristics of the two 'donors' meant that different conflicts came to the fore in different shapes and were addressed in different ways.

Self-determination vs. donor interests: For the US, the political deviance of the Bolivian government was particularly relevant in connection to specific US interests in the 'War on Drugs'. Officially, the US government reacted in line with democracy promotion by respecting self-determination and ownership. In fact, the US continued (and, as far as the Bolivian government allows, still continues) to cooperate in Bolivian counter-narcotics efforts. However, the US made it clear from the outset that certain issues were non-negotiable because they were considered to be vital to US security interests. The certification process and the actual 'de-certification' of Bolivia is the clearest sign of such explicit limits to the principle of self-determination. The US government clearly prioritized counter-narcotics-related interests over the respect for self-determination.

With regard to the change in economic policies, both the US and Germany proved rather flexible and pragmatic, perhaps because it was obvious that the administration in Bolivia enjoyed such broad support that a general attitude of objection would have no effect, or perhaps because no major economic interests were involved. The rather intense efforts by the German Embassy and even the Chancellor to secure the interests of the one German company affected by nationalization (including the decision to suspend a minor development cooperation project) suggest a prioritization of economic interests. The German reaction to Morales's claim to self-determination probably would have been much less benign and tolerant had there been significant danger to German economic interests.

Self-determination vs. universalist donor conceptions: With regard to the self-determined and democratically legitimized deviance from (and, in part, open breach of) mainstream standards of liberal democracy and good governance, both the US and Germany officially reacted with an attitude of respect for alternative paths and models. Both governments continued their development cooperation with Bolivia, and although there were some changes in US priorities (away from central government support), the US maintained a rather cooperative posture. In fact, USAID proved willing to make significant concessions in order to adapt to official Bolivian preferences, that is, to accept a self-determined path of political development even when this implied a partial deviation from the US conception of liberal (market) democracy. Germany even provided direct support to the political changes driven by the Morales government, including the Constituent Assembly.[54]

This partial deviance from what was perceived by both German and US representatives as universal standards, however, was still seen as problematic. Alignment with Bolivian decisions therefore represented a pragmatic and, in fact, reluctant adjustment, rather than a sign of principled respect for self-determination. This adjustment was driven by the recognition of broad majority support in Bolivia, the hope to have some moderating influence on the Bolivian government, and the strong desire to remain somehow engaged in Bolivia (stemming either from the self-interest of the various development agencies to continue their work or from the general political assessment that a withdrawal from the country would be the worst option). In this sense, the donors' reactions can be interpreted as attempts to balance the recognition of self-determination with the aim to minimize deviance from universally conceived standards. A degree of adaption to official Bolivian demands was the dominant strategy in this regard, even on the part of US foreign assistance. Negative reactions by the US were arguably driven not by considerations related to intrinsic conflicts of objectives but by (extrinsic) disagreements in the area of counter-narcotics and by what was seen as provocation by the Bolivian government.

Empowerment vs. protection of democracy: Regarding the tension between the deepening of democracy (in terms of political empowerment) and its protection (in terms of the stability of existing democratic institutions), the unambiguous majority support for and the democratic legitimization of every major step in Bolivia's political transformation have proved to be crucial factors. These made it almost impossible for external actors emphasizing the importance of democracy to openly reject the political changes promoted by the Bolivian government. As a result, the US remained more or less neutral, with some explicit assistance to the government, some open help for political and societal counterweights, and some dubious support for the departmental opposition. Germany openly supported the dismantling of existing democratic institutions in favour of 're-founding' Bolivian democracy. However, in cases where the breach of the democratic/constitutional rules of the game were perceived as overly dramatic, the German government decided to suspend its cooperation, but only temporarily and only in connection to specific projects. Even in these cases, the German decisions to suspend, end, or resume cooperation were driven more by concerns related to conflict resolution and intra-state peace than by an adherence to the established institutional order.

Political empowerment vs. intra-state peace: This final observation relates to the fourth conflict of objectives where democracy promotion and the aim to uphold intra-state peace collide. Germany de facto prioritized conflict prevention and thus intra-state peace. This is not to say that Germany tried to limit political empowerment; however, its main aim was not to promote the strengthening of formerly marginalized social groups and actors, but rather to secure inclusive processes of dialogue and consensus-building. In this regard, Germany favoured constraining the emancipatory project of the MAS in order to include the (former) elites and middle sectors as much as possible. The idea behind this strategy was that the empowerment of the indigenous and poor majority was real and ongoing, but that intra-state peace was what was truly at risk.

The US was not in a position to meaningfully contribute to intra-Bolivian dialogue; in fact, at least some US policies in Bolivia only increased polarization, since the US government was seen as a party to the internal conflict. However, in terms of official statements, the US, even if it generally welcomed the growing political inclusion of the indigenous and the poor, aimed more at limiting the powers of the newly empowered by supporting counterweights to the central government in political parties, civil society, and at the subnational level of the state. In general, it seems that neither empowerment nor peace have been priorities of the US government since the election of Morales.

Conclusion

The case of Bolivia suggests that the *problematique* of conflicting objectives is not limited to difficult cases of coerced regime change, the democratization of authoritarian regimes, or the implementation of democracy in post-conflict societies; rather, it is also an issue democracy promoters must deal with in the relatively benign context of post-transition countries. In particular, four conflicts of objectives associated with self-determination and empowerment in post-transition countries were shown to be relevant: the aim to promote self-determination may clash with donor interests or universalist donor conceptions, and the support for empowerment can collide with donor objectives related to the protection of democracy and intra-state peace. However, the recent and ongoing transformation of Bolivian democracy is a unique case, and broader comparative work is therefore required in order to systematically identify the types of conflicting objectives, the conditions that give rise to their emergence, the ways in which various democracy promoters react, and the effects this can have on democracy in recipient countries.

With these caveats in mind, the analysis shows that conflicts of objectives in democracy promotion cannot be reduced to the well-known tension between norms and interests. The question of whether external democracy promoters prioritize their particular (economic or security) interests or whether they are really willing to promote democracy is surely important, but it is only one question among a series of difficult issues. Conflicting objectives affect the very business of 'genuine' democracy promotion as well: the principles, norms, conceptions, and strategies that guide the whole endeavour. A general consequence is that critical and decidedly normative reflections on the normative premises and conceptual guidelines of democracy promotion are needed. This includes reconsideration of the basic assumptions regarding political development that underlie current democracy promotion policies. In the aftermath of recent experiences with forced regime change in countries including Iraq and Afghanistan, such reconsideration has begun. However, as this article has shown, there are more general problems of democracy promotion that can also affect supposedly easier cases.

Acknowledgments

This article presents selected results of the research project 'Determinants of Democratic States' Handling of Conflicting Objectives in Democracy Promotion' conducted by the Peace Research Institute Frankfurt (PRIF) and Goethe University Frankfurt and supported by the German Research Foundation (DFG). Previous versions were presented at the 2010 Convention of the International Studies Association, at the 2010 Conference of the ECPR Standing Group on International Relations, and in the Carnegie Papers series (Wolff, 'Challenges to Democracy Promotion'). The author thanks Hans Agné, Thomas Carothers, Arthur Goldsmith, Diane de Gramont, Annika Poppe, Laurence Whitehead, Richard Youngs, the members of the German Research Network 'External Democratization Policies', the editors of this special issue, and two anonymous reviewers for comments. All translations into English are those of the author.

Notes

1. Huntington, *Political Order*; Snyder, *From Voting to Violence*; Chua, *World on Fire*.
2. Cf. Burnell and Youngs, *New Challenges*; Goldsmith, 'Making the World Safe'; Smith, *A Pact with the Devil*.
3. See the general debate on conflicting objectives in democracy promotion in the introduction to this special issue (Grimm and Leininger, 'Not All Good Things Go Together').
4. Cf. Diamond, *The Spirit*; McFaul, *Advancing Democracy*; but see also Hobson and Kurki, *The Conceptual Politics*.
5. Grimm and Leininger, 'Not All Good Things Go Together'.
6. Cf. Mayorga, 'Bolivia's Silent Revolution'.

7. Interviews were conducted in April/May 2009 (Bolivia), in May 2010 (Washington, DC), and between 2008 and 2011 (Germany).
8. There are, of course, many different definitions of both democracy and democratization. However, it is generally accepted that democracy connotes a political regime that is meant to somehow realize the self-determination or sovereignty of the people. In the same basic way, democratization describes processes that entail political empowerment of the people, whether in terms of formal empowerment (for example, institutionalizing equal political rights) or in a more substantial sense (for example, increasing capabilities to exercise equal political rights). Cf. Coppedge and Gerring, 'Conceptualizing', 248, 253; Rueschemeyer, Huber Stephens, and Stephens, *Capitalist Development*, 10–11.
9. On diverging conceptions of democracy, cf. Coppedge and Gerring, 'Conceptualizing'. On the relevance of democracy's 'conceptual contestability' for democracy promotion, see Kurki, 'Democracy'.
10. Cf. O'Donnell and Schmitter, *Transitions*; Rueschemeyer, Huber Stephens, and Stephens, *Capitalist Development*.
11. Cf. Spanger and Wolff, 'Universales Ziel', 267.
12. Cf. Romero, Böhrt, and Peñaranda, *Del conflicto al diálogo*. While the Constituent Assembly had been specifically elected to draft a new constitution, Congress – the regular national parliament – had no formal authority to revise the constitutional draft. Under the new constitution, the national parliament is no longer called Congress but 'Plurinational Legislative Assembly'.
13. Cf. Wolff, 'New Constitutions'.
14. White House, 'Press Briefing'.
15. Cf. Wolff, 'Challenges', 8.
16. Cf. Gratius and Legler, 'Latin America', 207. However, apart from the official rhetoric and general diplomacy, US government actions were not always fully cooperative. Cf. Wolff, 'Challenges', 28.
17. Franco, 'Statement', 19.
18. White House, 'Presidential Determination [2006]'.
19. Negroponte, 'Annual Threat Assessment [2007]', 9.
20. Cf. La-Razon.com, September 13, 2006; August 31, 2007.
21. Gray, 'The United States', 171–6.
22. White House, 'President Bush'.
23. Cf. Wolff, 'Challenges', 10.
24. For comprehensive data on German development assistance, see Wolff, 'Challenges', 10–14.
25. US Department of State, CBJ 2009, 659; CBJ 2008, 603; CBJ 2007, 538.
26. US Department of State, CBJ 2007, 538.
27. USAID, 'USAID/OTI'.
28. Indeed, such cooperation went beyond assistance in counter-narcotics and socio-economic issues and included democracy assistance. For example, support for the Integrated Justice Centres (IJCs) was continued in close cooperation with the Bolivian Ministry of Justice. The US was apparently favourably disposed towards prolongation of this programme (see below).
29. US Department of State, CBJ 2008, 603–4.
30. Wolff, 'Challenges', 14.
31. Franco, 'Statement', 19.
32. US Department of State, 'Bolivia 2007', 13.
33. Cf. Wolff, 'Challenges', 14.
34. US Embassy La Paz, 'Scenesetter'.
35. US Department of State, CBJ 2010, 573, 575, 576.

36. For example, the programme designed to strengthen municipalities is mentioned in a USAID document from February 2008 (quoted in Wolff, 'Challenges', 31). This document identifies potential new activities for different budget scenarios and demonstrates USAID's willingness to adjust democracy promotion activities, at least in part, to official Bolivian preferences.
37. US Department of State, CBJ 2011, 658.
38. BMZ, 'Wieczorek-Zeul'.
39. BMZ, 'Bundesministerin'.
40. Bundesregierung, 'Verhandlungen', 9–10; BMZ, *Länderkonzept*.
41. *Die Welt*, May 12, 2006, 5.
42. *Der Spiegel*, May 8, 2006, 19.
43. Cf. Wolff, 'Challenges', 18.
44. BMZ, *Länderkonzept*, 1, 8, 3.
45. For comprehensive data on German development assistance, see Wolff, 'Challenges', 19–22.
46. Cf. GTZ, *Asesoramiento*. PADEP's initial decision to support the preparation of a Constituent Assembly was taken at the end of 2003, and GTZ (together with the German political foundations) contributed to the preparatory process during Mesa's interim government.
47. Cf. Wolff, 'Challenges', 22.
48. This emphasis was only partially a reaction to the new government; it was more generally a response to the conflict escalation since 2000. It also was part of a global trend in German development cooperation.
49. Cf. GTZ, *Asesoramiento*; Wolff, 'Challenges', 23.
50. GTZ, *Asesoramiento*, 50.
51. FES reportedly even supported an initiative to build a new oppositional social democratic party.
52. KAS has been hesitant to engage with the new regional opposition; for example, it has backed away from supporting the Santa Cruz-based political organization *Autonomía para Bolivia*.
53. Between the end of the Constituent Assembly and the negotiations in Congress, FES supported a dialogue between individual representatives of the government and the parliamentary opposition. Cf. Romero, Böhrt, and Peñaranda, *Del conflict al diálogo*.
54. In terms of political ideology, the German government was not as distant from Morales as the Bush administration was. Germany was then governed by a coalition between the conservative Christian Democrats (CDU/CSU) and the centre-left Social Democrats (SPD), and it was the latter party that controlled both the Foreign Office and the Development Ministry (Development Minister Wieczorek-Zeul belonged to the left wing of the SPD).

Notes on contributor

Jonas Wolff is senior research fellow at the Peace Research Institute Frankfurt (PRIF), Germany, and Chairman of PRIF's Research Council. His current research focuses on Latin American politics and international democracy promotion.

Bibliography

BMZ (Bundesministerium für wirtschaftliche Zusammenarbeit und Entwicklung). 'Bundesministerin Wieczorek-Zeul trifft bolivianischen Staatspräsidenten Morales'. Press Release, April 22, 2006. http://www.bmz.de (accessed March 31, 2008).

BMZ. *Länderkonzept Bolivien*. Bonn: BMZ, 2007.
BMZ. 'Wieczorek-Zeul sagt Bolivien weitere Unterstützung zu'. Press Release, February 27, 2006. http://www.bmz.de (accessed March 27, 2008).
Bundesregierung. 'Verhandlungen über die zukünftige Entwicklungszusammenarbeit mit der neuen bolivianischen Regierung. Antwort der Bundesregierung'. Berlin: Bundestag (Drucksache 16/1047), March 24, 2006.
Burnell, Peter, and Richard Youngs, eds. *New Challenges to Democratization*. London: Routledge, 2010.
Chua, Amy. *World on Fire: How Exporting Free Market Democracy Breeds Ethnic Hatred and Global Instability*. New York: Doubleday, 2003.
Coppedge, Michael, and John Gerring. 'Conceptualizing and Measuring Democracy: A New Approach'. *Perspectives on Politics* 9, no. 2 (2011): 247–67.
Diamond, Larry. *The Spirit of Democracy: The Struggle to Build Free Societies Throughout the World*. New York: Times Books, 2008.
Franco, Adolfo. 'Statement of the Honorable Adolfo Franco, Assistant Administrator, Bureau for Latin America and the Caribbean, U.S. Agency for International Development'. In *Democracy in Latin America: Successes, Challenges and the Future*, Hearing before the House Committee on International Relations, 14–21. Washington, DC: GPO, 2006.
Goldsmith, Arthur A. 'Making the World Safe for Partial Democracy? Questioning the Premises of Democracy Promotion'. *International Security* 33, no. 2 (2008): 120–47.
Gratius, Susanne, and Thomas Legler. 'Latin America Is Different: Transatlantic Discord on How to Promote Democracy in "Problematic" Countries'. In *Promoting Democracy and the Rule of Law. American and European Strategies*, ed. Amichai Magen, Thomas Risse, and Michael A. McFaul, 185–215. Houndmills: Palgrave Macmillan, 2009.
Gray Molina, George. 'The United States and Bolivia: Test Case for Change'. In *The Obama Administration and the Americas: Agenda for Change*, ed. Abraham F. Lowenthal, Theodore J. Piccone, and Laurence Whitehead, 167–82. Washington, DC: Brookings Institution Press, 2009.
Grimm, Sonja, and Julia Leininger. 'Not All Good Things Go Together: Conflicting Objectives in Democracy Promotion'. *Democratization* 19, no. 3 (2012): 391–414.
GTZ (Deutsche Gesellschaft für Technische Zusammenarbeit). *Asesoramiento en contextos altamente políticos. Experiencia del PADEP/GTZ en el proceso Constituyente en Bolivia*. La Paz: GTZ, 2008.
Hobson, Christopher, and Milja Kurki, eds. *The Conceptual Politics of Democracy Promotion*. London: Routledge, 2012.
Huntington, Samuel P. *Political Order in Changing Societies*. New Haven, CT: Yale University Press, 1970.
Kurki, Milja. 'Democracy and Conceptual Contestability: Reconsidering Conceptions of Democracy in Democracy Promotion'. *International Studies Review* 12, no. 3 (2010): 362–86.
Mayorga, René Antonio. 'Bolivia's Silent Revolution'. *Journal of Democracy* 8, no. 1 (1997): 142–56.
McFaul, Michael. *Advancing Democracy Abroad: Why We Should and How We Can*. Lanham: Rowman & Littlefield, 2010.
Negroponte, John D. 'Annual Threat Assessment of the Director of National Intelligence', January 11, 2007. http://www.dni.gov (accessed November 16, 2009).
O'Donnell, Guillermo, and Philippe C. Schmitter. *Transitions from Authoritarian Rule: Tentative Conclusions about Uncertain Democracies*. Baltimore, MD: The Johns Hopkins University Press, 1986.
Romero, Carlos, Carlos Böhrt, and Raúl Peñaranda. *Del conflicto al diálogo: Memorias del acuerdo constitucional*. La Paz: fBDM, FES-ILDIS, 2009.

Rueschemeyer, Dietrich, Evelyne Huber Stephens, and John D. Stephens. *Capitalist Development and Democracy*. Cambridge: Polity Press, 1992.

Smith, Tony. *A Pact with the Devil: Washington's Bid for World Supremacy and the Betrayal of the American Promise*. New York: Routledge, 2007.

Snyder, Jack. *From Voting to Violence: Democratization and Nationalist Conflict*. New York: WW Norton, 2000.

Spanger, Hans-Joachim, and Jonas Wolff. 'Universales Ziel – partikulare Wege? Externe Demokratieförderung zwischen einheitlicher Rhetorik und vielfältiger Praxis'. In *Schattenseiten des Demokratischen Friedens*, ed. Anna Geis, Harald Müller, and Wolfgang Wagner, 261–84. Frankfurt: Campus, 2007.

USAID. 'USAID/OTI Bolivia Field Report Apr–June 2007'. http://www.usaid.gov (accessed January 8, 2009).

US Department of State. 'Bolivia 2007 Performance Report', 2007. http://pdf.usaid.gov/pdf_docs/PDACL057.pdf (accessed January 8, 2009).

US Department of State. *Congressional Budget Justification: Foreign Operations*. Washington, DC: US Department of State, various Fiscal Years (CBJ for FY 2009 is quoted as CBJ 2009, etc.).

US Embassy La Paz. 'Scenesetter: Bolivia's August 6 Transition, the Challenges Ahead, and the U.S. Role', 2002 (Unclassified Document No. 2002LAPAZ02723). http://www.jeremybigwood.net (accessed January 6, 2010).

White House. 'President Bush Signs H.R. 7222, the Andean Trade Preference Act Extension', 2008. http://georgewbush-whitehouse.archives.gov (accessed November 17, 2009).

White House. 'Presidential Determination on Major Drug Transit or Major Illicit Drug Producing Countries for Fiscal Year 2007', 2006. http://georgewbush-whitehouse.archives.gov (accessed November 17, 2009).

White House. 'Press Briefing by Scott McClellan', December 20, 2005. http://georgewbush-whitehouse.archives.gov (accessed November 17, 2009).

Wolff, Jonas. 'Challenges to Democracy Promotion: The Case of Bolivia'. Carnegie Paper. Washington DC: Carnegie Endowment for International Peace, 2011.

Wolff, Jonas. 'New Constitutions and the Transformation of Democracy in Ecuador and Bolivia'. In *New Constitutionalism in Latin America: Promises and Practices*, ed. Detlef Nolte and Almut Schilling-Vacaflor. Aldershot: Ashgate, forthcoming.

Financing poverty alleviation vs. promoting democracy? Multi-Donor Budget Support in Zambia

Jörg Faust[a], Stefan Leiderer[a] and Johannes Schmitt[b]

[a]*Deutsches Institut für Entwicklungspolitik/German Development Institute, Bonn, Germany;* [b]*Institute of Political Science, University of Duisburg-Essen, Duisburg, Germany*

Many approaches to supporting democracy in developing countries have been affected by recent international reforms geared towards improving aid effectiveness through better harmonizing interventions and greater alignment to recipient countries' strategies. The paradigmatic instrument for these attempts has been direct budget support, whereby donors attempt not only to promote poverty reduction but also to achieve the institutional modernization conducive to public sector reforms and democratic accountability. However, based on empirical evidence from a recent evaluation of budget support in Zambia, this article argues that attempts at harmonization among donors can be easily hampered by varying interpretations of the goal hierarchy of budget support. In the course of the Multi-Donor Budget Support process in Zambia, some donors have prioritized the financing function of the instrument, while others have emphasized its potential influence on institutional reforms. While some harmonization efforts proved successful at fostering a number of public-sector reforms, the remaining harmonization deficiencies hampered the realization of the instrument's full potential to craft a coherent incentive system for facilitating improvements in democratic accountability.

Introduction[1]

The success of external democracy promotion with non-military means depends on the receptiveness of the recipient country's political system. Success also hinges on the coherence of the incentive system created by external actors for the relevant actors in the recipient country. A coherent and well-communicated incentive system generates consistent signals to the recipient country's political actors, clearly indicating which actions provoke positive or negative sanctions and thus enhances the leverage of external actors' measures to support democratic participation and accountability.[2]

Against this background, our primary research question focuses on the emergence of goal conflicts in the process of harmonizing aid interventions, which potentially are supportive for democratization. More concretely, we identify how competing objectives can influence the harmonization attempts of foreign aid donors in their attempts to provide Multi-Donor Budget Support (MDBS), a paradigmatic aid intervention intended not only to finance poverty reduction but also to promote democratic accountability. We illustrate these challenges by drawing on evidence from a recent evaluation of MDBS in Zambia – a developing country with a high (albeit decreasing) level of aid dependence, whose electoral democracy is confronted with a weak administrative apparatus in conjunction with disproportionate power of the executive branch in comparison to the legislature and civil society.

Our analysis of this typical case for MDBS underlines the potential benefits of improved donor harmonization. At the same time, the Zambian experience also demonstrates the difficulties Western donors have in adhering to their own harmonization agendas. Our analysis shows an intrinsic goal conflict between the broader agenda of democracy support and more narrowly defined public-sector reforms. In addition, the Zambian case also provides evidence of a more extrinsic goal conflict between budget support's function as a financing mechanism for poverty reduction and its function of promoting more profound institutional reforms.[3] These conflicts have been fomented by varying interpretations among donors with regard to the goal hierarchy of an instrument that is meant to be implemented in a highly harmonized fashion. Furthermore, we conclude that these different interpretations and approaches are often related to the particular constellations of donors' domestic constituencies that drive aid implementation strategies on the ground.

Our analysis proceeds as follows: In the analytical section, we briefly review the literature on aid effectiveness and democracy aid, which allows us to link the challenges of successfully promoting democracy to the broader reform agenda of international development assistance. Thereafter, we explain the intervention logic of MDBS, which seeks to simultaneously finance poverty reduction and promote democratic accountability through a combination of financial inputs, conditionality, and dialogue mechanisms. We also describe the coordination challenges for donors, should they wish to implement this multiple-objective aid instrument on the ground. The empirical part of our analysis begins by providing the rationale for case selection and by presenting crucial features of this aid instrument in Zambia. We then describe the achievements of budget support implementation, but also the difficulties of implementing the instrument in the highly harmonized manner necessary to craft a coherent incentive system capable of promoting the institutional reforms conducive to increasing democratic accountability. As the Zambian government's interest in pro-democratic reforms had been declining since 2008, MDBS donors were faced with the challenge of how to respond to the deteriorating political environment in a harmonized way. However, donors disagreed over the relative importance of democracy support in comparison to the financing objective of budget support. This absence of a shared goal hierarchy inhibited achieving a harmonized incentive system capable of supporting democratic accountability. As a result, MDBS in Zambia has been relatively successful in its financing function and in supporting the 'supply side' of public-sector accountability. However, support has been less effective than it might have been regarding more politically sensitive reforms related to the 'demand side' of democratic accountability.

Democracy promotion and Multi-Donor Budget Support
Democracy promotion and the aid effectiveness debate

Western foreign aid seeks not only to promote economic development and poverty reduction, but also to support institutional reforms that will strengthen the rule of law and the political institutions that facilitate democracy. Unfortunately, none of these goals are easy to achieve, and the empirical evidence of the effects of aid on economic development and good governance is sobering. There is no robust evidence that the amount of aid has had a statistically significant impact on a country's economic growth.[4] Moreover, econometric analysis reveals that official development assistance (ODA) in the last four decades of the twentieth century did not result in one-directional impacts on democracy levels in recipient countries,[5] but instead produced an amplification effect[6]; that is, foreign aid strengthened the existent political system to which it was channelled, regardless of whether the recipient was an autocracy or a democracy. In addition, increasing the aid dependency of a recipient country had negative effects on the rule of law, political transparency, and administrative quality.[7]

However, the effectiveness of aid focused on strengthening the political institutions conducive to democracy has been more positively assessed. Recent research has found that such aid has had a positive effect on the levels of democracy in recipient countries.[8] Although part of this effect is reduced when matching techniques to control for endogeneity are applied, this kind of aid still seems to be effective, at least in emerging democracies[9]; this finding is compatible with the notion that democracy aid is only effective in countries that have already undergone some transformation towards democracy. The two main explanations for these seemingly paradoxical findings point to the potential tensions between mainstream anti-poverty aid and foreign assistance explicitly aimed at improving political conditions.

The first explanation of why overall development assistance has been so ineffective is related to the fungibility of aid, a factor that can be particularly problematic in illiberal and non-transparent political settings.[10] Whether in the form of earmarked project aid for certain sector-specific purposes or unconditional financial flows: aid can always affect the opportunity costs for government allocation of domestic resources in development-oriented sectors. For instance, if a corrupt and autocratic government receives aid for a specific purpose in a given social sector, it can reallocate at least part of its own resources that were originally budgeted for this purpose and instead spend those funds on issues related to other political priorities. Thus, even earmarked aid projects in social sectors can indirectly finance clientele networks, a repression apparatus, or military arms races.[11]

The second explanation is related to the generally fragmented and uncoordinated delivery of foreign aid in the past; this lack of coordination is thought to adversely affect the quality of a recipient's governance.[12] Not only does the absence of donor coordination obstruct the creation of a coherent incentive system conducive to institutional reforms,[13] it also prevents coordinated dialogues with recipient governments that could steer more aid towards the self-defined developmental priorities of the recipients. In recipient countries with many donor agencies, state administrations suffer because they are burdened with the transaction costs of many different projects; in addition, the presence of many competing donor agencies amplifies the crowding-out effect of qualified bureaucrats from the state apparatus to donor agencies.[14] As a consequence, the potential effect of aid on economic development is also constrained in the presence of many uncoordinated donor activities, because donor fragmentation tends to undermine the state structures necessary for achieving sustainable economic development.[15]

The absence of coordinated aid interventions and the problem of fungibility can thus demonstrate how traditional aid geared primarily towards economic dimensions of development has proven to be ineffective in reducing poverty, increasing growth, and strengthening democracy. These issues have featured prominently in the discussions leading up to the recent international reform attempts. In several high-level summits in Rome (2003), Paris (2005), and Accra (2008) and Busan (2011), politicians from developed and developing countries agreed on the need for substantial improvements regarding donor harmonization and recipient country ownership.[16] To overcome the fragmentation problem, it was determined that donors should harmonize their procedures regarding disbursements, conditionality, monitoring, and evaluation. Moreover, aid should be better aligned with partner countries' priorities as formulated in national development plans and with existing administrative processes, in order to make use of domestic reform intentions and to avoid the emergence of parallel structures and excessive transaction costs created by isolated aid projects. Ideally, this harmonization and the recipient ownership of reforms would converge in a well-coordinated relationship between donors and recipients, thereby avoiding aid fragmentation and external conditionality unrelated to the domestic reform context.

This reform strategy implies that the linkages between promoting poverty alleviation and supporting public sector reforms and democracy should be strengthened and potentially merged into a single strategy. In the fragmented world of aid projects, measures of democracy support can be implemented relatively independently of measures primarily aimed at economic development.[17] In contrast, the new focus on highly coordinated and harmonized aid interventions at least conceptually attempts to reconcile into a single strategic approach the goals of promoting institutional change with those of poverty alleviation. While the underlying rationale for this strategic shift has been rooted in problems such as fungibility and donor fragmentation, the conceptual debate has not addressed the issue of potential conflicting objectives between poverty alleviation and the promotion of good governance, nor has it considered the subsequent implications of such conflict for donor harmonization and the incentive system. Thus, as we will illustrate, MDBS – the most prominent aid instrument of this reform agenda – is conceptually sound only to the extent that the implementing donors operate in accordance with the same underlying goal hierarchy.

Multi-Donor Budget Support: financial and democracy assistance?

Multi-Donor Budget Support (MDBS) is considered to be the paramount instrument of the envisaged reform agenda. The method can be traced back to the debt relief initiative for Heavily Indebted Poor Countries (HIPC) launched by the World Bank and the International Monetary Fund (IMF) in 1996. To be eligible for debt relief, HIPCs had to develop broad-based Poverty Reduction Strategy Papers and demonstrate the implementation of key reforms, including improvements in public financial management (PFM) and corruption.[18] Later, several donors including the European Commission (EC) and the United Kingdom (UK) began to provide additional financial resources in line with this conceptual approach.[19] With an increasing focus on donor coordination, harmonization, and the use of local systems, other donors soon followed suit, resulting in today's 'standard model' of MDBS with formalized harmonization and alignment mechanisms.[20] As a result of these developments, the intervention logic of MDBS attempts to combine financing and governance objectives within one conceptual approach.

The financing function of MDBS is intended to provide predictable financial flows to the recipient government's budget, in support of the country's national development and poverty reduction strategy based on the Millennium Development Goals (MDGs). In this way, MDBS is meant to increase the financial resources in sectors especially relevant to poverty alleviation and inclusive economic development. By using the recipient government's own systems, MDBS seeks to avoid the negative externalities that can arise from an uncoordinated project approach to channelling aid resources.

With respect to the governance function of MDBS, many donors perceive the use of the recipient country's own structures as an entry point for strengthening the recipient's public financial management systems and for promotion of a more effective, transparent, and accountable process of financial planning and implementation.[21] At the same time, MDBS is also intended to provide an opportunity for dialogue between donors and recipients regarding sector-specific institutional reforms (for example, health and education). In addition, MDBS has been increasingly perceived as a suitable instrument for promoting political processes conducive to democracy. This latter objective is thought to be supported by the strengthening of civic participation and democratic accountability in the formulation and implementation of the government's development strategies and annual budgets.[22] To achieve these governance functions, the financial disbursements of MDBS are accompanied by non-financial contributions, namely conditionality, policy dialogue, and technical assistance.

With regard to the conditionality of MDBS, one can differentiate between two levels. The entry conditionality for providing MDBS is typically formulated in so-called Underlying Principles, which generally include the government's commitment to (i) macro-economic stability, (ii) the implementation of a national development and poverty reduction strategy, (iii) the implementation of financial management reforms, and (iv) the principles of democratic accountability, participation, and human rights. In the case of a violation of the Underlying Principles, donors can suspend planned disbursements or entirely discontinue use of the instrument. In addition to this more general conditionality, donors and the recipient government regularly negotiate a more specific Performance Assessment Framework, which includes sets of concrete performance indicators measuring progress in specific sectors, financial management, or in other administrative fields. Donor disbursements can be linked in different ways to these indicators, for example, as a fixed tranche based on the overall assessment framework or as performance (or 'floating') tranches linked to specific process and performance indicators.

In addition to the financial resources and the two levels of conditionality, donors routinely provide technical assistance and capacity-building to the recipient government. The complex task of combining heterogeneous (yet ideally harmonious) disbursement strategies and a multidimensional conditionality scheme is accompanied by a formal dialogue mechanism for donors and the government. This dialogue mechanism is intended to ensure a continuous information exchange and a mechanism for conflict resolution; it is also meant to ensure that donors will align the sector-specific conditionality requirements with the reform priorities of the recipient government.

The interaction of these financial and non-financial components of MDBS is crucial for achieving the instrument's financing and governance objectives: Ideally, the non-financial contributions work to enhance the effectiveness and impact of the financial contributions. In turn, by linking disbursements to specific performance measures, the financial contributions create incentives that will increase the effectiveness of the non-financial contributions. Through this interaction, MDBS donors hope to achieve systemic improvements in the quality of the recipient administration. The channelling of resources through the recipient's budget aims to avoid the negative effects on the administration that can be generated by uncoordinated projects. An additional focus of MDBS is on improving the supply side of fiscal accountability. By conditioning financial flows on the implementation of reforms aimed at increasing the transparency, efficiency, and other core dimensions of public financial management – such as effective oversight institutions – MDBS seeks to strengthen 'good financial governance'. This conditionality is often accompanied by technical assistance geared towards the same objectives.[23]

Democracy support, harmonization, and the potential for conflicting objectives

While there is an explicit consensus among donors on the intervention logic of budget support regarding its financing function and its public financial management objectives, the prospect of democracy promotion through MDBS is often less explicitly stated.[24] Donors can have varying priorities regarding this political – and perhaps most ambitious – objective of the instrument. During the past decade, several bilateral donors – for example Germany – have expressed their intentions to use budget support as an instrument for democracy and human rights objectives. During the same period, other (in particular, multilateral) donors have been less forthcoming on this issue, tending to emphasize the financing objectives and the instrument's potential for improving PFM. More recently, however, several bilateral and multilateral donors have changed their positions; both the UK and the European Union are now increasing their investment in the political objective of MDBS.[25]

There are several arguments in support of the analytical link between MDBS and democracy promotion. First, the financial disbursements of MDBS are contingent upon the implementation of development plans, which are meant to be the basis for developing the indicators of the Performance Assessment Framework and which (presumably) have been developed in a participatory approach compatible with democratic principles.[26] In this capacity, MDBS can function as a catalyst for the participation of civil society and the legislature in the formulation of national and sector-specific development strategies.[27] Second, a harmonized incentive system is intended to strengthen democratic accountability with regard to the budget process and beyond. Furthermore, a harmonized incentive system based on the Underlying Principles, requiring the government's commitment to democratic principles and human rights, can function as a potential 'firewall' in the case of democratic deterioration.

Overall, the interaction between financial and non-financial components of MDBS described above is expected to be particularly advantageous in countries that are poor, aid-dependent, and whose governments exhibit a critical level of receptiveness regarding democratic participation and accountability. However, the effective implementation of MDBS in such countries also faces the significant challenge of donor coordination and harmonization. This challenge is especially relevant when MDBS is provided to countries with weak administrative capacities that have serious difficulties in formulating coherent development plans and subsequently aligning donors to their priorities. Consequently, donors must at least partially compensate for such typical deficiencies of low-income countries by strengthening their own harmonization efforts in accordance with the reform-oriented priorities defined by the recipient.

Especially in such contexts, a joint financing mechanism alone is not sufficient to realize the potential of MDBS. Effective harmonization is also required in the application of the non-financial inputs of MDBS, in particular with regard to conditionality. A resulting harmonized incentive system does not necessarily imply uniform behaviour, but it does require that unambiguous and coordinated messages be conveyed to the recipient government to signal the relative weight of budget support's strategic goals. However, the financing objective and the democracy objective of MDBS could come into conflict, at least in the short run. Donors might have varying preferences as to the level of democratic deterioration at which they should suspend disbursements that would otherwise be channelled to social sectors. They also can easily have differing expectations regarding sufficient improvements in parliamentary oversight functions for sustainable poverty-oriented budgeting. If budget support-providing donors cannot agree on a common position regarding these issues, their divergent priorities for the financing and the governance objectives of MDBS can lead to severe harmonization problems. Critical political events can then generate varying responses from the different donors based on their individual interpretations of the various dimensions of MDBS conditionality. Such uncoordinated behaviour can then negatively affect the interactions between the financial and non-financial contributions of the instrument and thus obstruct the emergence of a coherent incentive system (a prerequisite for supporting gradual improvements in democratic accountability). Conflicting objectives resulting from different goal hierarchies are more likely to affect the broader governance objectives than the financial function of the instrument. Thus, when a complex aid instrument such as MDBS attempts to achieve several goals simultaneously, the emergence of a coherent incentive system conducive to institutional reforms will suffer unless a clear goal hierarchy is established.

Democracy promotion and budget support in Zambia

Case selection and democratization in Zambia

In many respects, Zambia represents a typical recipient of MDBS in sub-Saharan Africa, and is thus appropriate for illustrating our conceptual arguments related to the instrument's intervention logic and the relevance of conflicting objectives for the implementation of a coherent incentive system suitable for democracy support. In 2005, the Zambian government and four donors (the EC, the World Bank, and the governments of the United Kingdom and the Netherlands) signed a Memorandum of Understanding (MoU) on the provision of Poverty Reduction Budget Support (PRBS). Later, other governments – including those of Finland, Germany, Norway and Sweden – and the African Development Bank followed suit.[28] Between 2006 and 2010, Zambia received roughly US$1 billion of budget support from these multilateral and bilateral donors.

Despite its increasing profits from raw material exports, Zambia is a country with extreme levels of poverty – the nation ranked 150th out of 169 countries in the 2010 Human Development Index.[29] Zambia has received enormous amounts of foreign assistance, largely due to the government's reliable compliance with the conditionality attached to IMF and World Bank programmes.[30] During the mid-1990s, Zambia ranked among the most aid-dependent countries. Although aid dependency has subsequently decreased substantially because of debt relief and economic growth, the reliance on aid resources is still important for the public sector.[31]

In addition, the political structures of Zambia make the country an interesting case for the analysis of the implementation of MDBS. As is typical for a least developed country, Zambia has limited administrative capacities for the formulation and implementation of a unified and coherent development strategy. Despite the existence of a comprehensive five-year development plan, the government lacks the strategic and programmatic capacity to effectively manage the fragmented aid portfolios of multiple donors. Moreover, while Freedom House indicators classify the country as an electoral democracy and levels of corruption are slightly below the sub-Saharan average, political conditions are far from approximating a consolidated democracy and a meritocratic state apparatus.[32]

The Zambian democratization process began in 1991, when President Kenneth Kaunda's one-party dominant regime was peacefully brought to an end by the clear electoral victory of the opposition Movement for Multi-Party Democracy (MMD).[33] However, the new administration under President Frederick Chiluba did not initiate a process of democratic consolidation. Especially during the second half of the 1990s, political rights and civil liberties were curtailed to the extent that Zambia almost re-established an authoritarian, one-party dominant regime. Economic reforms proved to be a mechanism of privilege distribution to powerful interest groups. Political power again became concentrated in the executive branch, and patterns of patronage and neo-patrimonial governance persisted in a hybrid regime.[34] However, intra-party conflicts and growing civil protests in urban centres forced President Chiluba to forgo running for a third presidential term. Instead, Levy Mwanawasa (MMD), Chiluba's hand-picked successor, won a highly disputed election in 2001. Political rights and civil liberties improved under his presidency, and Mwanawasa was returned to office in 2006, following elections that were widely judged to be both free and fair.[35] After Mwanawasa's death in August 2008, the then-vice president, Rupiah Banda, succeeded him; Banda won the following competitive and fair presidential contest in October 2008.

During the presidency of Rupiah Banda (2008–2011), the democratic process entered a period of stagnation, if not regression. The decision by Freedom House to downgrade Zambia's score in civil liberties in 2010 reflects this deterioration.[36] Political reforms such as the decentralization process and those affecting the civil service did not advance. Several more progressive elements of a long-awaited constitutional reform such as for example the direct elections of mayors were removed from the original agenda. The ruling party and its supporters systematically attempted to intimidate the opposition and civil society actors.[37] After the disclosure of several sizable cases of corruption, the government tried to constrain the freedom of the press and the fiscal manoeuvring room for civil society organizations. In 2009, another bureaucratic obstacle was created when the parliament passed a law requiring non-governmental organizations (NGOs) to register and re-register every five years.[38] The Zambian judiciary has also increasingly come under pressure from the incumbent government, as seen in the run-up to an anti-corruption policy launched in July 2009.[39]

Economic growth, although above 5% per annum since 2005, was only marginally translated into poverty alleviation. Instead, economic and political elites benefited from export-led growth while popular support for the MMD began to decline. In spite of temporary increases in intra-party rivalry, President Banda was nonetheless able to secure his place on the ballot for the 2011 election. Although the government's commitment to democratic principles seems to have declined, the 2011 elections successfully represented the voice of the populace: Banda lost, putting an end to almost two decades of MMD rule. By a margin of 183,100 votes, Banda was beaten by his rival Michael C. Sata from the Patriotic Front who obtained 42% of the total vote.[40]

Zambia has often been aptly characterized as a 'country at the crossroads'.[41] On the one hand, the country experienced a peaceful transition to electoral democracy in the early 1990s and since then has overcome several threats to democratic order. Competitive elections have been successfully instituted, and civil society has become actively involved in demanding greater democratic accountability. On the other hand, the dominance of the executive branch has often extended 'beyond the stipulations of the constitution',[42] and the deep-seated connections between the governing MMD party and the state apparatus have been substantial.[43] Most civil society organizations are only weakly rooted in Zambian society and are heavily dependent on external support. As in many other African democracies, the combination of a relatively weak civil society and limited checks and balances have impeded significant improvements in democratic accountability and have facilitated the persistence of neo-patrimonial structures. Thus, in this hybrid political context, implementing budget support could be a promising approach for democracy promotion, if financial disbursements represented significant political leverage that could be utilized by a harmonized donor strategy providing a coherent incentive system.

Budget support implementation: leverage, dialogue and conditionality

Overall, the financial weight of budget support in the Zambian government's development-oriented expenditures has been substantial. Although budget support disbursements as a percentage of the overall government budget have been less than 10% in the past decade, the government has relied almost entirely on external funding for its discretionary expenditures; statutory expenditures (such as personal salaries and interest payments) have amounted to more than two-thirds of the budget.[44] This means that the budget support disbursements have been of much greater significance for the development-oriented investments of the Zambian state than the relatively small size of these disbursements in relation to the overall budget might suggest. Thus, budget support has been highly valued by the president and the finance ministry because it has secured a critical fiscal space for the implementation of strategic public investments. From the perspective of Western donors, budget support has also become increasingly relevant.[45] While not dominating the overall aid portfolio, budget support almost tripled as a share of all aid provided by Western donors between 2004 and 2010, amounting to roughly 30% in 2010.[46]

As a consequence of its financial importance, budget support has become the politically most visible aid instrument in the Zambian public debate. Zambia's civil society and media perceive budget support as an important indicator of how the government is performing in terms of economic and political challenges. As such, for financial and political reasons, the financial component of budget support has a high leverage potential for tipping the scale in favour of pro-democratic reforms in the hybrid political context.[47]

Against this background, budget support donors and the government have been successful in building a formal framework of dialogue and conditionality in order to link the financial and non-financial components of the instrument. The structure for the policy dialogue was fixed in a joint Memorandum of Understanding (MoU); it consists of several fora in which the nine budget support donors and the Zambian government regularly meet at different technical and political levels to monitor the overall reform process and the requirements of conditionality.[48] This dialogue is closely linked to the other working groups at the sector level as well as to a High-Level Policy Dialogue, which also includes Organization for Economic Co-operation and Development (OECD) donors that do not provide budget support. The financial component of the MDBS process is thus accompanied by a well-institutionalized dialogue structure to harmonize and align donors with the development priorities of the government, to allow the parties to agree upon conditions and performance indicators, and to discuss different perceptions of political and economic reforms.

Like the dialogue structure, the conditionality attached to financial disbursements also follows the general intervention logic of the instrument. The MoU lays out the basic conditionality in the form of the Underlying Principles, which are defined as a mutually agreed-upon basis for cooperation. Accordingly, budget support has been provided on the precondition of the government's commitment to broadly defined economic and political objectives. The economic objectives are mainly related to sound macro-economic policies – as demonstrated by a positive IMF assessment – and the fight against poverty, to be accomplished through a national development plan. The political objectives focus upon the government's commitment to peace, democratic principles, the rule of law, the fight against corruption, and financial management reforms.[49] However, the periodic assessment of the Underlying Principles is based to a large degree on the individual judgement of each donor; donors can unilaterally initiate a High-Level Policy Dialogue in the case of a perceived violation. In addition, donors condition their budget support disbursements on the implementation of concrete institutional reforms, in particular in the area of public financial management. Progress in both the implementation of the country's National Development Plan and in governance-related reforms is measured by the indicators of the

Performance Assessment Framework, which evolved between 2006 and 2010 into a comprehensive framework with a growing number of targets, policy measures, and outcome indicators.

Achievements of MDBS in Zambia

In addition to the successful implementation of the framework described above, both the financing objective of the instrument and its objective to strengthen public financial management have also been accomplished in a satisfactory manner. The financial inflows provided by budget support are intended to contribute to the country's anti-poverty strategy, but generally face the challenge of aid fungibility. However, in Zambia, no fungibility-related problems could be observed for MDBS. On the contrary, the substantial increase in expenditures between 2006 and 2009 was primarily caused by increased domestic spending. More importantly, the additional expenditures went mainly to sectors that are arguably of particular relevance for poverty reduction, and the total increases in these sectors were higher than the total amount of MDBS.[50] Also, on the revenue side of the budget, there is no evidence for any substantial crowding-out of domestic resources by budget support: domestic revenue grew by 50% in real terms between 2002 and 2008, whereas external grants (including MDBS) fell by 35%.[51] Thus, there has been no sign that the fungibility of aid has led the government to reallocate resources away from poverty related areas, as the resources spent in these sectors have increased. The absence of evidence for a crowding-out effect is, of course, no proof that in the absence of budget support inflows, the government would not have allocated even more of its own resources to the social sectors or would not have augmented its own revenues to a greater extent. However, even from a defensive position, one could argue that the remaining fungibility problems have at least not been more serious than those of traditional earmarked aid projects, which are implemented outside of the government's budget. Moreover, the disproportional increases in sectors related to poverty alleviation and economic development suggest that MDBS did indeed augment the government's resources for these policy fields.

However, the increase in development-oriented public spending is not necessarily accompanied by the efficient use of disbursed financial resources. In contrast to the traditional off-budget project approach, donors providing budget support rely heavily on the government's financial management mechanisms. This implies serious fiduciary risks other than crowding-out, namely inefficiencies and misappropriation of funds. Thus, it has been in the budget support providers' own interests to strengthen the supply side of budget accountability through improved public financial management and corruption control.[52] Not surprisingly, budget support donors in Zambia uniformly put particular emphasis on including PFM indicators in their conditionality framework and on strengthening the PFM system and especially the Auditor General's Office through targeted technical assistance programmes.[53] Consequently, donors have had a relatively harmonized approach, consistently demonstrating their definite interest in public financial management issues as crucial to the reduction of fiduciary risk for their financing objective.[54] However, although public financial management reforms have been constantly discussed in the different dialogue and progress review forums, the broader agenda regarding the demand side of accountability has been less of a priority for most budget support donors.

This general focus on public financial management seems to show results. Standard corruption indicators for Zambia (such as the World Bank Governance Indicators) are slightly below the sub-Saharan Africa average, and showed slight improvements between 2005 and 2008 (followed by a minor decline in 2009).[55] According to several assessments, public financial management in Zambia has demonstrated progress (at least until 2008) in many dimensions: the comprehensiveness of fiscal information, the systematic reporting of arrears, and improvements in the Auditor General's internal audit external budget oversight, accomplished by expanding the coverage and the methodological expertise of the agency.[56]

Conflicting objectives during normal times

With respect to its financing function and the related aim of improving public financial management and the supply side of accountability, the budget support process in Zambia has functioned in an acceptable even if not in an entirely satisfactory manner. Nevertheless, since late 2008, a number of bilateral donors have become increasingly unsatisfied with the broader political process. More politically sensitive reforms such as the decentralization policy, the budget cycle reform, and the constitutional reform process have stagnated. As mentioned before, the government has attempted to constrain the free press and independent NGOs. However, not all donors felt equally dissatisfied. While some bilateral donors were concerned about the government's compliance with the fundamental conditionality of the Underlying Principles, others (such as the Department for International Development (DFID), the European Union (EU) and the African Development Bank) viewed the relative success regarding the financing function and the related financial management agenda as sufficient progress to merit continued disbursements.[57] In essence, the various donors assigned different weights to the different objectives related to MDBS. As one representative of a bilateral aid agency directly stated:

> We have different constituencies, different incentives and do respond to different political masters back home. I get demoted when I overlook a corruption scandal; others get promoted when they meet their disbursement targets.[58]

Until mid-2009, these different interpretations of the fundamental conditionality have been reflected in the difficulties experienced by donors attempting to engage in the dialogue process with a coherent strategy regarding the broader political process in Zambia. As a consequence, the policy dialogue has been dominated by operational issues, since a more political dialogue would have revealed the varying importance donors placed on the broader political objectives. For instance, whereas the Danish International Co-operation Agency – which only participated as an observer in the Zambian MDBS process – includes the importance of strengthening parliamentary oversight in its budget support guidelines, the original guidelines of the EC did not mention such aspects and concentrated only on state oversight institutions.[59] Other bilateral donors in Zambia (such as the governments of Germany, Norway, and Sweden) have also frequently mentioned the importance of a government's democratic accountability to parliament and civil society; this has not been an equally important issue for the World Bank and the African Development Bank.[60]

With regard to the Performance Assessment Framework, there has been a tendency for donors to overload this framework with a diverse set of sector-specific indicators and to limit the related discussion to the technical level. Moreover, a lack of consensus among donors regarding the political scope of the assessment framework and the appropriate type of indicators has undermined the coherent incentive structure required to induce the policy changes donors had hoped to see.[61] More importantly, however, donors have often overloaded the assessment framework with sector indicators, a tendency caused by a classic collective action problem. Overloading the assessment framework can reflect the interests of individual donors (providing additional political leverage for their specific sector activities) rather than the collective objectives of the donor group as a whole.[62] Even more problematic than the oversized assessment framework has been the incoherence between donors over how to link their disbursements to policy performance. Some donors disbursed only one fixed tranche that depended on the overall assessments of the performance framework and the Underlying Principles (the governments of Germany and Finland), while others split their disbursements into a variable and a fixed tranche (for example, the EU, the governments of Norway, Sweden, and the United Kingdom). However, the relative size of the variable tranche also differed substantially among the latter group of donors: the governments of Norway and Sweden reserve 50% for the variable tranche, but the United Kingdom allocates only 13%; the EU substantially reduced its variable tranche from its original 90% to 25% in 2010. In contrast, the World Bank and the African Development Bank operated with floating tranches, which were disbursed only once a set of selected indicators had been achieved. Overall, these individual and unrelated disbursement mechanisms seemed not to have hampered the financing objective, but may well have hindered the emergence of a clear incentive system for policy and political reforms. Furthermore, the combined fixed tranches have often added up to more than 80% of the overall budget support commitments, thereby reducing incentives for the Zambian government to invest particular effort in achieving specific indicators.[63] Finally, the coherency of the financial incentive system was further reduced because the disbursements of individual donors are each linked to different (sub-sets of) indicators.[64]

Thus, the described deficiencies of the political dialogue, the PAF indicators, and the disbursement strategy have further exacerbated the harmonization problem among budget support-providing donors. Overall, the lack of a joint dialogue focused on the political process together with the incoherent incentive scheme has meant that signals to the the Zambian government were not co-ordinated, demonstrating the lack of a common position among donor agencies regarding governance dynamics and how they should be addressed.

Donors have also not consistently demanded or motivated more systematic or consistent participation of civil society groups or legislators in sector-specific dialogue mechanisms. Neither a majority of donor agencies nor the government have been interested in moving beyond a government-to-government dialogue, a process that has a natural tendency to avoid purely political arguments whenever possible in order to facilitate technical progress. Thus, the sector dialogues of the MDBS process have not contributed to broader governance goals of budget support, such as promoting democratic inclusiveness and accountability through strengthening actors other than the executive.[65] Similarly, although much emphasis has been placed on the supply side of budget accountability to safeguard the financing objective, MDBS donors have not succeeded in building a common political strategy to focus their individual activities related to the strengthening of the oversight functions of civil society and the parliament.[66] Again, different interpretations of the relative importance of the instrument's democracy goals were at least partially responsible for this phenomenon. For instance, the Swedish government tried to focus its governance assistance on strengthening this kind of democratic accountability in all of its budget support-receiving countries (including Zambia) because it wanted explicitly to link its democracy agenda with the instrument of budget support.[67] In contrast, the EC's approach to MDBS was criticized for not placing sufficient importance on national accountability mechanisms outside of the core state apparatus.[68]

Overall, the absence of a harmonized political dialogue and an incentive set linking financial disbursements to issues of democratic accountability and participation has undermined coherent signalling to the Zambian government. Thus, despite the high potential leverage effects of the instrument, at least at the collective level, the providers of MDBS shied away from politicized issues due to internal dissent. This meant that the Zambian government had not encountered a clear and harmonized incentive system, which could have helped to promote political reforms.

Attempts at harmonization during times of crisis

When substantial instances of misappropriation and corruption were uncovered in the health sector in 2008 and 2009, the unease among donors regarding political performance increased, demanding a common response.[69] The most important donors in the health sector immediately suspended or delayed aid disbursements and requested an investigation by the Auditor General's Office. Resumption of disbursements was made dependent on an action plan that demanded further strengthening of the Auditor General's Office and the improvement of the health ministry's financial management.[70] Throughout 2009, the MDBS group complained about the limited efforts by the Zambian government to address this misappropriation case, increasing pressure on the government to implement delayed political reforms through the initiation of a High-Level Dialogue. This sudden 'ganging up' by the budget support donors as a response to a critical event placed the general political context at the centre of the policy dialogue[71]; some subsequent reforms by the Zambian government can be at least partly attributed to this attempt at collective action. One day before the budget support review in November 2009, a public service salary reform measure was approved by the Zambian cabinet. An overdue reform of the budgetary cycle, which would allow the parliament significantly more time to study the government's budget proposals, was also pushed through at the end of 2009.[72] Finally, the long-awaited (since 2006) cabinet approval of the Decentralization Implementation Plan was announced in early 2010.

Thus, in 2009, budget support-providing donors were able to set up an emergency dialogue and at least temporarily focus on core political issues.[73] On the one hand, these efforts can be evaluated as a temporarily successful attempt to create a firewall to protect against the further deterioration of the democratization process in Zambia. On the other hand, these politically visible achievements did not translate into sustainable improvements in democratic participation or democratic accountability, partly because of the Zambian government's resistance, but also because donors were unable to transform this initial phase of coordination into a more sustainable solution for their collective action problems.

Although the scandal in the health sector and the subsequent discovery of widespread misuse of funds in the road sector were followed by substantial efforts on the parts of budget support donors to maintain a harmonized approach, these events nevertheless highlighted the significant differences between those actors. This again relates to their different interpretations of MDBS, either primarily as an instrument of democracy support and good governance or as an instrument focused on financing poverty alleviation measures. Despite their initial harmonization attempts, these variations in interpretation among donors became apparent throughout 2009 and 2010 because of the critical political context.

More sceptical bilateral donors have argued that these scandals were a result of the overall deterioration of democracy and good governance. Like the analysts critical of the follow-up measures resulting from the corruption scandal,[74] this group of budget support-providing donors (including the governments of Germany and Sweden) also perceived the Zambian government as investing insufficient effort into technical examinations and as unwilling to suffer the politically sensitive consequences of the scandals. Consequently, these donors were in favour of at least temporarily suspending budget support and increasing pressure on the government to implement pending structural reforms in key areas related to corruption control and democratic accountability. However, at the same time, other donors (including the EU and the United Kingdom) took a more moderate position on these issues. They avoided making direct links to the overall democratization process, interpreting the disclosure of the scandals as the result of the successful strengthening of national supervisory bodies (namely, the Auditor General). These donors also perceived the process of dealing with the scandals to be slow and rocky, but pointed to the improved procedures and agencies within the Zambian administration that drove the process. Moreover, this group of donors did not want to create an explicit link between disbursements and the overall political context in Zambia.

These different interpretations led to internal conflicts within the group of budget support-providing donors regarding the objectives of the instrument and how to adequately respond to similar critical events. The different reactions of Sweden and the EC to the corruption case in late 2009 illustrate this argument. The Swedish decision to suspend disbursements was based on the interpretation that the Underlying Principles had been violated; the EC, in contrast, assessed the situation as a positive sign that the domestic institutions were capable of fighting corruption, and as a result even augmented its budget support disbursements in 2009 with additional resources from its Vulnerability Flex Support.[75] For the Zambian government, these varying interpretations and the subsequent opposite actions regarding disbursements made it difficult to anticipate the reaction of MDBS donors as a whole.

Thus, the budget support-providing donors in Zambia did not develop a harmonized fall-back scenario for times of political crisis; rather, they attempted to jointly respond in an ad hoc manner, a strategy that at best only partially functioned. Most importantly, the varying perceptions of donors regarding the scandals in the health and road sector revealed the heterogeneity of their expectations of what MDBS in Zambia should achieve.[76] It became clear that budget support donors had different perceptions regarding the potential of budget support as an instrument to shield democracy and to support democratic consolidation. Moreover, donors were also operating under different goal hierarchies with respect to the relative priority of the financing and political objectives. The subsequent failure to agree upon a joint position resulted in an incoherent incentive system that did not send clear signals to the recipient.

Interpretation and conclusions

For several years, MDBS has been the paradigmatic aid instrument of a more harmonized aid agenda. The intervention logic of the instrument is based on the coordinated combination of financial and non-financial contributions that aim to mitigate the traditional problems of project fragmentation and the existence of parallel structures to the recipient state administration. Using this combination of contributions, MDBS seeks to finance poverty alleviation by financially supporting the recipient's own anti-poverty strategy. Moreover, the combination of financial resources, conditionality, and political dialogue can also be perceived as an important instrument to strengthen the recipient country's administrative structures as well as to promote democratic accountability and participation.

As the Zambian experience suggests, the success of the instrument's democracy objectives critically hinges on the existence of a harmonized goal hierarchy among budget support-providing donors. The evidence from Zambia reveals that the instrument has performed relatively well regarding its financing function and no major problems of fungibility have arisen. Moreover, supervisory institutions such as the Auditor General's Office have at least technically been strengthened, as this entity's response to the scandals in the health and transportation sectors has shown. However, the instrument has not realized its full potential with regard to its broader democracy objectives, because MDBS donors have not shared a common interpretation of the intervention logic. Some donors have highlighted the democracy objectives, justifying the use of budget support by pointing to the instrument's potential to strengthen the oversight functions of the parliament and civil society and to shield democratic achievements from illiberal tendencies. Others have placed more importance on the financing objectives of the instrument; with regard to governance objectives, these donors only intend to use the instrument to strengthen public financial management within the state apparatus.

This disagreement over the broader political goals of MDBS has led to an extrinsic goal conflict among budget support-providing donors and has hampered the emergence of a common goal hierarchy. As a consequence of this goal conflict, donors have shied away from entering into a more political dialogue with the Zambian government; they could have sent clearer messages regarding the deterioration of the democratization process and the importance of the Underlying Principles as a prerequisite for receiving budget support. The lack of a joint goal hierarchy has also contributed to a weakly harmonized conditionality regarding the performance assessment framework and the disbursement mechanisms, which have also failed to realize their potential to send clear signals to the Zambian government. Although the donors tried to construct a harmonized approach during times of crisis and were thereby able to incentivize the Zambian government to realize certain highly visible, long-awaited reform steps, this attempt was again severely hampered by the donors' varying interpretations of the instrument's intervention logic. Whereas some bilateral donors perceived the Underlying Principles as a potentially powerful entry point for explicitly pursuing their objectives related to democratic accountability, others did not follow this approach at all. This led to an extreme contrast, in which some donor agencies suspended their disbursements while others augmented their financial contributions.

On the one hand, the example of the Zambian budget support process should not lead us to conclude that if donors were only harmonized enough in their objectives they could simply 'buy' political reforms related to the key features of a recipient country's political system. On the other hand, however, recipient governments do respond to coherent external incentives for political reform, as the European Union's enlargement process has shown.[77] And, even in Zambia, the government responded to donors when they temporarily overcame their collective action problems. Thus one could argue that a common goal hierarchy with a higher priority on the instrument's political objectives would have improved the harmonization of political conditionality and the related political dialogue. Of course, Zambia would not have emerged as a full-fledged democracy after only a few years of a harmonized provision of budget support focusing more on the political objectives of the instrument. At the same time, given the financial and political leverage of MDBS during the investigation period, such a harmonized approach probably could have been more effective in supporting democratic consolidation regarding the supervisory roles of parliament and civil society.

Overall, our findings do not contradict the intervention logic of the instrument in principle. Instead, they point to deeply-rooted challenges that must be faced: donors must overcome their collective action problems and implement complex aid instruments in accordance with a common goal hierarchy.

Finally, these collective action problems among budget support-providing donors in Zambia point out the domestic incentive systems for donors that have contributed to their difficulties in determining a common goal hierarchy. Not surprisingly, multilateral donors such as the World Bank and the African Development Bank have assigned less weight to the more political objectives of the instrument, as they have no strict mandate for explicit democracy support. In contrast, when the individual budget support operations of donor governments (such as those of Denmark, Germany, or Sweden) are closely tracked or must even be approved by powerful parliamentary commissions, these governments have strong incentives to highlight the instrument's political objectives related to democratic accountability. The Zambian case also reflects how changes in European governments have impacted donor agencies' harmonization attempts on the ground. When more conservative governments came to power in countries including Finland, Germany, the Netherlands, and the United Kingdom in 2009 and 2010, these newly elected governments soon began to assign more importance to political conditionality and the democracy objectives of the instrument.

One example of how such a domestic change in donor countries can affect the underlying – sometimes implicit – goal hierarchies of budget support is the United Kingdom: since the change of administration, 5% of any given budget support operation is now explicitly to be used for strengthening the oversight functions of parliaments and civil society. Even more striking has been the recent policy shift by the EC as documented in its 2011 budget support communication. Pressured by the increasing number of conservative governments among budget support providers, the commission has substantially increased the role of democracy in its budget support guidelines,[78] which previously were primarily oriented towards the financing objective of budget support. Thus, embassies and aid offices on the ground have had to respond to these unsynchronized changes of political contexts by adapting their case-specific interpretations of the goal hierarchy. Not surprisingly, this interference has done little to advance donor harmonization, a necessary condition for achieving the more political dimension of budget support.

Notes

1. This article is based on a joint international evaluation of budget support in Zambia covering the years 2005–2010. The evaluation was commissioned by the evaluation department of the German Ministry of Economic Co-operation and Development (BMZ), the independent evaluation office (IOB) of the Dutch Foreign Ministry, and the evaluation department of the Swedish International Development Agency (SIDA). Field research for the political economy section of the evaluation was conducted from February–May 2010, in July 2010, and in May 2011. For the official synthesis report, see De Kemp, Faust, and Leiderer, 'Between High Expectations and Reality'.
2. The typical example for this argument is the European Union. In the case of the EU, a coherent incentive system that offers membership status to the EU's neighbouring countries in combination with political conditionality based on pro-democratic changes has proven to have had a definite effect on political reforms (see Schimmelfennig and Scholtz, 'EU Democracy Promotion in the European Neighbourhood').
3. On extrinsic and intrinsic goal conflicts of democracy promotion see the introduction by Grimm and Leininger, 'Not All Good Things Go Together: Conflicting Objectives in Democracy Promotion'.
4. On aid's effects on economic growth and poverty, see Easterly, Levine, and Roodman, 'Aid, Policies, and Growth: Comment'; Roodman, 'The Anarchy of Numbers'; and Chong, Gradstein, and Calderón, 'Can Foreign Aid Reduce Income Inequality and Poverty?'.
5. Compare Knack, 'Does Foreign Aid Promote Democracy?'.
6. See Dutta, Leeson, and Williamson, 'The Amplification Effect'.
7. See Knack, 'Aid Dependence and the Quality of Governance', Bräutigam and Knack, 'Foreign Aid, Institutions and Governance'.
8. See Finkel, Pérez-Liñán, and Seligson, 'The Effects of U.S. Foreign Assistance on Democracy'; and Kalyvitis and Vlachaki, 'Democratic Aid and the Democratization of Recipients'.
9. See Nielson and Nielsen, 'Triage for Democracy'.
10. For an overview of the research on aid fungibility, see Kelly, 'Moving Money: Aid Fungibility in Africa', for empirical evidence regarding effects of fungibility across different sectors, see Feyzioglu, Swaroop, and Zhu, 'A Panel Data Analysis'.
11. For instance, Knack, 'Aid Dependence and the Quality of Governance'; Collier and Höffler, 'Unintended Consequences'.
12. See Morss, 'Institutional Destruction'.
13. See Emmanuel, 'Undermining Co-operation'.
14. See Knack and Rahman, 'Donor Fragmentation and Bureaucratic Quality'.
15. See Djankov, Montalvo, and Reynal-Querol, 'Aid with Multiple Personalities'.
16. For a discussion of this reform process and its implications for the organization of development assistance, see, for example, Hyden, 'After the Paris Declaration'; Meyer and Schulz, 'Ownership with Adjectives'; and Faust, 'Policy Experiments'.
17. Consequently, such an approach tends to anchor individual measures of democracy support even more deeply into the international aid system, a fact that has only recently gained recognition from scholars of foreign aid and democracy promotion (for example, Carothers, 'Democracy Support and Development Aid'; Faust, 'Policy Experiments'; and Burnell, *Promoting Democracy Abroad*).
18. For instance Booth, 'Are PRSPs Making a Difference?'.
19. See Koeberle and Stavreski, 'Budget Support: Concept and Issues'.
20. The following description of the intervention logic of budget support is related to an emerging consensus among aid practitioners and aid researchers concerning the potential effects of the financial and non-financial components of the instrument

(for example, Cordella and Dell'Ariccia, 'Budget Support Versus Project Aid'; and IDD and Associates, *Evaluation of General Budget Support*).
21. See IDD and Associates, *Evaluation of General Budget Support*.
22. See Hayman, 'Budget Support and Democracy'. With special reference to the World Bank's Budget Support (Policy Reform Credits). see Limpach and Michaelowa, 'The Impact of World Bank and IMF Programs on Democratization in Developing Countries'.
23. For example, IDD and Associates, *Evaluation of General Budget Support*.
24. See Horner and Power, *The Democratic Dimension of Aid*, 16; and Hayman, 'Budget Support and Democracy'.
25. For instance, in its 2008 strategy paper on programme-based approaches, the German ministry for development cooperation identified the objectives of budget support – the first being governance objectives strongly related to democracy and human rights improvements (see BMZ, 'Budget Support'). In contrast, the World Bank has avoided explicitly linking budget support to the objective of democracy support. In the UK, the explicit importance given to the strengthening of democratic accountability is a more recent phenomenon (DFID, 'Strengthening Accountability in Budget Support Countries'). Similarly, the EC, which had focused on the financing objective in the past, announced in October 2011 that its future budget support initiatives would be oriented more towards political objectives, such as support for democracy and 'good' governance.
26. See Booth, 'Are PRSPs Making a Difference'; and Horner and Power, *The Democratic Dimension of Aid*, 16.
27. In this regard, the intervention logic has been criticized as being too technocratic, as it places only limited emphasis on the iterative and highly political process of crafting a common development strategy among actors who might have different perspectives on how to solve a country's urgent development plans (for example, Lazarus, 'Participation in Poverty Reduction Strategy Papers'; and Faust, 'Policy Experiments').
28. In line with the ongoing international debate on aid effectiveness, the harmonization process in Zambia began to take shape in 2002. In response to the Declaration on Harmonization formulated at the first high-level meeting on aid effectiveness in Rome in 2003, seven donors agreed to launch a Harmonization in Practice initiative, which was later joined by all major donors to Zambia. In 2005, the government launched the Zambia Aid Policy and Strategy, which indicated the government's preference for budget support as the main instrument of aid. In response, donors formulated the Joint Assistance Strategy, thereby explicitly acknowledging the government's preference for the new aid modality and committing 'to the extent possible [to] increasingly deliver aid to the government sector through this modality to the extent that GRZ's [Government of the Republic of Zambia] systems meet established guidelines and standards, and that Co-operating Partners policies support such assistance' (Co-operating Partners, *Joint Assistance Strategy*, 38).
29. See UNDP, *Human Development Report*, 142.
30. Bertelsmann Stiftung, *BTI 2010 – Zambia Country Report*, 20.
31. For example, Fraser, 'Zambia: Back to the Future?'.
32. On the limited state capacity regarding donor management see Saasa, 'Political Economy of Budget Support in Zambia'. For comparative indicators of corruption see Kaufmann, Kraay, and Mastruzzi, 'The Worldwide Governance Indicators'. For limits of democratization see for example the 2010 country report of the Bertelsmann Foundation's Transformation Index: Bertelsmann Stiftung, *BTI 2010 – Zambia Country Report*, 2; and Freedom House, *Country Report Zambia – 2010*.
33. On democratization in Zambia during the 1990s, see, for example, Burnell, 'Taking Stock of Democracy in Zambia'; and Rakner and Svåsand, 'Stuck in Transition'.

34. Burnell, 'Taking Stock of Democracy in Zambia'; Burnell, 'Does Economic Reform Promote Democratisation?'.
35. Bertelsmann Stiftung, *BTI 2010 – Zambia Country Report*, 6.
36. See Freedom House, *Country Report Zambia – 2010*. The decision to downgrade Zambia on the score of Civil Liberties from 3 to 4 in 2010 was justified by non-legal restrictions on activities of non-governmental organizations. In 2011, 'due to political violence against the opposition and civil society groups, as well as the judiciary's failure to demonstrate substantial independence in key decisions throughout the year', Zambia received a downward trend arrow with unchanged scores in Political Rights (3) and Civil Liberties (4) (Freedom House, *Country Report Zambia – 2011*).
37. Freedom House, *Country Report Zambia – 2010*.
38. Ibid.
39. A minister in Banda's administration who was found guilty of inappropriate behaviour by a judicial tribunal was eventually re-appointed to the cabinet. Additionally, although he was declared guilty of corruption by the British High Court, former President Chiluba was rehabilitated in a subsequent corruption trial by the Zambian High Court (Freedom House, *Country Report Zambia – 2010*).
40. Electoral Commission of Zambia, 'Public Notice'.
41. Simon, *Countries at the Crossroads*.
42. Bertelsmann Stiftung, *BTI 2010 – Zambia Country Report*, 7.
43. This dominance of the executive branch is reflected in the composition of the parliament: about 40% of MPs hold positions as ministers or vice-ministers. This considerable overlap of the executive branch with the legislative branch prevents the assembly from fulfilling its oversight functions and controlling the government.
44. See Ngoma and Sichinga, *A Policy and Sectoral Analysis of Zambia's Fiscal Policies*; and Whitworth, 'Zambian Fiscal Performance'.
45. According to OECD/DAC statistics, Zambian aid dependency – measured as ODA in % of Gross National Income (GNI) – declined from roughly 25% at the beginning of the last decade to only 10% in 2009.
46. De Kemp, Faust, and Leiderer, 'Between High Expectations and Reality', 36.
47. Rakner and Svåsand, 'Stuck in Transition', 86.
48. The main forums for this policy dialogue are the Joint Steering Committee (JSC) and the Joint Executive Committee (JEC). In addition to quarterly JSC and JEC meetings, the government and MDBS donors meet twice a year for a structured annual review process. The latter meetings are jointly called by the government and donors and are open to the participation of legislators and representatives of civil society groups (De Kemp, Faust, and Leiderer, 'Between High Expectations and Reality').
49. GRZ and PRBS Group, *Memorandum of Understanding*, 5.
50. Economic Affairs represented the largest share of total expenditure growth between 2006 and 2008, accounting for more than 20% of the total increase. The second largest contributor was Social Protection, which accounted for almost another fifth of total expenditure growth, followed by Health (14.2%) and Education (12.8%).
51. De Kemp, Faust, and Leiderer, 'Between High Expectations and Reality'.
52. Hedvall et al., *Mid Term Review*, 6.
53. De Kemp, Faust, and Leiderer, 'Between High Expectations and Reality', 34.
54. The major budget support-related programme has been the programme on Public Expenditure Management and Financial Accountability (PEMFA), which was supported by all MDBS donors plus the US. In addition to the technical assistance on PFM related directly to MDBS, several bilateral donors including Norway and Germany developed additional technical assistance programmes regarding PFM reforms and the strengthening of external auditing.

55. This trend is revealed when taking the comparative indicators of corruption from Kaufmann, Kraay, and Mastruzzi, 'The Worldwide Governance Indicators'.
56. GRZ, *Zambia Public Financial Management Performance Report*; IMF, 'Zambia: 2009 Article IV Consultation'; and De Kemp, Faust, and Leiderer, 'Between High Expectations and Reality', 68.
57. This is backed by many confidential interviews held with representatives of different donor agencies during the first half of 2010 in Lusaka. For a list of the interviews see De Kemp, Faust, and Leiderer, 'Between High Expectations and Reality', 277.
58. Confidential interview, March 2010, Lusaka.
59. Koch and Morazan, *Monitoring Budget Support in Developing Countries*, 23, 25.
60. Confidential interviews in Lusaka, April and March 2010.
61. De Kemp, Faust, and Leiderer, 'Between High Expectations and Reality'.
62. While it could be argued that all indicators measure aspects of the national development plan, a more coherent alignment was inhibited by the fact that only 19 of the 36 indicators have concrete equivalents in the development plan (De Kemp, Faust, and Leiderer, 'Between High Expectations and Reality'). In several cases, it seems that sector-specific indicators were introduced to the assessment framework in order to give more leverage to the principle off-budget aid activities of specific donors.
63. Gerster and Chikwekwe, 'Poverty Reduction Budget Support (PRBS) in Zambia', 17.
64. De Kemp, Faust, and Leiderer, 'Between High Expectations and Reality'.
65. Ibid., 11, 76.
66. Ibid., 46. Mostly through projects not directly linked to Budget Support, several donors (including Finland, Germany, Norway, the UK, and USAID) implemented – often through NGOs – training measures for parliamentarians; the EU's support primarily focused on providing hardware and office construction (De Kemp, Faust, and Leiderer, 'Between High Expectations and Reality').
67. Koch, *Support to Domestic Accountability in Developing Countries*, 26.
68. Koch and Morazan, *Monitoring Budget Support in Developing Countries*, 23.
69. Molenaers, Cepinskas, and Jacobs, *Budget Support and Policy/Political Dialogue*, 431.
70. De Kemp, Faust, and Leiderer, 'Between High Expectations and Reality', 59.
71. See Molenaers, Cepinskas, and Jacobs, *Budget Support and Policy/Political Dialogue*.
72. Prior to the reform, the annual budget used to be approved only in March or April of a given year. Thus, in the first quarter of a year, budget allocations could only be made by direct presidential approval, which potentially expanded the government's discretionary leeway on budget allocations. The reform substantially reduced this leeway, because it forced the government to hand in its budget proposal draft months earlier for parliamentary approval.
73. Molenaers, Cepinskas, and Jacobs, *Budget Support and Policy/Political Dialogue*, 32.
74. Mwangala, 'Review of Oversight Institutions in Zambia'.
75. The Vulnerability FLEX mechanism (V-FLEX) has been a short-term instrument intended to support the most vulnerable African, Caribbean and Pacific Group of States (ACP) countries as they cope with the impact of the global financial and economic crisis of 2009 in order to mitigate its social consequences.
76. Molenaers, Cepinskas, and Jacobs, *Budget Support and Policy/Political Dialogue*.
77. For instance, Schimmelfennig and Scholtz do show in a panel analysis that political conditionality of the EU did have a positive effect on democracy levels in those neighbourhood countries who had a prior membership perspective but not on others. See Schimmelfennig and Scholtz, 'EU Democracy Promotion in the European Neighbourhood'.
78. European Commission, *The Future Approach to EU Budget Support*.

Notes on contributors

Jörg Faust is head of the governance department at the German Development Institute in Bonn. His current work is focused on the link between political institutions and development as well as on democracy support and the political economy of aid. He also works on comparative methods and evaluation and was a co-lead for the evaluation of budget support in Zambia.

Stefan Leiderer is an economist at the German Development Institute in Bonn. His current work is focused on public financial management, programme-based approaches in development cooperation with a special focus on budget support as well as on evaluation methods. He was a co-lead for the evaluation of budget support in Zambia.

Johannes Schmitt is a researcher and PhD candidate at the Institute of Political Science at the University of Duisburg Essen. He was part of the evaluation team evaluating budget support in Zambia. His research is on politics in Africa, budget support and democracy promotion, aid relations and political conditionality.

References

Bertelsmann Stiftung. *BTI 2010 – Zambia Country Report*. Gütersloh: Bertelsmann Stiftung, 2009.
BMZ. 'Budget Support in the Framework of Programme-Oriented Joint Financing (PJF)'. Strategies 181. Bonn: Bundesministerium für wirtschaftliche Zusammenarbeit und Entwicklung (BMZ) [German Federal Ministry for Economic Co-operation and Development], 2008.
Booth, David, ed. 'Are PRSPs Making a Difference? The African Experience'. Special issue, *Development Policy Review* 21, no. 2 (2003): 131–59.
Bräutigam, Deborah A., and Stephen Knack, 'Foreign Aid, Institutions and Governance in Sub-Saharan Africa'. *Economic Development and Cultural Change* 52, no. 2 (2004): 255–85.
Burnell, Peter. 'Does Economic Reform Promote Democratisation? Evidence from Zambia's Third Republic'. *New Political Economy* 6, no. 2 (2001): 191–212.
Burnell, Peter. *Promoting Democracy Abroad: Policy and Performance*. New Jersey: Transaction, 2011.
Burnell, Peter. 'Taking Stock of Democracy in Zambia'. In *Democratic Consolidation in the Third World: Problems and Prospects*, ed. Jeff Haynes, 132–51. London: Routledge, 2001.
Carothers, Thomas. 'Democracy Support and Development Aid: The Elusive Quest for Synthesis'. *Journal of Democracy* 21, no. 4 (2009): 12–26.
Chong, Alberto, Mark Gradstein, and Maria Calderón. 'Can Foreign Aid Reduce Income Inequality and Poverty?'. *Public Choice* 140, no. 1 (2009): 59–84.
Collier, Paul, and Anke Höffler. 'Unintended Consequences: Does Aid Promote Arms Races?'. *Oxford Bulletin of Economics and Statistics* 69, no. 1 (2007): 1–27.
Co-operating Partners. *Joint Assistance Strategy for Zambia (JASZ) 2007–2010*. Lusaka: Co-operating Partners, 2007.
Cordella, Tito, and Giovanni Dell'Ariccia. 'Budget Support versus Project Aid'. International Monetary Fund Working Paper 88/03. Washington, DC: IMF, 2003.
De Kemp, Antonie, Jörg Faust, and Stefan Leiderer. 'Between High Expectations and Reality: An Evaluation of Budget Support in Zambia'. The Hague: Policy and Operations Evaluation Department (IOB), Dutch Foreign Ministry, 2011.
DFID. 'Strengthening Accountability in Budget Support Countries: DFID's 5% Commitment'. Briefing Note for Country Offices. London: DFID, 2011.

Djankov, Simeon, Jose G. Montalvo, and Marta Reynal-Querol. 'Aid with Multiple Personalities'. *Journal of Comparative Economics* 37, no. 2 (2009): 217–29.

Dutta, Nabamita, Peter T. Leeson, and Claudia R. Williamson. 'The Amplification Effect: Foreign Aid's Impact on Political Institutions'. 2010 (unpublished manuscript).

Easterly, William, Ross Levine, and David Roodman. 'Aid, Policies, and Growth: Comment'. *American Economic Review* 94, no. 3 (2004): 774–80.

Electoral Commission of Zambia. 'Public Notice – Presidential Election Results', http://www.elections.org.zm/election_results.php (accessed January 9, 2012).

Emmanuel, Nikolas. 'Undermining Co-operation: Donor-patrons and the Failure of Political Conditionality. *Democratization* 17, no. 5 (2010): 856–77.

European Commission. *The Future Approach to EU Budget Support to Third Countries. Communication from the Commission to the European Parliament, the Council, the European Economic and Social Committee and the Committee of the Regions.* Brussels: European Commission, October 13, 2011.

Faust, Jörg. 'Policy Experiments, Democratic Ownership and Development Assistance'. *Development Policy Review* 28, no. 5 (2010): 515–34.

Feyzioglu, Tarhan, Vinaya Swaroop, and Min Zhu. 'A Panel Data Analysis of the Fungibility of Foreign Aid'. *World Bank Economic Review* 12, no. 1 (1998): 29–58.

Finkel, Steven E., Aníbal Pérez-Liñán, and Mitchell A. Seligson. 'The Effects of U.S. Foreign Assistance on Democracy Building, 1990–2003'. *World Politics* 59, no. 3 (2007): 404–39.

Fraser, Alastair. 'Zambia: Back to the Future?'. In *The Politics of Aid: African Strategies for Dealing with Donors*, ed. L. Whitfield, 299–328. Oxford: Oxford University Press, 2009.

Freedom House. *Country Report Zambia – 2010*. Washington, DC: Freedom House, 2010.

Freedom House. *Country Report Zambia – 2011*. Washington, DC: Freedom House, 2011.

Gerster, R., and M. Chikwekwe. 'Poverty Reduction Budget Support (PRBS) in Zambia. Joint Annual Review 2007: Learning Assessment'. Final Report. Lusaka, 2007.

Grimm, Sonja, and Julia Leininger. 'Not All Good Things Go Together: Conflicting Objectives in Democracy Promotion'. *Democratization* 19, no. 3 (2012): 391–414.

GRZ. *Zambia Public Financial Management Performance Report and Performance Indicators: 2008 Assessment and Update Report.* Lusaka: Government of the Republic of Zambia, 2008.

GRZ and PRBS Group. *Memorandum of Understanding between the Government of the Republic of Zambia and Co-operating Partner Agencies Concerning Poverty Reduction Budget Support.* Lusaka: GRZ and PRBS Group, April 1, 2005.

Hayman, Rachel. 'Budget Support and Democracy: A Twist in the Conditionality Tale'. *Third World Quarterly* 32, no. 4 (2011): 673–88.

Hedvall, F., L. Ljung, K. Sinclair, G. Steen, P. Søndergaard, and P. Tegwa. *Mid Term Review of the Public Expenditure Management and Financial Accountability (PEMFA) Programme in Zambia.* Stockholm: SIPU, International Swedish Institute for Public Administration, 2007.

Horner, Lisa, and Greg Power. *The Democratic Dimension of Aid: Prospects for Democracy Building within the Contemporary International Architecture of Development Co-operation. Literature Review for International IDEA.* Stockholm: Global Partners and Associates, 2009.

Hyden, Goran. 'After the Paris Declaration: Taking on the Issue of Power'. *Development Policy Review* 26, no. 3 (2008): 259–74.

IDD and Associates. *Evaluation of General Budget Support: Synthesis Report: Note on Approach and Methods.* Birmingham: University of Birmingham, 2006.

IMF. 'Zambia: 2009 Article IV Consultation, Third Review Under the Three-Year Arrangement Under the Poverty and Reduction and Growth Facility, and Request for

Modification of Performance Criteria'. IMF Country Report 10/17. Washington, DC: IMF, 2010.
Kalyvitis, Sarantis, and Irene Vlachaki. 'Democratic Aid and the Democratization of Recipients'. *Contemporary Economic Policy* 28, no. 2 (2010): 188–218.
Kaufmann, Daniel, Aart Kraay, and Massimo Mastruzzi. 'The Worldwide Governance Indicators: Methodology and Analytical Issues'. World Bank Policy Research Working Paper no. 5430. Washington, DC: World Bank, 2010.
Kelly, Jones. 'Moving Money: Aid Fungibility in Africa'. *SAIS Review* 25, no. 2 (2005): 167–80.
Knack, Stephen. 'Aid Dependence and the Quality of Governance: Cross-country Empirical Tests'. *Southern Economic Journal* 68 (2001): 210–329.
Knack, Stephen. 'Does Foreign Aid Promote Democracy?'. *International Studies Quarterly* 48, no. 2 (2004): 251–66.
Knack, Stephen, and Aminur Rahman. 'Donor Fragmentation and Bureaucratic Quality in Aid Recipients'. *Journal of Development Economics* 83, no. 1 (2007): 176–97.
Koch, Svea. *Support to Domestic Accountability in Developing Countries: Taking Stock of the Approaches and Experiences of German Development Co-operation. Case study: Tanzania*. Maastricht: ECDPM, 2011.
Koch, Svea, and Pedro Morazan. *Monitoring Budget Support in Developing Countries: A Comparative Analysis of National Control Mechanisms*. Brussels: Policy Department DG External Policies, 2010.
Koeberle, Stefan, and Zoran Stavreski. 'Budget Support: Concept and Issues'. In *Budget Support as More Effective Aid? Recent Experiences and Emerging Lessons*, ed. S. Koeberle, Z. Stavreski, and J. Walliser, 3–26. Washington, DC: The World Bank, 2006.
Lazarus, Joel. 'Participation in Poverty Reduction Strategy Papers: Reviewing the Past, Assessing the Present and Predicting the Future'. *Third World Quarterly* 29, no. 6 (2008): 1205–21.
Limpach, Sophia, and Katharina Michaelowa. 'The Impact of World Bank and IMF Programs on Democratization in Developing Countries'. Working Paper 62/2010. Zürich: University of Zürich, Center for Comparative and International Studies (CIS), 2010.
Meyer, Stefan, and Nils-Sjard Schulz. 'Ownership with Adjectives: Donor Harmonisation: Between Effectiveness and Democratization. Synthesis Report'. Working Paper 58. Madrid: FRIDE, 2008.
Molenaers, Nadia, Linas Cepinskas, and Bert Jacobs. *Budget Support and Policy/Political Dialogue: Donor Practices in Handling (Political) Crisis*. Antwerp: University of Antwerp, 2010.
Morss, Elliott R. 'Institutional Destruction Resulting from Donor and Project Proliferation in Sub-Saharan African Countries'. *World Development* 12, no. 4 (1984): 465–70.
Mwangala, Petronella. *Review of Oversight Institutions in Zambia*. Lusaka, 2010 (unpublished manuscript).
Ngoma, Isaac, and Robert Sichinga. *A Policy and Sectoral Analysis of Zambia's Fiscal Policies and Performance Trends 2006–2010*. Lusaka: Civil Society for Poverty Reduction, 2010.
Nielson, Richard, and Daniel Nielson. 'Triage for Democracy: Selection Effects in Governance Aid'. 2010 (unpublished manuscript).
Rakner, Lisa, and Lars Svåsand. 'Stuck in Transition: Electoral Processes in Zambia 1991–2001'. *Democratization* 12, no. 1 (2005): 85–105.
Roodman, David. 'The Anarchy of Numbers: Aid, Development and Crosscountry Empirics'. *World Bank Economic Review* 21, no. 2 (2007): 255–77.
Saasa, Oliver. 'Political Economy of Budget Support in Zambia', 2010 (unpublished manuscript).

Schimmelfennig, Frank, and Hanno Scholtz. 'EU Democracy Promotion in the European Neighbourhood: Political Conditionality, Economic Development and Transnational Exchange'. *European Union Politics* 9, no. 2 (2008): 187–215.

Simon, David. *Countries at the Crossroads – Country Report Zambia*. Washington, DC: Freedom House, 2007.

United Nations Development Programme (UNDP). *Human Development Report*. New York: Oxford University Press, 2010.

Whitworth, Alan. 'Zambian Fiscal Performance, 2002–2008'. 2010 (unpublished manuscript).

Coerced transitions in Timor-Leste and Kosovo: managing competing objectives of institution-building and local empowerment

Nicolas Lemay-Hébert

International Development Department, University of Birmingham, UK

Institution-building under the aegis of international administration has faced various hurdles and obstacles in Kosovo and Timor-Leste. One particular hurdle is related to the mandates of the United Nations Interim Administration Mission in Kosovo and United Nations Transitional Administration in East Timor, which created a conflict of objectives for the external actors – specifically, between institution-building and local empowerment. This article analyses the strategies of international administrators and local elites in this context. After attempting to prioritize institution-building while paying lip-service to imperatives of empowerment, international officials were forced to readjust their strategy as a result of opposition and resistance from local partners. In light of the practical consequences of the conflict of objectives, international officials proceeded to prioritize local empowerment, reducing their institution-building role. The article concludes by identifying the implications of these experiences for the debate concerning democracy promotion, and highlights the attributes of the 'participatory intervention' framework put forward by Chopra and Hohe.

Introduction

UN-led peace-building is now increasingly coming under scrutiny. As new-found dilemmas emerge, the literature on the subject is paying more attention to the inherent limits of international involvement in war-torn societies.[1] One of the major dilemmas of external involvement is linked to the dual objectives of institution-building and empowerment of local actors. After a string of interventions in the 1990s, which did not meet local and international expectations, and where the international community's involvement in institution-building was minimal, the United Nations Security Council pushed for more robust interventions. The end of the 1990s provided the perfect 'petri-dish', in the words of Sergio Vieira de Mello, for the international community to experiment with a new type of peace-building mission, namely international protectorates.[2] However, as Philip Roeder and Donald Rothchild assert, protectorates do not eliminate the problems of external intervention and power-sharing; on the contrary, they can exacerbate such problems as well as introduce entirely new dilemmas.[3] This article highlights the difficulties arising from external administrations in the context of Kosovo and Timor-Leste.

The international involvement in Timor-Leste and Kosovo – which took the form of international administration including executive, legislative, and judicial authority – reflected international preconceptions about the territories, the state of infrastructural destruction, and the perceived absence of capability on the part of indigenous authorities.[4] Two human-made catastrophes of enormous proportions occurred only months apart in 1999,[5] eliciting similar responses from the international community, despite the fact that the two territories have virtually nothing in common with each other. Timor-Leste and Kosovo are geographically separated by nearly 10,000 kilometres and are culturally distinct. Timor-Leste's local context was that of a mostly ethnically and religiously homogenous society unified behind its leader, Xanana Gusmão, and the umbrella organization that had supported the cause of independence during the final years of Indonesian occupation (the National Council of Maubere Resistance, which became the National Council of Timorese Resistance in 1998); Kosovo's circumstances were drastically different, its society being deeply divided over ethnic, religious, and linguistic lines. Furthermore, the local Kosovar-Albanian leadership was split between the pacifist political party led by Ibrahim Rugova, which had assured a certain degree of health and education services in the Albanian language when Serbia's Milošević had drastically restricted such services in the 1980s and 1990s, and Hashim Thaci's Kosovo Liberation Army (KLA). The two parties established their own institutional apparatuses following the Federal Republic of Yugoslavia (FRY)'s withdrawal from Kosovo, as did Belgrade in the region along the northern part of the Ibar River. In Kosovo, the final resolution of the territory's status was not clear from the outset, and there was intense international wrangling over the fate of the territory, led notably by Serbia but also by Serbia's traditional political ally and permanent Security Council member, Russia, among other recalcitrant states. In the case of Timor-Leste, Security Council politics did not impede the work of the international administration, and the final status of the territory had been clarified from the outset by an internationally recognized referendum in August 1999. Moreover, the former occupying power, Indonesia, recognized the referendum's result, even if its armed forces and associated militias proceeded to punish the Timorese population for rejecting its proposal of an autonomous status within Indonesia.

The study of two nearly identical peace missions taking place in two very different geographical and socio-political settings allows us to isolate the role of international practice from other variables (ethnic, religious, or linguistic divisions, cohesion of the UN Security Council, politics of the state that had previously controlled the territory, etc.). For this reason, this contribution will focus exclusively on the period from 1999–2004 in Kosovo (when the mission de facto began its exit strategy),[6] and on the period between 1999 and 2002 in Timor-Leste (in 2002, the Timor-Leste mission officially withdrew, only to resume some of its executive competencies four years later following the collapse of Timorese security institutions).[7]

In addition, examination of the international experiences in Kosovo and Timor-Leste can provide valuable insight for future peace missions. The idea of direct governance of war-torn or 'dysfunctional' societies by an outside organization retains a pervasive influence in certain segments of academia and in policy circles, despite the controversial outcomes in Kosovo and Timor-Leste. Although the Brahimi report casts the tenets of international administration in a harsh light, there are still pundits who plead the case for new international administrations to be deployed in post-conflict contexts to exercise direct governance on behalf of the local population.[8] The actual cases of direct governance by international organizations have perhaps been too few to analyse in quantitative studies[9]; however, there is still a need to review the experiences of Kosovo and Timor-Leste using qualitative methods,[10] building on and complementing the existing literature on the subject.[11] There is a further need to clarify the lessons learned from these two international administrations,[12] especially given the fact that the state-building legacies in the cases of Kosovo and Timor-Leste can be distorted and manipulated in different ways to justify specific agendas in international relations.[13]

In this context, this article demystifies the state-building experiences of Kosovo and Timor-Leste while contributing to this special issue on 'conflicting objectives in democracy promotion' by specifically focusing on the intrinsic conflict of objectives between institution-building and empowerment imperatives in the conduct of public affairs 'from the outside-in'.[14] Following the 'canons' of literature on the subject, *institution-building* is defined as an integral part of state-building, understood as 'the creation of new government institutions and the strengthening of existing ones'.[15] In this regard, state-building can be seen as intertwined with the concept of *peace-building*, defined by Boutros Boutros-Ghali in *An Agenda for Peace* as 'an action to identify and support structures that will tend to strengthen and solidify peace in order to avoid a relapse into conflict'.[16] The article's main argument is that the initial focus on institution-building in Kosovo and Timor-Leste and the centralization of authority in the hands of international officials led these officials to marginalize empowerment imperatives and to exclude the local population from the governance framework, creating new problems on the ground and fuelling a wave of popular opposition to the international administration. Although outside intervention can help avoid a return to the initial conflict by local parties, it can also create a new set of dilemmas for the external actors. As such, this article contributes to the discussion of the 'institutionalization before liberalization' strategy, defined as actions aiming to build 'the foundations of effective political and economic institutions *before* the introduction of electoral democracy and market-oriented adjustment policies'.[17] This theory can be interpreted as privileging a restricted notion of institution-building to the detriment of local empowerment, especially when the process is understood as 'limit[ing] political and economic freedoms in the short run, in order to create conditions for a smoother and less hazardous transition to market democracy – and durable peace – in the long run'.[18] For Roland Paris, 'pursuing this strategy will require international agencies and their principal backers – the industrialized democracies – to behave in ways that may be viewed as illiberal or even imperialistic', but as he adds 'this, it seems to me, is the short-term price of an effective peacebuilding policy'.[19] In that regard, the international administrations of Kosovo and Timor-Leste are clear examples of a progressive shift in the international community towards this strategy.[20]

This article offers new insights into the limits of the 'institutionalization before liberalization' strategy, when understood as limiting local empowerment in favour of externally-controlled institution-building. It should be emphasized that this interpretation does not convey perfectly the original intent presented by Paris in *At War's End*, but it is an interpretation that nevertheless has come to be associated more globally with the strategy.[21] In fact, for Roland Paris, international state-building should not delay local participation: 'decisionmaking authority should be transferred to indigenous institutions as quickly as possible, and locals should be trained in public administration and prepared to take over the management of governmental agencies immediately'.[22] By focusing on the strategies implemented by internal and external actors in Kosovo and Timor-Leste, this article sheds light on the third research question asked by Grimm and Leininger (that is, how local and international actors deal with the specific conflict of objectives). This article focuses mainly on the strategy-building aspects of the conflicts of objectives (see Figure 1 in the introduction to this special issue[23]), since norm-building aspects have been analysed in a previous contribution.[24]

First, the article examines the intrinsic conflict of objectives between institution-building and empowerment by analysing the architectures created by the United Nations Security Council in Kosovo and Timor-Leste. Second, I analyse the policy of prioritizing institution-building over local empowerment put in place by international officials by focusing on the international administrations' internal process of institution-building, which led to the policy of co-opting certain political elites while marginalizing the overall population. Faced with local opposition to their policies, international officials decided to compromise, and thus reduced their institution-building presence in order to reinforce local empowerment. The article finally explores what role democracy promotion and local empowerment understood more broadly could play in such a context, and what other avenues could be explored in order to mitigate the conflicts of objectives in the future.

International architecture in Kosovo and Timor-Leste

In 1999, the state of violence and institutional destruction in Kosovo and in Timor-Leste led the United Nations Security Council to establish fully-fledged international administrations with executive, legislative, and judicial powers to preside over the two territories – the United Nations Interim Administration Mission in Kosovo (UNMIK, active since 1999) and the United Nations Transitional Administration in Timor-Leste (UNTAET, 1999–2002). In both cases, the international apparatus was headed by a Special Representative of the Secretary-General (SRSG), who acted as the legal head of state of these territories and enjoyed 'virtually unlimited powers'[25] in the process. This specific institutional architecture differed from that of previous international interventions, such as the administration of the Saar Basin and Danzig by the League of Nations and the UN peace missions in West New Guinea, Namibia, Cambodia, and Eastern Slavonia.[26] No other peace mission had ever been endowed with so much authority; more precisely, no previous peace mission had translated its mandate into such a degree of authority on the ground. The SRSG in Timor-Leste, Sergio Vieira de Mello, described his job as amounting to 'benevolent despotism'.[27] The two missions affirmed their respective authorities by enacting virtually identical decrees stating that 'all legislative and executive authority with respect to Kosovo [Timor-Leste], including the administration of the judiciary, is vested in UNMIK [UNTAET] and is exercised by the SRSG [Transitional administrator]'.[28]

While the political situation in Kosovo precluded any direct transfer of authority to local institutions, there was a certain degree of support for an interim administration in Timor-Leste directed by the leader of the independence movement, Xanana Gusmão, with Sergio Vieira de Mello in the role of international adviser.[29] The unprecedented centralization of authority in the hands of UN officials in Kosovo and Timor-Leste, combined with a poor understanding of and a disregard for the local context, fuelled a political backlash by local actors, who resented their subjugation to the excessive authority of an international administration 'whose decisions cannot be challenged by the local population, whose actions are not always transparent, and who cannot be removed from power by the community in whose interests he or she exercises authority ostensibly'.[30] Deprived of a meaningful and democratic outlet to express complaints within the system, opposition grew outside the system.

There was thus a bona fide conflict of objectives in the mandates entrusted to the international actors. In the words of Grimm and Leininger (introduction to this special issue), a *conflict of objectives* is a 'clash of two competing goals whereby the achievement of one goal is impaired by the achievement of the other goal'.[31] Although the obligation to consult the local population was recognized by the UN in both cases – the principle was even enshrined from the start in Resolution 1272, which states 'the need for UNTAET to consult and cooperate closely with the East Timorese people in order to carry out its mandate effectively' – the UN nevertheless chose to enforce its authority to an unprecedented degree, showing a 'preoccupation with control at the expense of the local community's involvement in government'.[32] Specifically, the UN administrators found themselves facing a serious conflict of objectives between local empowerment and institution-building with international officials, at first prioritizing the latter to the detriment of the former. As will be shown in the following sections, the procedural democracy and co-option practices promoted by international officials fell short of local expectations in terms of local empowerment, and it was only when faced with opposition and resistance that they finally modified their policies.

Putting institutions first in Kosovo and Timor-Leste: the international policy of co-option of local elites and its limits

While it was expected that the UN would quickly take control of the territories in the immediate aftermath of the 1999 crises in Timor-Leste and Kosovo, the UN faced formidable difficulties in its deployment of forces. In face of the practical challenges posed by parallel structures and the lack of personnel, the UN had to recognize and negotiate with the de facto institutions. Direct opposition to the parallel institutions proved to be an impracticable policy. Bernard Kouchner, the second SRSG in Kosovo, astutely managed these initial challenges by co-opting the local political elite in order to consolidate UN authority over the region. The Kosovo Transitional Council (KTC), with only advisory and consulting authority, initially brought together local actors from various backgrounds, but it was plagued by serious logistical problems and eventually lost all its usefulness. In December 1999, Kouchner took a different approach, brokering an agreement between three Kosovar Albanian leaders (Hashim Thaçi, Ibrahim Rugova, and Rexhep Qosja) that led to the creation of the representative structures of self-government in Kosovo, designated the Joint Interim Administrative Structure (JIAS). The objective was to create a 'consultative body [...] in order to incorporate individuals who participate in parallel structures in the municipal administration'.[33] In return for inclusion in the administrative structures of Kosovo, in particular a seat in the newly created Interim Administrative Council (IAC), the Kosovar leaders were required to give up their earlier titles and claims and to dissolve all parallel structures, with a deadline of 31 January 2000.

The JIAS included the creation of the IAC, an expansion of the KTC, and the establishment of 20 administrative departments and municipal councils to be jointly co-headed by international and local representatives. All members of these bodies were appointed by the SRSG. The enlarged KTC, whose 36 members represented the pluralistic nature of Kosovar society, was nothing more than a forum in which the members discussed issues of general political interest in an ad hoc fashion. The mandate of the IAC was to 'make policy recommendations, serve as an advisory cabinet for the SRSG and act as an executive board for the JIAS'.[34] The Kosovar members of the IAC frequently complained that the 'real decisions were made behind their backs and without them being consulted'.[35] The new structure was quickly understood by Kosovar Albanians to be a way for UNMIK to enforce its authority over the territory of Kosovo, at least south of the Ibar River, rather than a genuine system of sharing authority.[36] As David Marshall, who acted as head of the Legal Systems Monitoring Section for the Organisation for Security and Co-Operation in Europe (OSCE) Mission in

Kosovo between 2000 and 2001, and Shelley Inglis note, 'despite vocal protest from all members of the JAC, regulations were provided to the JAC as a token gesture. By the end of 2001, it was clear that what had begun as one of the only high-level forums for international and local consultation and cooperation on legal issues had become an empty shell.'[37]

Municipal and legislative elections could have modified the status quo in Kosovo. However, even after the first municipal elections in October 2000, in which the JIAS structure began to be replaced by elected Municipal Assemblies and Presidents, UNMIK retained all of its discretionary powers, as reaffirmed by UNMIK Regulation 2000/45 on the Self-government of Municipalities in Kosovo.[38] The Constitutional Framework for Provisional Government, which created the Provisional Institutions of Self-Government (PISG), reproduced the same political arrangement, this time at the 'national' level. Although it was a major step towards a transfer of certain competencies to local institutions, the framework did not fundamentally alter the architecture of power in Kosovo, in the sense that UNMIK still held the keys of power. For King and Mason, the constitutional framework 'did not endow its democratically members (sic) with ultimate authority in any area'.[39] Following the legislative election of 17 November 2001, tensions between UNMIK and local institutions grew, leading to public clashes fuelled by the gap between the 'legitimacy [of elected bodies] and actual political power'.[40] The policy of 'Standards before Status' adopted in 2002 also frustrated domestic actors by demonstrating UNMIK's propensity to control the political agenda. Jock Covey, who acted as Deputy Special Representative of the Secretary General (DSRSG) in Kosovo, says 'ambiguity about the goals that had to be met and the absence of a working partnership with the PISG to attain them created a widespread popular perception that this policy should really be called "Standards to Prevent Status."'[41] UNMIK's prioritization policy, which favoured institution-building over local empowerment imperatives, began to foster resentment among the local population and elites who felt excluded from decision-making processes. Only the violent incidents of March 2004, which saw incensed Kosovars taking on ethnic minorities and international forces, compelled a radical change in the power dynamic in Kosovo; subsequently, the UN downsized its mission and presence in the Kosovar political landscape.[42]

International administrators used a similar strategy of prioritization of institution-building objectives over local empowerment goals in Timor-Leste, co-opting certain elements of the political elite while marginalizing local power structures and the local population in general. After the 1999 international intervention in Timor-Leste, village and *suco* (cluster of villages) chiefs took part in cooperative efforts with the National Council of Timorese Resistance (CNRT), the vast political umbrella revered by the Timorese for its role in the resistance against Indonesia. According to Rod Nixon, 'this organization [CNRT] overlapped extensively with local administrative and ritual structures',[43] which gave it particular legitimacy in Timor-Leste. As early as the end of October 1999, a couple of weeks before the arrival of Sergio Vieira de Mello in Dili, the CNRT began to create political structures through village elections. In most districts, the CNRT was already conducting repatriation efforts and channelling militia members accused of war crimes to traditional judicial systems when UNTAET finally arrived. The CNRT appointed representatives at every level, establishing a shadow administration. While the efficiency and legitimacy of the CNRT was recognized from the outset by UNTAET, senior officials in the international administration decided to make a priority of imposing their authority over the territory. At both local and national levels, Timorese leaders could have been part of the administration from the outset,[44] but the UNTAET's senior leadership decided otherwise.

UNTAET created the National Consultative Council (NCC) in order to incorporate some Timorese leaders into the decision-making process. However, the NCC had, as its title indicates, only consultative powers. UNTAET Regulation 1999/2 establishing the NCC made clear that it 'shall in no way prejudice the final authority of the Transitional Administrator in exercising the responsibilities vested in UNTAET'.[45] Although the NCC was supposed to be a 'unique means for UNTAET to hear and to respond to the needs of the East Timorese and for the latter to participate in important policy decisions',[46] it became clear that the council could be transformed into merely a Timorese chamber for legitimizing decisions taken by UNTAET. As UNTAET official Peter Galbraith notes, 'the Timorese thought they had little choice but to ratify whatever was put in front of them. They were essentially told "if you don't do this, there'll be dire consequences with no money to follow".'[47] According to Samantha Power, the Nobel Prize Winner Jose Ramos-Horta laughed off the UN's invitation to join the NCC and he told de Mello that 'I was powerless outside of ET for long enough', while adding that 'the last thing I need is to be powerless inside Timor'. Moreover, Gusmão said 'we felt we were being used. We realized we weren't there to help the UN make decisions or to prepare ourselves to run the administration, We were there to put our rubber stamp on Sergio [Vieira de Mello]'s regulations, to allow the UN to claim to be consulting.'[48] From the beginning, UNTAET described its purpose as 'not so much an interim administration as a co-architect, with the East Timorese people, of a national administration that would serve long after UNTAET's departure'[49]; however, local perception of the UN effort was clearly quite different.

Dealing with conflicting objectives: a necessary compromise by UNTAET and UNMIK officials

The events in Kosovo in 2004 drastically changed international perceptions of the costs associated with the conflicting goals of institution-building and local empowerment, perceptions that had originally led the UN to prioritize the former over the latter in the first stages of the intervention. In the midst of the most violent incidents in Kosovo since the 1999 war, 19 people died and more than 1000 were wounded in clashes between Kosovar Albanian demonstrators, who were infiltrated by radical elements, and ethnic minorities in Kosovo, most notably the Serbian community. The crisis stemmed not only from ethnic divisions but also from the contentious relationship between Kosovars and international officials.[50] Although the UN's consultation with and co-option of political elites at first helped gave some legitimacy to the international administration, this was not in itself sufficient. As correctly forecast by the International Crisis Group (ICG) in 2001, 'the newly elected officials will be unlikely to accept for long the straightjacket imposed by the unelected international administration'.[51] Indeed, as the Independent International Commission on Kosovo concurrently stated, 'the extensive powers accorded the SRSG mean that, instead of the substantial self-government promised the Kosovars under Resolution 1244, they will instead get very limited autonomy. They will have the illusion of self-rule rather than the reality.'[52] The Commission goes on to say that 'a pervasive distrust of the administrative and political capacity of the population appears to underlie the constitutional provisions. If the population is distrusted, it is likely to repay like with like.'[53]

Former UNMIK officials King and Mason observed that after the events of March 2004, the level of satisfaction with UNMIK's action was so low that 'if UNMIK had been up for election, it would have needed to campaign hard to win votes from anybody in Kosovo other than its own staff'.[54] The Secretary General of the UN subsequently dispatched the Norwegian Ambassador Kai Eide to conduct a 'comprehensive review of the policies and practices of all actors in Kosovo', and to prepare an additional report on the 'comprehensive review of the situation in Kosovo'.[55] The first Eide report was clear: there should be an ambitious policy of transfer of authority to the institutions of Kosovo, coupled with a restructuring of UNMIK. Eide clarified in his second report that, 'while standards implementation in Kosovo has been uneven, the time has come to move to the next phase of the political process'.[56] It was clear that 'after administering Kosovo for six years and four months, the UN accepted that its usefulness had come to an end'.[57] The Eide reports shaped Martti Ahtisaari's mission as Special Envoy of the Secretary General on Kosovo's future status. In accordance with the reports, international officials jump-started the transfer of competencies to local institutions, prioritizing local empowerment over institution-building objectives.

In Timor-Leste, SRSG Sergio Vieira de Mello began attempting to change UNTAET's policy in the spring of 2000. He engaged in a policy of compromise in the face of growing criticism over the lack of participation of the local elite and general population in the governing process. With Timorese unrest boiling over, he sent half a dozen trusted members of his staff on a two-day retreat, asking them to return with proposals for overhauling the mission.[58] The group came up with a system of co-governance with Timorese officials. In July 2000, Vieira de Mello introduced what would be described as the 'First Transitional Government', consisting of a National Council (NC) and a Cabinet, together with the office of the Transitional Administrator; these developments were met with some resistance from UN Headquarters. The Cabinet, along with the office of the Transitional Administrator, was meant to act as the executive power; the expanded Council, consisting of 33 members (later 36), was to constitute a sort of 'legislative forum', in order to provide a separation of powers that was completely new to Timor-Leste.[59] Vieira de Mello offered a mea culpa in the National Congress of the CNRT, admitting that the National Council 'came under increasing scrutiny for not being representative enough of East Timorese society, and not transparent enough in its deliberations. Faced as we were with our own difficulties in the establishment of this mission, we did not, we could not involve the Timorese at large as much as they were entitled to.'[60] The local elite maintained their pressure on the international administration, continuing to denounce UNTAET's centralizing tendencies. As Jean-Christophe Cady, deputy head of UNTAET, made clear from the outset: 'while the role of the president of the CNRT is essential in the consultative process, the proposal for shared executive power is not within UNTAET's capacity to grant'.[61] Gusmão accused the UN of tokenism, adding that he 'did not wish to inherit the heavy decision-making and project implementation mechanisms in which the role of the East Timorese is to give their consent as observers rather than the active players we should start to be'.[62] Timorese ministers even threatened to resign, noting that 'the East Timorese Cabinet members are caricatures of ministers in a government of a banana republic. They have no power, no duties, no resources to function adequately.'[63] Furthermore, discontent with the UN policy toward the East Timorese was not restricted to local officials; certain high-ranking international officials offered their resignations over disagreement with the tendencies toward centralization exhibited by UNTAET. However, with the 30 August 2001 Constituent Assembly Elections, the government became 'all East Timorese'; this was the beginning of the 'second Timorization'. The NC and the Cabinet were supplanted by a Second Transitional Government, consisting of a Council of Ministers and an elected Constituent Assembly. The Constituent Assembly was sworn in, and a 'Second Transitional Government' consisting entirely of East Timorese ministers, vice-ministers, and secretaries was appointed by Sergio Vieira de Mello. On 14 April 2002, Gusmão was elected president of Timor-Leste with an overwhelming majority of 82.7%. Timor-Leste declared its independence one month later, on 20 May 2002. As Charles Scheiner notes, 'it took UNTAET two years to realize that *Transitional*, not *Administration*, was the most important word in their name'.[64]

From democracy promotion to participatory intervention: finding new ways to increase local empowerment in international interventions

The discussion above could lead one to believe that an early democratization process is key, hence favouring the prioritization of democracy over institution-building. Indeed, one of the most common prescriptions for avoiding (or at least mitigating) the effects of the legitimacy dilemma,[65] and for fostering legitimacy on the ground is to make democracy promotion a priority. To a certain extent, this was what Roland Paris warned practitioners about when he put forth the 'institutionalization before liberalization' strategy. Fostering legitimacy requires more than simply the promotion of procedural democracy; rather, state-building necessitates genuine participation by the local population in the democratic process, with locals experiencing the externally guided process as an endogenous one. For Jarat Chopra and Tanja Hohe, 'the blunt approach of international interventions has been to rely on "free and fair" electoral exercises as a single event, and to promote global standards of political rights and North Atlantic concepts of democracy that do not resonate with local communities'. For them, the problem with such an approach lies in the disconnection between external and local sources of legitimacy. Thus, 'individuals may turn out to vote en masse, but their understanding of the ballot may be defined according to a parallel cosmos. A democratically elected power holder may be recognized internationally though not locally.'[66]

The prevailing paradigm of democratization in state-building is certainly not enough by itself to bridge the legitimacy gap in most state-building interventions. For Chopra and Hohe, 'other than reflecting the familiar ingredients of the Western state, the idea of participation among the democratization and peace-building cognoscenti is still at the stage of labels or headlines, and the notion lacks clear definition, any kind of effective strategy, or as much appreciation of the local mind-set as of the model to be imported'.[67] Democracy is too often seen as an event rather than a process leading to the implementation of a top-down approach. The democratization expert Thomas Carothers notes that 'as with the problem of ownership, the problem of knowledge of the local context has been endemic in all foreign aid but is especially common in democracy assistance'. The goal of outside intervention should be 'a productive marriage of external and internal efforts in which outside expert help and experience join with internal ideas, commitment, and initiative'.[68] Charles Call and Susan Cook argue that 'the shortcomings of the democratic reconstruction model require that more attention be paid to specific and local context and to integration of appropriate external governance models with local, legitimate practices in war-torn societies'.[69] The crucial aspect here is the ability to build up a genuine local process that consolidates the legitimacy of the state in the eyes of its citizens. This was an argument duly recognized by the UN, or at least by Boutros Boutros-Ghali, as expressed in his *Agenda for Democratization*. This report states that 'while democratization is a new force in world affairs (...) it is not for the United Nations to offer a model for democratization or democracy (...). Indeed, to do so could be counter-productive to the process of democratization which, in order to take root and to flourish, must derive from the society itself.' The report adds that 'imposition of foreign models (...) may generate resentment among both the government and the public, which may in turn feed internal forces inimical to democratization (...)'.[70] The top-down understanding of democracy promotion in this regard makes sense only if one accepts that 'an externally driven "social (re)engineering" project can accelerate or substitute for a more "organic" historical process of state-building that would otherwise be driven by local actors'.[71] This perspective seems elusive at best, as this study has highlighted in the contexts of Timor-Leste and Kosovo. Similarly, Bueno de Mesquita and Downs argue that democracy promotion conducted from the outside tends to lead to erosion in the trajectory of democracy development, even in the accepted Western sense of the concept.[72]

The 'participatory intervention' framework proposed by Chopra and Hohe requires 'granting space for local voices to be expressed and for communities to get directly involved in the evolution of their own cultural or political foundations'. This means 'giving time for an indigenous paradigm to coexist with, or to gradually transform during the creation of, modern institutions. Integral to the process is the design of mechanisms for genuine popular participation in administrative bodies at the local level.'[73] Kofi Annan, in a report on peacekeeping missions, refers to 'participatory governance'. One year after the deployment of the peace missions in Kosovo and Timor-Leste, he clearly states that a 'sustainable domestic peace' becomes sustainable 'not when all conflicts are removed from society, but when the natural conflicts of society can be resolved peacefully through the exercise of State sovereignty and, generally, *participatory governance*'.[74] The report adds that sustainable peace 'can only be achieved by the local population itself; the role of the United Nations is merely to facilitate the process'.[75] Robert Orr writes that 'while seeking to build up local governance and participation capacity, the international community must observe the cardinal rule of governance: indigenous ownership of the process is key'.[76] He continues, 'even when local actors are disorganized and disempowered in the wake of conflict, they must be given a leadership role in the rebuilding process. Likewise, even when international actors must assume certain functions temporarily, they should always train and empower indigenous counterparts.'[77]

Conclusion

As this study has demonstrated institution-building has significant limits when it is disconnected from the needs and perceptions of the local society targeted by the intervention, encompassed here under the concept of local empowerment. The goal here is to prevent the establishment of what David Chandler has dubbed 'phantom states', whose governing institutions may have extensive external resources but lack social or political legitimacy.[78] Moreover Marina Ottaway argues that outsiders can set up governmental organizations, but 'such organizations will only become significant and established – hence institutions – when the relevant actors believe that they provide solutions to real problems'.[79] The political experiences of both Kosovo and Timor-Leste show the inherent limits of international strategy when such strategy promotes institution-building in early stages without any meaningful participation from the local population. The imposition of solutions from a top-down perspective can be effective only to a certain extent: It can certainly contribute to the restoration of peace and order (a negative peace, to use Galtung's terminology[80]), but has definite limitations in terms of state-building in the broader sense of the word.

This article has analysed the conflict of objectives between institution-building and local empowerment that existed in the first stages of the international interventions in Kosovo and Timor-Leste. It started by reviewing the international strategy, which is a mix of the co-option of certain political elites and the wider marginalization of the local population in the externally imposed structures of governance. Then the article described the local reactions of opposition and resistance. The international response in Timor-Leste, which was devised by the SRSG Sergio Vieira de Mello, was courageous: It induced structural changes in the international architecture to allow greater participation while hastening the exit of the UN mission. In Kosovo, the UN faced a dramatic explosion of violence in March 2004, which forced the organization to change its stance toward the status of the territory and future negotiations. However, more than 12 years after the NATO intervention, the UN is still present in Kosovo, due in large part to the uneven recognition of Kosovo's unilateral independence and to Security Council politics. In the final section, the article has described other possible avenues for balancing the objectives of institution-building and local empowerment in a post-conflict context. There is a genuine need to find a durable solution by which local concerns of legitimacy and representation can be taken into account, instead of international organizations simply imposing 'democracy promotion' goals from the outside.

The conflict of objectives between institution-building and local empowerment is of paramount importance in the specific context of an international administration. Direct governance of war-torn territories is virtually incompatible with the objective of fostering and nurturing legitimacy in an externally guided state-building project. As Chesterman observes, 'political structures created for foreign control (benevolent or not) tend to be unsuited to local rule. The reason for this, in part, is that the "limited goals" of foreign control (benevolent or not) are generally determined with limited regard to local circumstances.'[81] The legitimacy aspects related to institution-building, if initially discarded in the setting-up and exercise of the peace mission's mandate, will find a way to reaffirm themselves throughout the mission. The dilemmas in terms of policy prescription are quite real. William O'Neill, who worked for the UNMIK, demonstrates the difficulty of the situation when he states that 'the UN should avoid acting like the "ugly imperialist" but also should not be reluctant to be assertive, even overriding local decisions'.[82]

A number of other avenues for conflict resolution and democracy promotion exist. The importance of national ownership was underlined by Ban Ki-Moon in 2007 at the Peace-building Commission[83] and in his report on peace-building submitted to the General Assembly and the Security Council.[84] It is also one of the lessons of Timor-Leste identified by Vieira de Mello himself: 'there must be the will to cede power as soon as possible. The United Nations, the keenest of proponents of decolonisation, has in East Timor and Kosovo found itself accorded neo-colonial powers. The result was initially unsettling.'[85] In order to provide an alternative to direct governance by UNMIK, the Independent International Commission on Kosovo proposed what it calls 'conditional independence', which is 'quite distinct from limited self-rule under UNMIK'. It proposes to allow Kosovo to control the entire range of powers now reserved by the SRSG, but under conditions that would ensure stability in the region: explicit renunciation of any changes in borders, a constitutional guarantee of human rights for all citizens, the renunciation of violence in settling internal or external disputes, and a commitment to regional cooperation.[86] Richard Caplan argues for a similar policy, stating that 'in many cases it is possible to devolve responsibility to the local population, insist on transparency and, as a safeguard, maintain control over the public purse, as was done in the case of the UN's Division of Health Services in East Timor: the only administrative division to be headed by an East Timorese nearly one year after the start of the UN operation'.[87] This seems also to be the preferred alternative by participants in regional round-tables in the aftermath of the Brahimi report, a project conducted by the International Peace Academy on the future of peace-building. Participants in African, Asian, and Latin American round-tables all expressed the need 'for greater local ownership of the processes of peace-building'. For these participants, 'emphasis should be on building the capacity for local governance, as in the *later stages of the East Timor mission*, rather than on deploying a vast number of international staff of highly uneven quality'.[88] As Kreilkamp notes, 'it suggests that there are potential alternatives to the hard-line approach that has been adopted by the Security Council'.[89] These are alternatives that could be planned and implemented in future peace-building missions in order to mitigate the most glaring effects of international interventions on local societies.

Acknowledgements

My thanks go to Sonja Grimm, Julia Leininger, and Tina Freyburg for their invitation to contribute to this special issue and for their helpful comments throughout the writing process, as well as two anonymous reviewers for their comments on previous versions of this article. Earlier versions of this article were presented at the annual meeting of the International Studies Association (ISA), New Orleans, 17 February 2010, and at an author's workshop at the ETH-Zurich, 24–25 March 2011. I would also like to thank the participants in the Zurich and New Orleans meetings for their helpful comments and suggestions as well as Roland Paris, for his thoughtful criticism of the manuscript, and Claire Bacher for careful language editing. This work was supported by project PEACE – 'Local Ownership and Peace Missions', financed by the Marie Curie Actions (FP7).

Notes

1. Paris and Sisk, 'Introduction: Understanding the Contradictions of Postwar State-building'; Newman, 'Liberal Peacebuilding Debates'; Aoi, de Coning, and Thakur, 'Unintended Consequences, Complex Peace Operations and Peacebuilding Systems'; Lidén, Mac Ginty, and Richmond, 'Introduction: Beyond Northern Epistemologies of Peace: Peacebuilding Reconstructed?'.
2. Power, *Chasing the Flame*, 303.
3. Roeder and Rothchild, 'Conclusion: Nation-state Stewardship', 328.
4. Lemay-Hébert, 'The "Empty-shell" Approach'.
5. The armed conflict between the Kosovo Liberation Army (KLA) and the Federal Republic of Yugoslavia (FRY) that began in February 1998 proved to be the second major challenge facing Western Europe and the United States in less than a decade.

After the Rambouillet Agreement of 18 March 1999 was rejected by the Serbian leadership, military response took over from diplomacy in the Balkans; the NATO Operation Allied Force followed on 22 March 1999 with the aim of expelling FRY forces from Kosovo. In response, the Serb military and paramilitary groups stepped up their campaign against Kosovar Albanians. At the end of June 1999, more than 10,000 casualties had been attributed to Serbian forces in Kosovo; meanwhile, more than 1.5 million Kosovar Albanians had been forcibly expelled from their homes, representing an estimated 90% of the Kosovar Albanian population. In Timor-Leste, Indonesia agreed to a consultation process, whereby the population of East Timor would vote to accept or reject the idea of autonomy within Indonesia. Despite Indonesia's overt pressure on the Timorese, the results were overwhelming clear. The vote on 30 August 1999 showed that 78.5% of East Timorese voters (with 98% turnout) rejected the option of autonomy within Indonesia in favour of independence. However, following the vote, certain elements of the Indonesian armed forces in collaboration with local militias waged an operation termed Operation Clean Sweep, a three-week scorched-earth campaign meant to punish the East Timorese for their decision. In the course of this operation, an estimated 1500–2000 East Timorese were killed; the hostilities led to the displacement of three-quarters of the total population of 890,000, including an exodus of 250,000 Timorese.

6. The exit strategy is yet to be completed. An international civilian office was created to supervise the new Kosovar institutions, but any meaningful change in the UN mandate must come through a new United Nations Security Council Resolution that abrogates Resolution 1244. The international division over the fate of Kosovo stands in the way of such a change.
7. See: Lemay-Hébert, 'UNPOL and Police Reform in Timor-Leste'.
8. Poppen, 'Prospects for Securing Peace in Haiti Look Bleak'; Ward, 'The Case for International Trusteeship in Haiti'; Weiner, 'An Evolving Idea For Liberia Envisions UN Trusteeship'.
9. Fortna, 'Peacekeeping and Democratization', 43.
10. This article is based on semi-directive interviews conducted in Kosovo in 2007 and Timor-Leste in 2008 with international and local officials.
11. See, among others: Caplan, 'Partner of Patron?'; Narten, 'Dilemmas of Promoting Local Ownership'; Surkhe, 'Peacekeepers as Nation-builders'.
12. Berdal and Caplan, 'The Politics of International Administration', 2–3; Conflict Security and Development Group, *A Review of Peace Operations*, para. 53.
13. Boot, 'Pirates, Terrorism and Failed States'; Schwartz, 'UN Go Home'; Plantev, 'Assessing the Balkans Peacekeeping Experience'; Vaknin, 'Should UN Administer Iraq'.
14. Lemay-Hébert, 'State-building from the Outside-in'.
15. Fukuyama, *State-building*, ix. For a discussion of the institutionalist approach to state-building, see: Lemay-Hébert, 'Statebuilding Without Nationbuilding?'.
16. United Nations, *An Agenda for Peace*, 46.
17. Paris, *At War's End*, 179 (author's emphasis).
18. Ibid., 187–8.
19. Paris, 'Wilson's Ghost', 781.
20. Paris, *At War's End*, 211, 218; Bellamy and Williams, *Understanding Peacekeeping*, 261.
21. Ward, 'The Case for International Trusteeship in Haiti', 31.
22. Paris, *At War's End*, 210.
23. Grimm and Leininger, 'Not All Good Things Go Together', 402.
24. Lemay-Hébert, 'The "Empty-shell" Approach'.

25. Mertus, 'The Impact of Intervention on Local Human Rights Culture', 28; Independent International Commission on Kosovo, *Kosovo Report*, 259.
26. Chesterman, *You, the People*; Stahn, *The Law and Practice of International Territorial Administration*; Wilde, 'From Danzig to East Timor and Beyond'; Zaum, *The Sovereignty Paradox*.
27. Vieira de Mello, 'How Not to Run a Country', 4.
28. United Nations, *UNTAET Regulation 1999/1*, 1.1; United Nations, *UNMIK Regulation 1999/1*, 1.1.
29. Brahimi, 'L'ONU Entre Nécessité et Minimalisme', 305.
30. Caplan, *International Governance of War-torn Territories*, 196.
31. Grimm and Leininger, 'Not All Good Things Go Together', 397.
32. Chopra, 'The UN's Kingdom of East Timor', 30.
33. United Nations, *Report of the Secretary-General on the United Nations Interim Administration in Kosovo*, para. 35.
34. UNMIK Division of Public Information, 'UNMIK at 18 Months'.
35. Brand, 'The Development of Kosovo Institutions', 19.
36. Narten, 'Building Local Institutions and Parliamentarianism in Post-war Kosovo', 147.
37. Marshall and Inglis, 'The Disempowerment of Human Rights-based Justice in the United Nations Mission in Kosovo', 118.
38. United Nations, *UNMIK Regulation 2000/45*, para. 46.2.
39. King and Mason, *Peace at Any Price*, 119.
40. Brand, 'The Development of Kosovo Institutions', 52.
41. Covey, 'Making a Viable Peace', 121.
42. The events are generally believed to have been triggered by two separate incidents. The first was the shooting of a Kosovo Serb youth in the village of Caglavica (Pristina region) on 15 March, which led to a blockade by Kosovo Serbs of the main Pristina–Skopje road just outside Pristina. This road is seen as essential to the Kosovar economy, especially for the Albanian community. The second incident, on 16 March, was the death of three Albanian children by drowning in the Ibar River near the Serb community of Zubin Potok. The rumour spread that the children were chased by Serbs before their death; this sparked Albanian attacks on Serb enclaves. Though the circumstances of the second incident have not been clearly established, the cumulative effects of the two incidents precipitated spontaneous Albanian demonstrations. The demonstrations were quickly taken over by 'organized elements', and intense fighting erupted between the two communities, with the violence quickly spreading to other cities. In the course of these events, 19 people died and more than 1000 were wounded. See: Lemay-Hébert, 'State-building from the Outside-in'.
43. Nixon, 'The Crisis of Governance', 93.
44. Bowles and Chopra, 'East Timor: Statebuilding Revisited', 276.
45. United Nations, *UNTAET Regulation 1999/2*, para. 1.3.
46. United Nations, *Report of the Secretary General on the United Nations Transitional Administration in East Timor*, para. 70.
47. Quoted in: Steele, 'Nation Building in East Timor', 79.
48. Power, *Chasing the Flame*, 307.
49. United Nations, *Head of UN Transitional Administration in East Timor Briefs Security Council*.
50. Lemay-Hébert, 'State-building from the Outside-in'.
51. International Crisis Group, 'Kosovo: Landmark Election', ii.
52. Independent International Commission on Kosovo, *The Follow-up of the Kosovo Report*, 25.
53. Ibid., 20–1.

54. King and Mason, *Peace at Any Price*, 220.
55. United Nations, *Report of the Secretary General on the United Nations Interim Administration Mission in Kosovo*.
56. United Nations, *Letter Dated 7 October 2005 From the Secretary General Addressed to the President of the Security Council*.
57. King and Mason, *Peace at Any Price*, vii.
58. Power, *Chasing the Flame*, 328.
59. 'SRSG: Executive Authority Shared With the East Timorese'.
60. Quoted in: Chesterman, 'East Timor', 201.
61. 'UN Rejects Calls for Shared Executive Power in E. Timor'.
62. Dodd, 'Gusmão Gives UN Team a Serve'; McBeth, 'E Timorese Unhappy About Being Sidelined By UN'.
63. Dodd, 'Give Us a Free Hand or We Quit'.
64. Scheiner, 'Suggestions for the Next United Nations Mission in Timor-Leste'.
65. Lemay-Hébert, 'Everyday Legitimacy and International Administration: Global Governance and Local Legitimacy in Kosovo'.
66. Chopra and Hohe, 'Participatory Intervention', 291–2.
67. Ibid., 291. See also: Carothers, 'The End of the Transition Paradigm', 5–21.
68. Carothers, *Aiding Democracy Abroad*, 262–6.
69. Call and Cook, 'On Democratization and Peacebuilding', 234.
70. Boutros-Ghali, *An Agenda for Democratization*, 4.
71. Krause and Jütersonke, 'Peace, Security and Development in Post-conflict Environments', 451.
72. Bueno de Mesquita and Downs, 'Intervention and Democracy', 627.
73. Chopra and Hohe, 'Participatory Intervention', 289. For examples of 'participatory local governance', see: UNDP, 'Participatory Local Governance'.
74. United Nations, *No Exit Without Strategy*, para. 10 (italics added).
75. Ibid., para. 12.
76. Orr, 'Governing When Chaos Rules', 140.
77. Ibid., 140.
78. Chandler, *Empire in Denial*, 9.
79. Ottaway, 'Rebuilding State Institutions in Collapsed States', 248.
80. Galtung, *Peace: Research, Education, Action*, 245.
81. Chesterman, *You, the People*, 237.
82. O'Neill, *Kosovo: An Unfinished Peace*, 139.
83. United Nations, Secretary General Underscores National Ownership.
84. United Nations, *Report of the Secretary-General on Peacebuilding in the Immediate Aftermath of Conflict*, para. 7.
85. Vieira de Mello, 'Introductory Remark and Keynote Speech', 19.
86. Independent International Commission on Kosovo, *The Follow-up of the Kosovo Report*, 25–7.
87. Caplan, 'Partner or Patron?', 230.
88. International Peace Academy, 'Refashioning the Dialogue', 5 (italics added).
89. Kreilkamp, 'UN Postconflict Reconstruction', 652.

Notes on contributor

Nicolas Lemay-Hébert is a Marie Curie Experienced Researcher in the International Development Department, University of Birmingham (UK). He is additionally an Adjunct Professor, Department of Economics, University of Quebec at Montreal, and Associate Director, Statebuilding and Fragile States at the Center for Peace Missions and Humanitarian Studies, Raoul Dandurand Chair, University of Quebec at Montreal.

Bibliography

Aoi, Chiyuki, Cedric de Coning, and Ramesh Thakur. 'Unintended Consequences, Complex Peace Operations and Peacebuilding Systems', in *Unintended Consequences of Peacekeeping Operations*, ed. Chiyuki Aoi, Cedric de Coning, and Ramesh Thakur, 3–19. Tokyo: United Nations University Press, 2007.

Bellamy, Alex, and Paul Williams. *Understanding Peacekeeping*. Cambridge: Polity, 2010.

Berdal, Mats, and Richard Caplan. 'The Politics of International Administration'. *Security Governance* 10, no.1 (January/March 2004): 1–5.

Boot, Max. 'Pirates, Terrorism and Failed States'. *Wall Street Journal*, December 9, 2008.

Boutros-Ghali, Boutros. *An Agenda for Democratization*. New York: United Nations, 1996.

Bowles, Edith, and Tanja Chopra. 'East Timor: Statebuilding Revisited', in *Building States to Build Peace*, ed. Charles Call and Vanessa Wyeth, 271–302. Boulder, CO: Lynne Rienner, 2008.

Brahimi, Lakhdar. 'L'ONU Entre Nécessité et Minimalisme'. *Politique Etrangère* 2 (Summer 2005): 297–311.

Brand, Marcus. 'The Development of Kosovo Institutions and the Transition of Authority from UNMIK to Local Self-Government'. CASIN report. Geneva: CASIN, January 2003.

Bueno de Mesquita, Bruce, and George Downs. 'Intervention and Democracy'. *International Organization* 60, no. 3 (Summer 2006): 627–49.

Call, Charles, and Susan Cook. 'On Democratization and Peacebuilding'. *Global Governance* 9, no. 2 (April–June 2003): 233–46.

Caplan, Richard. *International Governance of War-torn Territories*. Oxford: Oxford University Press, 2005.

Caplan, Richard. 'Partner or Patron? International Civil Administration and Local Capacity-building'. *International Peacekeeping* 11, no. 2 (Summer 2004): 229–47.

Carothers, Thomas. *Aiding Democracy Abroad: The Learning Curve*. Washington, DC: Carnegie Endowment for International Peace, 1999.

Carothers, Thomas. 'The End of the Transition Paradigm'. *Journal of Democracy* 13, no. 1 (January 2002): 5–21.

Chandler, David. *Empire in Denial: The Politics of State-building*. London: Pluto Press, 2006.

Chesterman, Simon. 'East Timor', in *United Nations Interventionism 1991–2004*, ed. Mats Berdal and Spyros Economides, 192–216. Cambridge: Cambridge University Press, 2007.

Chesterman, Simon. *You, the People: The United Nations, Transitional Administration, and State-building*. Oxford: Oxford University Press, 2004.

Chopra, Jarat. 'The UN's Kingdom of East Timor'. *Survival* 42, no. 3 (Autumn 2000): 27–39.

Chopra, Jarat, and Tanja Hohe. 'Participatory Intervention'. *Global Governance* 10, no. 3 (July–September 2004): 289–305.

Conflict Security and Development Group. *A Review of Peace Operations: A Case for Change, Synthesis Report*. London: King's College, March 10, 2003.

Covey, Jock. 'Making a Viable Peace: Moderating Political Conflict', in *The Quest for Viable Peace: International Intervention and Strategies for Conflict Transformation*, ed. Jock Covey, Michael Dziedzic, and Leonard Hawley, 99–122. Washington, DC: United States Institute of Peace, 2005.

Dodd, Mark. 'Give Us a Free Hand or We Quit'. *Sydney Morning Herald*, December 5, 2000.

Dodd, Mark. 'Gusmão Gives UN Team a Serve: "We Don't Want a Legacy of Cars"'. *Sydney Morning Herald*, October 10, 2000.

Fortna, Virginia Page. 'Peacekeeping and Democratization', in *From War to Democracy: Dilemmas of Peacebuilding*, ed. Anna Jarstad and Timothy Sisk, 239–59. Cambridge: Cambridge University Press, 2008.
Fukuyama, Francis. *State-building*. Ithaca, NY: Cornell University Press, 2004.
Galtung, Johan. *Peace: Research, Education, Action. Essays in Peace Research, Vol. 1*. Copenhagen: Christian Ejlers, 1975.
Grimm, Sonja, and Julia Leininger, 'Not All Good Things Go Together: Conflicting Objectives in Democracy Promotion'. *Democratization* 19, no. 3 (2012): 391–414.
Independent International Commission on Kosovo. *The Follow-up of the Kosovo Report: Why Conditional Independence?* Independent International Commission on Kosovo, Solna, Sweden: Tryckeriet Åsbrink Grafiska, 2001.
Independent International Commission on Kosovo. *Kosovo Report: Conflict, International Response, Lessons Learned*. Independent International Commission on Kosovo, Oxford: Oxford University Press, October 2000.
International Crisis Group. 'Kosovo: Landmark Election'. Balkans Report No. 120 Pristina/ Brussels: ICG, November 21, 2001.
International Peace Academy. 'Refashioning the Dialogue: Regional Perspectives on the Brahimi Report on UN Peace Operations'. Regional Meetings, February–March 2001, Johannesburg, Buenos Aires, Singapore, London.
King, Iain, and Whit Mason. *Peace at Any Price: How the World Failed Kosovo*. Ithaca, NY: Cornell University Press, 2006.
Krause, Keith, and Oliver Jütersonke. 'Peace, Security and Development in Post-conflict Environments'. *Security Dialogue* 36, no. 4 (December 2005): 447–62.
Kreilkamp, Jacob. 'UN Postconflict Reconstruction'. *New York University Journal of International Law and Politics* 35, no. 3 (2002): 619–70.
Lemay-Hébert, Nicolas. 'The "Empty-shell" Approach: The Setup Process of International Administrations in Timor-Leste and Kosovo, Its Consequences and Lessons'. *International Studies Perspectives* 12, no. 2 (2011): 188–209.
Lemay-Hébert, Nicolas. 'Everyday Legitimacy and International Administration: Global Governance and Local Legitimacy in Kosovo'. *Journal of Intervention and Statebuilding* (forthcoming 2012).
Lemay-Hébert, Nicolas. 'State-building from the Outside-in: UNMIK and its Paradox'. *Journal of Public and International Affairs* 20 (Fall 2009): 65–86.
Lemay-Hébert, Nicolas. 'Statebuilding Without Nationbuilding? Legitimacy, State-failure and the Limits of the Institutional Approach'. *Journal of Intervention and State-Building* 3, no. 1 (2009): 21–45.
Lemay-Hébert, Nicolas. 'UNPOL and Police Reform in Timor-Leste: Accomplishments and Setbacks'. *International Peacekeeping* 16, no. 3 (2009): 393–406.
Lidén, Kristoffer, Roger Mac Ginty, and Oliver Richmond. 'Introduction: Beyond Northern Epistemologies of Peace: Peacebuilding Reconstructed?'. *International Peacekeeping* 16, no. 5 (2009): 587–98.
Marshall, David, and Shelley Inglis. 'The Disempowerment of Human Rights-based Justice in the United Nations Mission in Kosovo'. *Harvard Human Rights Journal* 16 (Spring 2003): 95–146.
McBeth, John. 'E Timorese Unhappy About Being Sidelined By UN'. *Far Eastern Economic Review*, November 1, 2000.
Mertus, Julie. 'The Impact of Intervention on Local Human Rights Culture: A Kosovo Case Study'. *The Global Review of Ethnopolitics* 1, no. 2 (December 2001): 21–36.
Narten, Jens. 'Building Local Institutions and Parliamentarianism in Post-war Kosovo: A Review of Joint Efforts by the UN and the OSCE from 1999–2006'. *Helsinki Monitor* 17, no. 2 (2006): 144–59.

Narten, Jens. 'Dilemmas of Promoting Local Ownership: The Case of Postwar Kosovo', in *The Dilemmas of Statebuilding: Confronting the Contradictions of Postwar Peace Operations*, ed. Roland Paris and Timothy Sisk, 252–84. London: Routledge, 2008.

Newman, Edward. 'Liberal Peacebuilding Debates', in *New Perspectives on Liberal Peacebuilding*, ed. Edward Newman, Roland Paris, and Oliver Richmond, 26–53, Tokyo: United Nations University Press, 2009.

Nixon, Rod. 'The Crisis of Governance in New Subsistence States'. *Journal of Contemporary Asia* 36, no. 1 (2006): 75–101.

O'Neill, William. *Kosovo: An Unfinished Peace*. London: Lynne Rienner, 2002.

Orr, Robert. 'Governing When Chaos Rules: Enhancing Governance and Participation'. *The Washington Quarterly* 25, no. 4 (Autumn 2002): 139–52.

Ottaway, Maria. 'Rebuilding State Institutions in Collapsed States', in *State Failure, Collapse and Reconstruction*, ed. Jennifer Milliken, 245–66. Oxford: Blackwell, 2003.

Paris, Roland. *At War's End: Building Peace After Civil Conflict*. Cambridge: Cambridge University Press, 2004.

Paris, Roland. 'Wilson's Ghost : The Faulty Assumptions of Postconflict Peacebuilding', in *Turbulent Peace: The Challenges of Managing International Conflict*, ed. Chester Crocker, Fen O. Hampson, and Pamela Aall, 765–84. Washington, DC: United States Institute of Peace, 2001.

Paris, Roland, and Timothy Sisk. 'Introduction: Understanding the Contradictions of Postwar Statebuilding', in *The Dilemmas of Statebuilding: Confronting the Contradictions of Postwar Peace Operations*, ed. Roland Paris and Timothy Sisk, 1–20. London: Routledge, 2008.

Plantev, Plamen. 'Assessing the Balkans Peacekeeping Experience: Lessons for Afghanistan, Iraq and Beyond'. Roundtable presented at the Future of Peace Operations Project, Henry Stimson Center, May 13, 2003.

Poppen, Jens-Ulrich. 'Prospects for Securing Peace in Haiti Look Bleak'. *Jane's Intelligence Review*, May 23, 2005.

Power, Samantha. *Chasing the Flame: Sergio Vieira de Mello and the Fight to Save the World*. New York: Penguin Press, 2008.

Roeder, Philip, and Donald Rothchild. 'Conclusion: Nation-state Stewardship and the Alternatives to Power Sharing', in *Sustainable Peace: Power and Democracy After Civil Wars*, ed. Philip Roeder and Donald Rothchild, 319–46. Ithaca, NY: Cornell University Press, 2005.

Scheiner, Charles. 'Suggestions for the Next United Nations Mission in Timor-Leste'. Timor-Leste Institute for Reconstruction Monitoring and Analysis [La'o Hamutuk], June 22, 2006.

Schwartz, Stephen. 'UN Go Home'. *Weekly Standard* 8, no. 30 (14 April 2003).

'SRSG: Executive Authority Shared With the East Timorese'. *Radio UNTAET [transcript]*, July 15, 2000.

Stahn, Carsten. *The Law and Practice of International Territorial Administration: Versailles to Iraq and Beyond*. Cambridge: Cambridge University Press, 2008.

Steele, Jonathan. 'Nation Building in East Timor'. *World Policy Journal* 19 (Summer 2002): 76–87.

Surkhe, Astri. 'Peacekeepers as Nation-builders: Dilemmas of the UN in East Timor'. *International Peacekeeping* 8, no.4 (2001): 1–20.

United Nations. *An Agenda for Peace*. UN Doc. S/24578, September 21, 1992.

United Nations. *Head of UN Transitional Administration in East Timor Briefs Security Council*. UN Doc. SC/6799, February 3, 2000.

United Nations. *Letter Dated 7 October 2005 From the Secretary General Addressed to the President of the Security Council*. UN Doc. S/2005/635, October 7, 2005.

United Nations. *No Exit Without Strategy: Security Council Decision-making and the Closure of Transition of United Nations Peacekeeping Operations*. UN Doc. S/2001/394, April 20, 2001.

United Nations. *Report of the Secretary-General on Peacebuilding in the Immediate Aftermath of Conflict*. UN Doc. A/63/881, S/2009/304, June 11, 2009.

United Nations. *Report of the Secretary-General on the United Nations Interim Administration in Kosovo*. UN Doc. S/1999/1250, December 23, 1999.

United Nations. *Report of the Secretary General on the United Nations Interim Administration Mission in Kosovo*. UN Doc. S/2004/613, July 30, 2004.

United Nations. *Report of the Secretary General on the United Nations Transitional Administration in East Timor*. UN Doc. S/2000/53, January 26, 2000.

United Nations. *Secretary General Underscores National Ownership, International Partnership in Consolidating Peace, As Peacebuilding Commission Ends First Session*. UN Doc. PBC/17, June 27, 2007.

United Nations. *UNMIK Regulation 1999/1, On the Authority of the Interim Administration in Kosovo*. UN Doc. UNMIK/REG/1999/1, July 25, 1999.

United Nations. *UNMIK Regulation 2000/45: On Self-government of Municipalities in Kosovo*. UN Doc. UNMIK/REG/2000/45, August 11, 2000.

United Nations. *UNTAET Regulation 1999/1: On the Authority of the Transitional Administration in East Timor*. UN Doc. UNTAET/REG/1999/1, November 27, 1999.

United Nations. *UNTAET Regulation 1999/2: On the Establishment of a National Consultative Council*. UN Doc. UNTAET/REG/1999/2, December 2, 1999.

United Nations Development Program (UNDP). 'Participatory Local Governance: LIFE's Method and Experience 1992–1997'. Technical Advisory Paper 1. UNDP: New York, 1997.

UNMIK Division of Public Information. 'UNMIK at 18 Months: Joint Interim Administrative Structure'. *UNMIK-JIAS Fact Sheet*, http://www.unmikonline.org/1styear/jias.htm (accessed February 14, 2011).

'UN Rejects Calls for Shared Executive Power in E. Timor'. *Kyodo News*, June 27, 2000.

Vaknin, Sam. 'Should UN Administer Iraq: Kosovo's Iraqi Lessons'. *Global Politician*, May 3, 2005.

Vieira de Mello, Sergio. 'How Not to Run a Country: Lessons from the UN in Kosovo and Timor-Leste'. Unpublished manuscript, 2000.

Vieira de Mello, Sergio. 'Introductory Remark and Keynote Speech', in *The United Nations Transitional Administration in East Timor (UNTAET): Debriefing and Lessons*, ed. Nassrine Azimi and Chang Li Lin, 15–24. London: Martinus Nijhoff, 2003.

Ward, Michael. 'The Case for International Trusteeship in Haiti'. *Canadian Military Journal* 7, no. 3 (Autumn 2006): 25–34.

Weiner, Tim. 'An Evolving Idea For Liberia Envisions UN Trusteeship'. *The New York Times*, August 17, 2003.

Wilde, Ralph. 'From Danzig to East Timor and Beyond: The Role of International Territorial Administration'. *American Journal of International Law* 95, no. 3 (July 2001): 583–606.

Zaum, Dominik. *The Sovereignty Paradox: The Norms and Politics of International Statebuilding*. Oxford: Oxford University Press, 2007.

Power-sharing and democracy promotion in post-civil war peace-building

Jai Kwan Jung

Department of Political Science and International Relations, Korea University, Seoul, South Korea

Why do peace and democracy not often go together in countries emerging from violent civil conflicts? If the promotion of peace and democracy are conflicting objectives, what are the sources of the problem? Based on the conceptual distinction between short-term peace-making and long-term peace-building that incorporates democracy promotion as an essential component, this article argues that peace-making and democracy promotion often constitute a conflictual relationship when external actors impose a particular set of institutional arrangements – namely, power-sharing agreements – in order to end civil war as quickly as possible. The sharing of power between governments and rebels can be effective at reducing the security dilemma and credible commitment problems in the transition from civil war to peace, but it is a short-term solution and a source of the conflict between peace-making and democracy promotion. This is because power-sharing builds wartime divisions into post-war political structures and provides a strong incentive for former warring parties to garner political support primarily from their own constituent groups. The persistence of wartime cleavages tends to lower public confidence in newly established governmental institutions. Thus, power-sharing is likely to function as an institutional barrier to the establishment of democracy in the long run. This article demonstrates the adverse effects of power-sharing on democracy promotion by analysing post-civil war electoral politics and public attitudes toward former warring parties and governmental institutions in Bosnia and Herzegovina.

Introduction

Civil war is frequently a recurrent problem. Once a country has been swept by violent conflict, residual hostilities can easily escalate into a new war. The repetitive nature of civil conflict suggests that it is very difficult to establish durable peace after civil war. Even more difficult is the building of democracy in such conflict-prone societies. Nonetheless, the United Nations (UN) and other international organizations consider democracy promotion essential for the creation of self-sustaining peace, as they believe that peace and democracy have mutually reinforcing effects in countries transitioning away from civil war.[1] This idea has been embraced as a policy package in the international community, which Marina Ottaway refers to as the 'democratic reconstruction model'; this includes such institutional proposals as the formulation of a new democratic constitution and the organization of elections.[2] In fact, international actors have often pushed civil war adversaries to agree on democratic rules and procedures during peace negotiations as a core part of their peace-building and democracy promotion efforts. However, the international community's record of democracy promotion is not particularly rosy. The UN has been involved in 19 post-civil war transitions since the end of the Cold War, but only five cases can be regarded as having established a democratic political system: Guatemala, Mozambique, Namibia, Nicaragua, and South Africa (see Table 1 for details).

Why do peace and democracy so rarely go hand in hand in countries emerging from violent civil conflicts? The UN defines *peace-making* as an active attempt to resolve an ongoing conflict, and *peace-building* as a coordinated action at the end of a conflict intended to consolidate peace and prevent a recurrence of fighting in the long run.[3] This conception is based on the understanding that short-term peace-making and long-term peace-building are sequential objectives that do not conflict with each other. In addition, peace-building has become a multidimensional concept incorporating democracy promotion as a critical component. However, a growing number of scholars question the underlying assumption of the multidimensional concept of peace-building: do all good things go together? If not, what are the conflicting objectives and the sources of the problem?[4]

In line with this growing scepticism and the main theme of this special issue, I propose a view of short-term peace-making and long-term democracy promotion as conflicting objectives. This extrinsic conflict is especially likely to occur when a civil war ends by external mediation that imposes a particular set of institutional arrangements, namely power-sharing institutions. The allocation of executive, legislative, territorial, and veto powers to civil war adversaries has been widely adopted to resolve ongoing conflicts as quickly as possible through peace negotiations and to establish democratic governments during post-conflict transition.[5] However, I argue that power-sharing is essentially a short-term solution to initiate negotiations and make peace deals, but one that is likely to generate long-term adverse effects on democracy promotion in post-civil war countries because of its institutional pathologies.

In the next section, I will specify the theoretical logic of why I argue that power-sharing is a source of the extrinsic conflict between peace-making and democracy promotion in civil war-torn countries. In the third section I will explain why I chose Bosnia and Herzegovina (hereafter BiH) to illustrate the extrinsic conflict between short-term peace-making and long-term democracy promotion. BiH is a crucial

Table 1. Negotiated settlements of civil wars after the Cold War.

Country	Peace lasted?	Five-year mark for democracy	UN PKO	Power-sharing
Angola (1991)	No	−2 (+1)	Yes	0
Angola (1994)	No	−3 (−2)	Yes	3
Angola (2002)	Yes	−2 (0)	Yes	3
Bosnia-Herzegovina (1995)	Yes	−66 (0)	Yes	4
Cambodia (1991)	Yes	1 (0)	Yes	2
Central African Rep. (1997)	Yes	5 (0)	Yes	0
Chad (1997)	No	−2 (0)	No	0
Congo-Brazzaville (1999)	Yes	−4 (+2)	No	0
Congo-Kinshasa (2002)	No	5 (+5)	Yes	2
Djibouti (1994)	Yes	2 (+9)	No	2
El Salvador (1992)	Yes	7 (0)	Yes	0
Guatemala (1994)	Yes	8 (+5)	Yes	0
Lebanon (1991)	Yes	−66 (0)	Yes	2
Liberia (1990)	No	0 (0)	No	2
Liberia (1996)	No	0 (0)	Yes	2
Mozambique (1992)	Yes	6 (+12)	Yes	1
Namibia (1989)	Yes	6 (+6)	Yes	1
Nicaragua (1990)	Yes	8 (+9)	Yes	0
Philippines (1992)	Yes	8 (0)	No	0
Rwanda (1993)	No	−6 (+1)	Yes	2
Sierra Leone (1996)	No	2 (−2)	No	1
Sierra Leone (1999)	No	5 (+5)	Yes	2
Sierra Leone (2001)	Yes	5 (+3)	Yes	0
South Africa (1994)	Yes	9 (+4)	Yes	3
Tajikistan (1997)	Yes	−1 (+4)	Yes	2

Source: Peace Agreement Digital Collection of US Institute of Peace; Polity IV; UCDP; Sambanis, 'What is Civil War?'.
Notes: In column 1, the numbers in parentheses indicate the year in which the war ended. In column 3, the numbers in parentheses indicate the change in the Polity IV democracy index five years after the war ended. The power-sharing index in column 5 was created by examining of the actual texts of peace agreements; provisions for sharing executive, electoral, territorial, and veto powers among civil war adversaries were evaluated using a five-point scale.

case; the international community has invested what amounts to its most comprehensive and expensive post-Cold War peace-building effort in this former Yugoslavian republic. If the degree of international commitment is proportional to the success of democracy promotion in post-civil war countries, BiH is one of the most likely candidates for democratization under external oversight. In light of current developments, however, it is still highly uncertain whether BiH will become a multi-ethnic democracy in the foreseeable future.[6] In the fourth section, I will explain how a rigid power-sharing system was devised to resolve the bloodiest conflict in Europe since World War II. In the fifth section I will analyse how this institutional design has contributed to stalled democratization in BiH by examination of post-conflict election results, public support for former warring parties, and public confidence in governmental institutions; this analysis will demonstrate fundamental problems facing the establishment of a multi-ethnic democracy in BiH. In the concluding section, I will draw implications for broader research on democracy promotion in war-torn societies.

The peace trap in the negotiated settlement of civil war

One of the most difficult issues in the negotiated settlement of civil war is the design of new political institutions. The conflicting interests of the government and rebel groups are not easy to reconcile, and warring parties can renew the fighting whenever negotiations favour one side over the other, since they retain their organizational power during peace talks. Thus, international mediators often propose a particular set of institutions as a bargain to obtain peace. The long-term consequences of these institutional arrangements for peace and democracy hinge on two factors: whether international intervention is solely based on a short-term purpose without long-term consideration, and whether the institutions are designed to effectively mitigate wartime divisions.

Drawing on the debate between the consociational and the integrative approach,[7] scholarly discussions on institutional design in the transition from civil war to peace and democracy have centred on power-sharing arrangements.[8] As Arend Lijphart identifies, power-sharing refers to allocating executive seats to former warring parties and arranging electoral proportionality, regional autonomy, and veto power.[9] The underlying logic is that sharing executive and electoral seats can reduce the security dilemma and problems of credible commitment among warring parties, because this ensures that all parties will have influence on governmental decision-making during the post-conflict transition. Granting significant autonomy to territorially concentrated rebels can also be an effective solution to stop fighting immediately, as it can address a main source of grievances. In brief, the power-sharing approach assumes that well-designed political institutions can encourage cooperative behaviour among warring factions in the short-run and generate a virtuous circle in post-conflict transitions in the long-run: power-sharing institutionalizes cooperation between warring parties, and this institutionalized cooperation will contribute to political stability and ultimately to sustainable democracy. The expected benefits of power-sharing have been supported by some empirical evidence. In Barbara Walter's analysis of civil war settlements between 1940 and 1992, for example, governments and rebels were 38% more likely to sign a peace treaty if it included a power-sharing provision.[10] Hartzell and Hoddie also demonstrate that power-sharing makes the recurrence of civil war less likely.[11] The international community in general, and the UN in particular, tends to consider power-sharing to be the only feasible institutional option for ending civil wars through peace negotiations and for establishing durable peace and democracy in war-torn societies.[12]

However, power-sharing does not automatically lead to democracy. First of all, it is not a fully democratic system, as it seeks to reduce the relevance of democratic contestation by a pre-determined formula of allocating power in the new government. Second, power-sharing is essentially a short-term solution to end civil war as quickly as possible and is likely to produce long-term adverse effects on democratization. At first glance, power-sharing seems to be an attractive option, as it promises an institutionalized security guarantee to civil war adversaries. It can also reduce the credible commitment problems inherent in the implementation of peace agreements. However, its long-term effects on democratization may not be desirable, since power-sharing does not mitigate but reinforces wartime cleavages in the structures of post-conflict politics. Power-sharing is thus a source, rather than a solution, of the conflict between the short-term objective of peace-making and the long-term goal of democracy promotion.

The tension between short-term and long-term objectives generally appears when civil war adversaries arrive at a mutually destructive stalemate.[13] To resolve such a stalemate, external mediators often propose or even impose a power-sharing deal that can balance the distribution of political power between warring parties and serve as a powerful incentive to sign a peace treaty. However, the power-sharing approach can also place civil war-torn countries in a peace trap. While power-sharing is effective for achieving peace through negotiation, it builds wartime divisions into post-war political structures and provides an incentive structure under which the perpetuation of wartime cleavages in post-conflict politics is beneficial to the former warring parties seeking to sustain the status quo of the initial institutional set-up. As a result, wartime cleavages are likely to become deeply entrenched in post-conflict electoral politics. Such institutionalized divisions can, in turn, prolong ordinary citizens' support for the former warring parties. Because key governmental positions are allocated to former warring parties, as agreed in power-sharing deals, and because institutionalized wartime cleavages can lead to frequent deadlocks in governmental decision-making, public confidence in post-conflict governmental institutions is likely to be low and opinions of the institutions are likely to reflect societal divisions. This persistence of wartime cleavages in post-civil war politics hinders the establishment of democratic governance. I argue that power-sharing arrangements are more likely to generate a vicious circle than a virtuous one in the long-run.

Another critical problem of power-sharing is its institutional rigidity. Once power-sharing is agreed upon, it becomes difficult to make changes to the initial set-up. This is because power-sharing assumes a coherent leadership in each warring party and does not take into account potential within-group divisions in the implementation of the power-sharing deal. Should dissatisfied factions within former warring parties threaten to derail the entire peace process, power-sharing institutions tend to be unable to adapt to the new political grievances. Thus, the end result would be either the collapse of power-sharing itself and a return to conflict, as seen in Cyprus and Lebanon, or the persistence of ineffective governmental institutions, as will be described below in the case of BiH. In summary, power-sharing has been applauded as the most effective institutional option for resolution of military stalemates and promotion of democracy in countries emerging from civil wars; however, in reality, power-sharing tends to transform military stalemates into political stalemates that can delay democratization in the long-run.

Why Bosnia-Herzegovina?

To illustrate the logic of selecting BiH as a case study for this article, Table 1 lists 25 civil wars in the post-Cold War period that were resolved through the signing of a peace agreement. The list of negotiated settlements was compiled by classifying the outcomes of a total of 64 civil wars ending between 1989 and 2002. [14] Of these 64 civil wars, 15 ended in clear, one-sided military victories for either the government or the rebels; in 13 cases, fighting was halted by a unilateral call for a ceasefire or truce; and 36 conflicts were resolved via negotiations. However, 11 of the 36 cases that ended in negotiated settlements were autonomy-seeking or separatist conflicts, such as the Kosovo war and the conflict in East Timor, which were resolved by the granting of regional autonomy or independence. These autonomy-seeking civil wars are excluded from the list in Table 1 to reduce the heterogeneity of cases in comparison.[15] The remaining 25 civil wars listed in Table 1 represent situations in which rebel forces sought to take over the central government (that is, centre-seeking civil wars) but the conflicts were ultimately resolved through peace negotiations.

In 16 of the 25 negotiated settlement cases, peace was maintained for the first five years after the end of civil war, while large-scale violence broke out in the remaining nine cases. However, democracy promotion in war-torn countries has been much more difficult than halting hostilities. Democracy is generally conceptualized as a political regime in which key executive and legislative seats are filled by contested elections and open participation.[16] In the post-civil war context, it should also mean a democratic regime sustained by the country's own citizens, not by external actors.[17] Considering this conception of post-civil war democracy, only seven of the 25 cases can be considered to have achieved democratic rule five years after the end of hostilities, in terms of a Polity IV democracy score higher than '5'.[18] To be fair, of these seven successful cases El Salvador and the Philippines should not be counted as cases of post-civil war democratization, because democratic transitions had begun before the civil war was officially resolved and there was no change in the level of democracy during the post-conflict period. The most spectacular change in the measure of democracy took place in Mozambique (+12 points). The other 18 cases remained in a state of anocracy (a hybrid regime with a Polity score between '-5' and '5'), autocracy (Rwanda), or non-independent polity (BiH and Lebanon).

The UN has carried out various types of peacekeeping operations (PKOs) in 19 of the cases of negotiated ends to hostilities: observer missions, traditional PKOs, multidimensional PKOs, and peace enforcement missions.[19] Power-sharing was arranged in 13 cases of UN involvement in negotiated settlements. The power-sharing index in the last column of Table 1 was created by examining the actual texts of peace agreements, calculating a five-point measure representing provisions for the sharing of executive, electoral, territorial, and veto powers among civil war adversaries.[20] The quantitative literature on UN PKOs suggests that a more powerful UN operation, such as a multidimensional PKO and enforcement mission, is likely to produce a better outcome in terms of peace and democracy promotion than a weakly mandated mission.[21] In the same vein, a more comprehensive power-sharing agreement is presumed to lead to more sustainable peace and democracy in post-civil war countries.[22] Thus, the most likely success case for the UN would be BiH, where a strong peace enforcement mission was conducted under Chapter VII of the UN Charter and a very thorough power-sharing system was agreed upon as a result of the Dayton Peace Agreement. However, no one would currently regard BiH as a success story of UN peace-building and democracy promotion efforts because a high degree of international support is still necessary for the maintenance of the country's political stability.

The Bosnian civil war broke out among Bosniaks, Serbs, and Croats directly following the declaration of independence from Yugoslavia in March 1992. The war lasted until November 1995, resulting in about 70,000 casualties and 2.5 million refugees. This bloody conflict ended in a negotiated settlement with the help of strong external mediation by the UN and various Western powers, including the United Kingdom. International actors have continued to engage in the country's post-conflict transition through various peace-building operations; establishment of a multi-ethnic democracy has been one of their explicit objectives. Although BiH had no prior experience with democracy, its socio-economic conditions were relatively favourable for democracy promotion in the early post-conflict period, in comparison to conditions in countries truly impoverished by civil war. The average per capita income of the 25 countries listed in Table 1 is $1868 in the first post-conflict year; in a majority of cases, per capita income is below $1000.[23] In this sense, BiH was relatively 'wealthy' when the transition from civil war began: its per capita income was $2188 in 1995, and the economy grew at an average annual rate of 22.3% for the first five years after the war. These appear to be conducive conditions for democracy building, considering the general relationship between economic development and democratization.[24]

More important than BiH's socio-economic conditions is the degree of international peace-building efforts. After achieving a cessation of conflict through strong external mediation, the international community has carried out its most expensive peace-building operations in BiH: The number of peacekeeping troops per 1000 inhabitants was 15.5 for the first five years after the war, the five-year average of international aid per capita was $312, and peace-building operations have cost $41 billion to date.[25] If the degree of international effort is critical for democracy promotion in countries emerging from civil wars, BiH is the most likely case for successful post-civil war democratization. However, the country is still classified as a non-independent polity because the Office of High Representative (OHR) created by the international community as part of the Dayton Agreement has been ruling the country de facto.

Why, then, have the enormous peace-building efforts in BiH failed to produce a desirable outcome in democracy promotion? The main argument put forward in the previous section suggests that an answer can be found by examining why and how power-sharing institutions were organized as a result of peace negotiations. BiH is a textbook case of rigid power-sharing; it is the only country that was given the highest possible score in the power-sharing index in Table 1. In other words, BiH is a crucial case, in the language of case study research methods. Cases that are extreme in particular dimensions of theoretical interest are generally regarded as *crucial* in the sense of being 'least likely' or 'most likely' cases.[26] A most likely case is ideally 'one that, on all dimensions except the dimension of theoretical interest, is predicted to achieve a certain outcome, and yet does not'.[27] Since a most likely case can disprove a theory, the BiH case could possibly put the power-sharing approach to a rigorous test and illuminate sources of the problems in long-term democracy promotion in the aftermath of violent civil conflict.

Institutional design for short-term peace-making

The Dayton Accords, formally known as the General Framework Agreement for Peace in Bosnia and Herzegovina, can be considered a success in short-term peace-making, as it ended the most violent and recalcitrant conflict in post-World War II Europe. Before Dayton, a series of international interventions had failed to stop the bloodshed. The first international mediation was led by the European Community and the Conference on Security and Co-operation in Europe between March and August 1992, and subsequent efforts were undertaken by the UN, the European Union (EU), the United States of America (hereafter US), Russia, and the Contact Group.[28] The international interventions prior to the Dayton Accords largely failed, but the US mediation led by Charles Redman generated a partial peace agreement between Bosnian Croats and Bosniaks in March 1994. Excluding Bosnian Serbs, the two warring parties agreed to form a federal government. This agreement became the constitutional framework of the Federation of Bosnia and Herzegovina (hereafter FBiH), which was later established as one of the two entities in BiH.

One distinctive feature of the Dayton Peace Agreement is that its 11 annexes cover a much broader set of military and constitutional issues than the previous failed agreements had.[29] In particular, Annex 1 specifies three phases of redeployment for armed forces along the inter-entity boundary and allows for the deployment of a 60,000-strong NATO-led Implementation Force (IFOR) acting under Chapter VII of the UN Charter. Annexes 2, 3, and 4 provide the structure for executive, electoral, and territorial power-sharing, with constitutionally guaranteed veto rights. In essence, these three annexes divide BiH into two entities: the FBiH, with 51% of the territory (10 cantons), and the Republika Srpska (hereafter RS), with 49%. BiH's central state institutions were designed as follows:
- A three-member rotating presidency representing each of the three constituent peoples (Bosniaks, Bosnian Croats, and Bosnian Serbs);

- The House of Peoples, which consists of 15 delegates selected by the upper house of the FBiH and by the National Assembly of the RS, with two-thirds from the FBiH (five Bosniaks and five Croats) and one-third from the RS;
- The House of Representatives, which consists of 42 members elected by proportional representation, with two-thirds elected from the FBiH and one-third from the RS; and
- The Council of Ministers nominated by the Chair of the Council of Ministers and approved by the House of Representatives, with no more than two-thirds appointed from the FBiH; Deputy ministers are appointed from a different ethnic group than their respective ministers.[30]

This comprehensive set of executive, electoral, and territorial power-sharing arrangements is supplemented by veto power vested in the collective presidency and the parliamentary assembly. Any policy decision can be declared destructive to a 'vital interest' of the Bosniak, Croat, or Serb people by a member of the presidency or by a majority of delegates representing each ethnic group in the House of Peoples and thereby vetoed. These provisions demonstrate that BiH's ethnic power-sharing system is an extreme example of rigid institutional design. Although Article X in Annex 4 stipulates that the Dayton Constitution may be amended by a two-thirds majority of votes in the House of Representatives, given the ethnic power-sharing arrangements in the lower house, it is impossible for a single ethnic group to win the super-majority required to amend the constitution.

This rigid system is further complicated by the establishment of equally elaborate power-sharing institutions at the regional level. The FBiH and RS have their own constitutions, parliaments, and presidencies. Although the FBiH constitution was not a direct creation of the Dayton Accords, it follows the same ethnic power-sharing model: (1) a joint presidency, with a Bosniak and a Bosnian Croat as president and vice-president; (2) the House of the Peoples, which includes 30 Bosniaks, 30 Bosnian Croats, and up to 14 'others', selected by the Cantonal Assemblies; (3) and the Federation House of Representatives, composed of 140 elected members based on proportional representation. The RS also elects its own president and vice-president, as well as the 83 members that make up the RS National Assembly.

One immediate problem of this ethnic-based federalism is how to define the relationship between the central government and the two entities. Article III in Annex 4 briefly assigns the central government of BiH responsibility for foreign policy, foreign trade policy, customs policy, monetary policy, the finances of central government institutions, immigration and refugee policy and regulations, international criminal law enforcement, establishment and operation of international communication facilities, regulation of inter-entity transportation, and air traffic control. The regional governments of FBiH and RS are responsible for all the other governmental functions, including powers not explicitly assigned to the central government, such as policy execution and revenue collection. As this constitutional allocation of powers is heavily weighted toward the entities, they hold far more significant decision-making authority and enjoy almost complete autonomy in implementing policies.

The boundary between the two entities is based on the ethnic division that was exaggerated by population displacement during the civil war; the Dayton Agreement was thus explicitly designed to lock the most significant wartime cleavage into BiH's political and legal structures, creating a number of paradoxes. First, the Dayton Constitution proclaims the goal of integrating the entire population into a unified BiH, but it bases this integration precisely on what divides BiH – ethnicity.[31] As a result, the central government institutions have remained dysfunctional and have further reinforced ethnic divisions during the post-conflict transition period, with few mechanisms in place to promote territorial integrity or unified sovereignty. Second, successful post-war peace-building and democracy promotion require a certain degree of state capacity, but the state institutions set out in the Dayton Accords appear to be designed to guarantee deadlock in the central government and parliament. The inability of central government institutions to function should thus come as no surprise. Third, although the former Yugoslavian system had already illustrated the institutional pathologies of ethnic federalism, the Dayton Constitution recreated most of those 'subversive institutions'.[32]

Why did the peace process forge such a paradoxical ethnic power-sharing system in BiH? The answer lies in the time horizons held by international mediators during the peace negotiations. The Dayton Agreement was essentially imposed by the international community as a whole and by the US in particular. The architect of the peace accords, Richard Holbrooke, tactically utilized several deadlines and the threat of NATO bombing to put substantial pressure on neighbouring Croatia and Serbia as well as on the warring parties in BiH. Since his primary objective was to stop the bloodshed as quickly as possible, Holbrooke followed a strictly deal-oriented strategy with little concern for its long-term implications. The first priority of the US was an immediate peace settlement; the actual terms were of secondary importance.[33] In this respect, one legal scholar has appropriately observed that the warring parties of the Bosnian civil war were largely bludgeoned and partly bribed into putting their signatures to the Dayton Accords without playing any significant roles in developing the settlement terms.[34] This has led to a consistent lack of commitment among the former warring parties regarding implementation of the settlement terms during the post-conflict transition period.

In summary, the primary goal of the Dayton Agreement was to put an immediate end to the war. Unfortunately, the agreement institutionalized the most significant wartime cleavage in the design of the power-sharing system: the tri-ethnic collective presidency, the ethnic-based federalism, the mutual veto systems, and the ethnic quotas in the parliament and bureaucracy. It has thus provided a strong incentive for the former warring parties to maintain the ethnic status quo, and a strong disincentive for cross-ethnic cooperation. This incentive structure has encouraged ethno-nationalist elites to manipulate the central government institutions and prevent the development of multi-ethnic governance. Trapped in the ineffective and unproductive workings of governmental institutions, international actors, already heavily involved in every post-conflict transition activity in BiH, have become much more powerful than they had originally intended.[35]

Long-term peace-building and democracy promotion

Although there is a growing concern that BiH will soon be on the verge of collapse yet again,[36] large-scale violence has not occurred since Dayton. Competitive elections have been held regularly throughout the post-conflict period, and the key executive and legislative offices have been filled through these elections. BiH can thus be regarded as having established, at the very least, an electoral democracy. However, BiH's fragile peace has not been self-sustaining; rather, it is maintained by a high degree of international commitment. The NATO-led IFOR successfully completed its demilitarization mission, separating each ethnic group's armed forces along the boundary of FBiH and RS and incapacitating heavy weaponry. IFOR was replaced by a 32,000-strong Stabilization Force (SFOR) in December 1996. The SFOR maintained peacekeeping troops until December 2005 and was itself replaced by the 7000-member European Union Force (EUFOR), which remains in BiH to keep the peace. More importantly, a careful examination of post-war election results and public support for political parties and governmental institutions reveals serious obstacles to the establishment of a multi-ethnic democracy in BiH. In particular, the data demonstrate how well the rigid power-sharing system has reinforced the main wartime divisions in post-war politics and hindered the development of democratic governance in the long-run.

The post-conflict electoral politics in BiH began with the rushed first elections in September 1996, just nine months after the Dayton Agreement was signed. The reason for this short time frame was that the IFOR was supposed to withdraw from BiH within one year. Given that hostilities among the three ethnic groups had been exacerbated during the war and because wartime ethnic cleansing had divided the country into ethnically homogeneous regions, it was not surprising that the results of the first elections were divided strictly on ethnic lines.[37] The three main ethnic parties who had been wartime adversaries – the Social Democratic Action (SDA), the Croatian Democratic Union in BiH (HDZ), and the Serbian Democratic Party (SDS) – won the three-member collective presidency with ease, as well as 86% of seats in the House of Representatives. As the rushed elections allowed little time for multi-ethnic opposition groups to organize, the multi-ethnic coalition party, the Joint List for BiH, won only two seats in the lower house elections.

The results of the first elections had profound political implications for the subsequent process of democratization. They lent political legitimacy to those who had led BiH into war and who shared little more than a common interest in sustaining ethnic divisions. Ethno-nationalist elites were able to take advantage of the institutional tools created by the Dayton Accords. The three main ethnic parties intentionally paralyzed the functioning of the central state institutions and prevented any policy decision potentially harmful to their ethnic interests. For instance, BiH's Parliamentary Assembly met just once and passed no legislation for six months after the first elections, and the Council of Ministers (composed of only three ministers) lacked staff, funding, and even office space. In short, the first election results fully realized every pitfall that could have been expected from the rigid power-sharing arrangements.[38]

The first elections served as a wake-up call for the international community. Alarmed by the strengthened political positions of the ethnic parties, the international community sought to remedy the governmental dysfunction by reducing the authority of the ethnic parties. To this end, at the Bonn Peace Implementation Council summit in December 1997, the already overwhelming mandate of the OHR was further empowered to dismiss elected representatives who obstructed the implementation of the Dayton Agreement, to keep radical ethnic parties from participating in elections, and to directly impose certain reform policies and legislation. For example, the OHR removed or suspended 115 elected and appointed officials from public office between 1997 and 2004 and banned the Serbian Radical Party of the RS (SRS) from the 2000 general elections.[39]

This heavy-handed international involvement, however, has resulted in 'capacity sucking-out' rather than 'capacity building' for the BiH central state institutions.[40] Trapped in Bosnia's fragile peace, external actors have continued to rule the country on the basis of short-term planning. For example, in the run-up to the 2002 elections, as public dissatisfaction was increasing with the inadequate economic reforms of the incumbent Alliance for Change – a coalition of 10 moderate parties formed by OHR pressure after the 2000 elections – Paddy Ashdown, the High Representative (HR), enacted one reform policy every three days for 150 days straight.[41]

The OHR has thus been closely involved in BiH's electoral politics by enforcing pre- and post-election coalitions among moderate parties and banning radical ethnic parties and politicians. Nevertheless, election results over the post-war period do not suggest a substantive shift in voter support from ethnic to multi-ethnic parties. The three former warring parties have always won the presidential elections, except in 2006. The lower house election results seem to suggest fading strength among the three main ethnic parties, as their seat share has decreased since the 1998 elections. However, other than the Social Democratic Party (SDP), the major political parties competing against the SDA, the HDZ, and the SDS are not multi-ethnic; they are essentially ethnicity-based parties as well, albeit slightly more moderate.

Moreover, a party-list PR with no electoral threshold, as agreed upon in Dayton, has produced a highly fragmented ethnic party system. For instance, 48 parties were registered for the 1996 elections. Of these, 31 parties ran for the House of Representatives, but only five independently gained one or more seats. This highly fragmented system has not been conducive to the creation of a stable coalition for multi-ethnic democracy. The Alliance for Change, a 10-party coalition government led by the SDP, was formed after the 2000 elections due to pressures from OHR. However, all 10 parties in the Alliance decided to run separately in the 2002 elections, and its second-strongest party, the Party for Bosnia and Herzegovina, even decided to rejoin forces with the SDA.[42] As a result, the three ethno-nationalist parties returned to power at all state- and entity-levels in the 2002 elections, while the SDP lost heavily in both national and local elections in comparison to the 2000 elections.

Thus, institutional incentives provided by rigid power-sharing have facilitated the ethnic entrenchment of BiH's electoral politics, offering no motivation for ethnic parties to appeal to voters in other ethnic groups. The OHR's frequent intervention in post-war elections has been based on short-term purposes, effectively hindering the development of the institutional capacity necessary for the establishment of a multi-ethnic democracy. Overall, the ethnic divisions in BiH have been reinforced not only by the war but also by the post-war elections. Changes in the rigid power-sharing arrangements that have shaped the incentive structure of ethno-nationalist elites may be necessary in order to promote multi-ethnic cooperation and democratic governance in BiH. Otherwise, the perpetuation of ethno-national divisions will not easily be attenuated. To date, under the current system, the three constituent groups have made little progress in achieving a consensus on constitutional reforms.[43]

Public attitudes toward political parties and post-war governmental institutions reveal another dimension of obstacles to the establishment of a multi-ethnic democracy in BiH. To examine how ordinary people perceive former warring parties that have evolved into political parties and to what extent they trust the governmental institutions that have been established in the post-conflict transition, I analyse the Bosnian responses from the World Values Surveys 2001.[44] Table 2 presents data on public support for former warring parties in BiH.

Table 2. Ethnic cleavage and individual party support in Bosnia-Herzegovina.

Ethnicity	SDA	HDZ	SDS	SDP	Others	Total
Bosniaks	130 30.23% 100%	0	0	136 31.63% 78.61%	164 38.14% 54.30%	430 100% 61.96%
Croats	0	38 44.19% 100%	0	24 27.91% 13.87%	24 27.91% 7.95%	86 100% 12.39%
Serbs	0	0	51 28.65% 100%	13 7.30% 7.51%	114 64.04% 37.75%	178 100% 25.65%
Total	130 18.73% 100%	38 5.48% 100%	51 7.35% 100%	173 24.93% 100%	302 43.52% 100%	694 100% 100%

Source: The World Value Surveys 2001.
Notes: Entries in each cell are the frequency, row percentage, and column percentage of total respondents, in that order. The χ-square statistic is 551.45 and is significant at the 0.001 level.

The World Values Surveys were conducted in BiH in 2001, when the Alliance for Change was in power and public dissatisfaction with its tepid political and economic reforms was on the rise. Respondents were asked, 'If there were a national election tomorrow, for which party on this list would you vote?' One clear result from Table 2 is that the three ethno-nationalist parties obtained zero support from respondents of other ethnic groups: all SDA supporters were Bosniaks, all HDZ supporters were Bosnian Croats, and all SDS supporters were Bosnian Serbs. Another way to detect tendencies toward moderation of ethnic voting is to investigate whether the supposedly multiethnic party, SDP, garnered significant support across different ethnic groups. However, the descriptive statistics in Table 2 show that almost 80% of SDP supporters were Bosniaks. This suggests that ethnic divisions are deeply entrenched, not only in BiH's party politics but also in the hearts and minds of ordinary people.[45]

What about public support for post-war political institutions? Table 3 presents data on public confidence in the key domestic and international institutions that have been created by or been involved in peace-building operations in BiH. The World Values Surveys asked Bosnian respondents: 'I am going to name a number of organizations. For each one, could you tell me how much confidence you have in them: is it a great deal of confidence, quite a lot of confidence, not very much confidence or none at all?' Entries in Table 3 are the percentages of respondents who had 'a great deal of' or 'quite a lot of' confidence in each institution. Clearly, a large majority of Bosnian people did not have confidence in the central government and parliament, but placed relatively higher trust in the police, an institution that had been established separately in each entity after the Dayton Accords. Ethnicity plays a certain role here as well: Bosniaks had a higher level of confidence in the central state institutions than did Bosnian Croats and Serbs. This ethnic difference makes sense in consideration of the fact that the Bosniaks essentially obtained most of what they had wanted through the peace negotiations leading up to Dayton, in comparison to the other two ethnic groups. Moreover, a much larger ethnic distinction can be found in public confidence in international institutions: while a majority of Bosniak respondents felt confident in NATO

Table 3. Institutional confidence in Bosnia-Herzegovina.

	Bosniaks	Croats	Serbs
Government	34.69% (588)	20.77% (183)	25.05% (393)
Parliament	23.41% (581)	17.59% (182)	16.45% (389)
Police	70.50% (590)	62.84% (183)	53.55% (394)
EU	57.07% (573)	53.55% (183)	32.04% (387)
NATO	52.88% (573)	44.81% (183)	12.95% (386)
UN	51.30% (573)	46.16% (182)	17.27% (388)

Source: The World Value Surveys 2001.
Notes: Entries represent the percentage of respondents who expressed confidence in each institution, with the number of total respondents in parentheses.

and the UN, only 13% and 17% of Bosnian Serbs trusted these two international institutions, respectively.

In summary, Bosnia's most significant wartime cleavage is deeply entrenched in the minds of individual citizens when they express their party support and level of trust in governmental institutions. Election results since Dayton have also shown that ethno-nationalist divisions have dominated post-conflict electoral politics, as the rigid ethnic power-sharing system provides a powerful incentive for former warring parties to garner political support primarily from their own constituencies. Considering that there is little institutional incentive for cross-ethnic coalitions (other than pressure from the OHR), the establishment of a multi-ethnic democracy in BiH is as yet illusory.

Conclusion

The UN and other international actors have envisioned short-term peace-making and long-term peace-building as sequential objectives, with democracy promotion as a critical component for multidimensional peace-building in civil war-torn countries. Such a view sounds logical, but this article has argued that peace-making and democracy promotion often constitute a conflictual relationship in the actual transition period after civil war. This extrinsic conflict is likely to arise when external actors mediate peace negotiations and propose power-sharing deals to end civil war as quickly as possible. Power-sharing can reduce the security dilemma of civil war adversaries and the credible commitment problems in the implementation of peace agreements, but it can also generate long-term adverse effects on democratization by locking wartime cleavages into post-war political structures. It is thus paradoxical that power-sharing, considered to be the most effective institutional option for peace- and democracy-building in post-conflict societies, is often a source of the tension between peace-making and democracy promotion. Power-sharing is essentially a short-term solution for when a choice must be made between immediate peace-making and longer-term considerations of democracy promotion. For the most part, the international community has adopted the short-term solution, as stopping violence and preventing massacres take top priority. However, the short-term solution does not guarantee achievement of the long-term objective.

While putting the power-sharing approach to a rigorous test through the case of BiH, this article suggests that the expected pitfalls of power-sharing should be addressed in democracy promotion in post-civil war countries. In this regard, two success stories from Table 1, Mozambique and South Africa, can offer recommendations. In South Africa, a series of agreements between the white minority government and the African National Congress resulted in the 1993 Interim Constitution Pact. This created comprehensive power-sharing institutions with a sunset clause that allowed the power-sharing system to expire after five years. Indeed, South Africa's formal power-sharing was in place just for three years (from 1993 to 1996) and successfully paved the way for the current majoritarian democracy.[46] Mozambique's 16-year-long civil war was also resolved through negotiations in 1992, but without a formal power-sharing arrangement. The peace agreement between the Mozambican Liberation Front and the Mozambican National Resistance provided only for an electoral system based on proportional representation. Informal bargaining between the former adversaries has been utilized to achieve compromises during Mozambique's post-civil war transition.[47] These two success cases share one commonality: much less rigid institutional arrangements than those developed in the course of the peace negotiations in BiH. Institutional design is, of course, just one of many factors that can shape the process and outcome of post-conflict democratization in various contexts. However, without creative endeavours to devise a long-term, customized approach more appropriate than the power-sharing approach, international efforts at democracy promotion will be much less effective than they aspire to be.

Acknowledgements

I thank Valerie Bunce, Jeff Checkel, Sonja Grimm, Anna Jarstad, Dong Sun Lee, Julia Leininger, Walter Mebane, Sidney Tarrow, Nicolas van de Walle, Christopher Way, and the anonymous reviewers for their helpful comments on earlier drafts. Any remaining errors are mine alone.

Notes

1. Boutros-Ghali, *An Agenda for Democratization*.
2. Ottaway, 'Promoting Democracy after Conflict'.
3. Ibid., 38.
4. See, for example, Flores and Nooruddin, 'Democracy under the Gun'; Hippler, 'Democratization after Civil Wars'; Jarstad and Sisk, *From War to Democracy*.
5. Lijphart, 'The Wave of Power-sharing Democracy'.
6. Since the Dayton Peace Agreement, one of the main objectives of international peace-building efforts has been establishing a stable democratic government run by the three ethnic groups of BiH together.
7. Lijphart, *Democracy in Plural Societies*; Horowitz, *Ethnic Groups in Conflict*.
8. Hartzell and Hoddie, 'Institutionalizing Peace'; Horowitz, 'Constitutional Design'; Linder and Bächtiger, 'What Drives Democratization in Asia and Africa?'; Mukherjee, 'Why Political Power-sharing Agreements Lead to Enduring Peaceful Resolution of Some Civil Wars, But Not Others?'; Norris, *Driving Democracy*; Roeder and Rothchild, *Sustainable Peace*.
9. Lijphart, 'Constitutional Design for Divided Societies'.
10. Walter, *Committing to Peace*, 80.
11. Hartzell and Hoddie, 'Institutionalizing Peace'.
12. Lijphart, 'Constitutional Design for Divided Societies', 96; Ottaway, 'Promoting Democracy after Conflict'.
13. Zartman, 'Ripeness'.
14. For the list of civil wars that ended between 1989 and 2002, I relied on Sambanis's (Sambanis, 'What is Civil War?') data, updating it through 2002 using the Uppsala Conflict Data Program (UCDP: http://www.ucdp.uu.se); Sambanis lists civil wars only up to 1999. In classifying the outcomes of civil war, one-sided military victory was coded when there was a clear winner. A unilateral call for ceasefire or truce

was coded when an armed conflict stopped with neither a clear winner nor a peace treaty. A negotiated settlement refers to an end to civil war through a peace agreement and requires that the fighting stopped for at least six months as a result of the agreement.

15. In terms of the root cause of conflict, autonomy-seeking civil war is qualitatively different from centre-seeking civil war. The resolution of autonomy-seeking civil war requires only a particular type of power-sharing (regional autonomy arrangements, or secession in some cases).
16. Alvarez et al., 'Classifying Political Regimes'.
17. Wantchekon, 'The Paradox of "Warlord" Democracy'.
18. The Polity IV democracy index ranges from −10 to 10, whereby a political regime with a score higher than 5 is labelled *democracy*, with a score lower than −5 *autocracy*, and with a score between −5 and 5 *anocracy* (Marshall and Jaggers, *Polity IV Project*).
19. Data sources are Doyle and Sambanis, *Making War and Building Peace*, and the UN Department of Peacekeeping Operations (http://www.un.org/Depts/dpko/dpko/index.asp).
20. Principal data sources are the Peace Agreement Digital Collection in the US Institute of Peace and the UCDP.
21. Doyle and Sambanis, *Making War and Building Peace*, Chapter 3.
22. Hartzell and Hoddie, 'Institutionalizing Peace'; Lemarchand, 'Consociationalism and Power Sharing in Africa'; Spears, 'Understanding Inclusive Peace Agreements in Africa'.
23. The data on per capita incomes are extracted from the Penn World Table 6.3.
24. Acemoglu and Robinson, *Economic Origins of Dictatorship and Democracy*; Boix and Stokes, 'Endogenous Democratization'; Epstein et al., 'Democratic Transitions'; Przeworski et al., *Democracy and Development*.
25. Zürcher, 'Building Democracy While Building Peace', 84.
26. Eckstein, 'Case Studies and Theory in Political Science', 119.
27. Gerring, *Case Study Research*, 115.
28. See Atiyas, 'Mediating Regional Conflicts and Negotiating Flexibility'.
29. Annex 1 focuses on the military aspects of the peace settlement, Annex 2 on the interentity boundary line, Annex 3 on elections, Annex 4 on constitutions, Annex 5 on arbitration mechanisms, Annex 6 on human rights issues, Annex 7 on refugee and internally displaced persons issues, Annex 8 on the formation of commissions to preserve national monuments, Annex 9 on the establishment of public corporations, Annex 10 on civilian implementation of the peace settlement, including the appointment and role of a High Representative (HR), and Annex 11 on the establishment of an international police task force. The full text of the peace agreement is available at http://www.usip.org/library/pa/bosnia/daytongfa.html.
30. Another form of executive power-sharing provided for in Annex 4 is the appointment of ambassadors and other international representatives of BiH, using the same ethnic quota: no more than two-thirds from the FBiH.
31. See Mansfield, 'Ethnic but Equal'.
32. Bunce, *Subversive Institutions*; Deets, 'Public Policy in the Passive-aggressive State'.
33. See Curran, Sebenius, and Watkins, 'Two Paths to Peace'; and Watkins and Rosegrant, 'Getting to Dayton'.
34. Szasz, 'The Dayton Accord'.
35. Each annex of the Dayton Accords specifies which international organizations shall guide and monitor the implementation of settlement terms. NATO is primarily responsible for all military aspects of the agreement; the Organization for Security and Cooperation in Europe for elections, regional stabilization, and human rights issues; the UN for the international police task force and civilian implementation of the

agreement, including the creation and operation of the OHR; the International Monetary Fund for the BiH Central Bank; and the European Court of Human Rights for the Constitutional Court and refugee issues.
36. Chivvis, 'Back to the Brink in Bosnia?'.
37. See Shoup, 'The Elections in Bosnia and Herzegovina'.
38. See Bieber, 'Power Sharing after Yugoslavia'; Hayden, *Blueprints for a House Divided*; Hayden, '"Democracy" without a Demos?'; McMahon, 'Rebuilding Bosnia'; Woodward, 'Bosnia and Herzegovina'.
39. Manning, 'Elections and Political Change in Post-war Bosnia and Herzegovina', 61.
40. Knaus and Cox, 'The "Helsinki Moment" in Southeastern Europe', 51; see also Chandler, *Bosnia*.
41. Knaus and Cox, 'The "Helsinki Moment" in Southeastern Europe', 47–49.
42. Burwitz, 'The Elections in Bosnia-Herzegovina, October 2002'.
43. See Hayden, 'The Continuing Reinvention of the Square Wheel'; Tuathail, O'Loughlin, and Djipa, 'Bosnia-Herzegovina Ten Years after Dayton'.
44. Inglehart et al., *World Values Surveys* and *European Values Surveys*, 1999–2001.
45. The 2001 data is the most recent wave of the World Values Surveys that includes BiH. More recent survey data that was collected in BiH and includes the question of party support is the 2008 European Values Study, but it does not provide information on respondents' ethnicity. If respondents' ethnicity is inferred from their religious denomination as ethnicity and religion generally, not perfectly, overlap in BiH, the same ethnic divisions can be found in the 2008 European Values Study as well: all SDA supporters are Muslim, all HDZ supporters are Catholic, 99% of SDS supporters are Orthodox, and more than two-thirds of SDP supporters are Muslim. It suggests that the ethnic entrenchment in BiH's party politics has not been reduced since 2001.
46. For details, see Sisk and Stefes, 'Power Sharing as an Interim Step in Peace Building'.
47. See Manning, *The Politics of Peace in Mozambique*.

Notes on contributor

Jai Kwan Jung is Assistant Professor at the Department of Political Science and International Relations at Korea University, Seoul, South Korea.

Bibliography

Acemoglu, Daron, and James A. Robinson. *Economic Origins of Dictatorship and Democracy*. New York: Cambridge University Press, 2006.
Alvarez, Michael, Jose Antonio Cheibub, Fernando Limongi, and Adam Przeworski. 'Classifying Political Regimes'. *Studies in Comparative International Development* 31, no. 2 (1996): 3–36.
Atiyas, Nimet Beriker. 'Mediating Regional Conflicts and Negotiating Flexibility: Peace Efforts in Bosnia-Herzegovina'. *Annals of the American Academy of Political and Social Science* 542, no. 1 (1995): 185–201.
Bieber, Florian. 'Power Sharing after Yugoslavia: Functionality and Dysfunctionality of Power Sharing Institutions in Post-war Bosnia, Macedonia and Kosovo'. In *From Power Sharing to Democracy: Post-conflict Institutions in Ethnically Divided Societies*, ed. Sid Noel, 85–103. Montreal, Kingston: McGill-Queens University Press, 2005.
Boix, Carles, and Susan C. Stokes. 'Endogenous Democratization'. *World Politics* 55, no. 4 (2003): 517–49.
Boutros-Ghali, Boutros. *An Agenda for Democratization*. New York: United Nations, 1996.

Bunce, Valerie J. *Subversive Institutions: The Design and the Destruction of Socialism and the State.* New York: Cambridge University Press, 1999.

Burwitz, Bernd. 'The Elections in Bosnia-Herzegovina, October 2002'. *Electoral Studies* 23, no. 2 (2004): 329–38.

Chandler, David. *Bosnia: Faking Democracy after Dayton.* London: Pluto, 2000.

Chivvis, Christopher S. 'Back to the Brink in Bosnia?'. *Survival* 52, no. 1 (2010): 97–110.

Curran, Daniel, James K. Sebenius, and Michael Watkins. 'Two Paths to Peace: Contrasting George Mitchell in Northern Ireland with Richard Holbrooke in Bosnia-Herzegovina'. *Negotiation Journal* 20, no. 4 (2004): 513–37.

Deets, Stephen. 'Public Policy in the Passive-aggressive State: Health Care Reform in Bosnia-Hercegovina 1995–2001'. *Europe-Asia Studies* 58, no. 1 (2006): 57–80.

Doyle, Michael, and Nicholas Sambanis. *Making War and Building Peace: United Nations Peace Operations.* Princeton, NJ: Princeton University Press, 2006.

Eckstein, Harry. 'Case Studies and Theory in Political Science'. In *Handbook of Political Science: Strategies of Inquiry, vol. 7,* ed. Fred Greenstein and Nelson W. Polsby, 79–137. Reading, MA: Addison-Wesley, 1975.

Epstein, David L., Robert Bates, Jack Goldstone, Ida Kristensen, and Sharyn O'Halloran. 'Democratic Transitions'. *American Journal of Political Science* 50, no. 3 (2006): 551–69.

Flores, Thomas Edward, and Irfan Nooruddin. 'Democracy under the Gun: Understanding Postconflict Economic Recovery'. *Journal of Conflict Resolution* 53, no. 1 (2009): 3–29.

Gerring, John. *Case Study Research: Principles and Practices.* New York: Cambridge University Press, 2007.

Hartzell, Caroline, and Matthew Hoddie. 'Institutionalizing Peace: Power Sharing and Post-civil War Conflict Management'. *American Journal of Political Science* 47, no. 2 (2003): 318–32.

Hayden, Robert M. *Blueprints for a House Divided: The Constitutional Logic of the Yugoslav Conflicts.* Ann Arbor: University of Michigan Press, 1999.

Hayden, Robert M. 'The Continuing Reinvention of the Square Wheel: The Proposed 2009 Amendments to the Bosnian Constitution'. *Problems of Post-Communism* 58, no. 2 (2011): 3–16.

Hayden, Robert M. '"Democracy" without a Demos? The Bosnian Constitutional Experiment and the Intentional Construction of Nonfunctioning States'. *East European Politics and Societies* 19, no. 2 (2005): 226–59.

Hippler, Jochen. 'Democratization after Civil Wars: Key Problems and Experiences'. *Democratization* 15, no. 3 (2008): 550–69.

Horowitz, Donald. 'Constitutional Design: Proposals Versus Processes'. In *The Architecture of Democracy: Constitutional Design, Conflict Management, and Democracy,* ed. Andrew Reynolds, 15–36. Oxford: Oxford University Press, 2002.

Horowitz, Donald. *Ethnic Groups in Conflict.* Berkeley: University of California Press, 1985.

Inglehart, Ronald, et al., *World Values Surveys* and *European Values Surveys, 1999–2001* [Computer file]. ICPSR version. Ann Arbor, MI: Institute for Social Research [producer], Ann Arbor, MI: Inter-university Consortium for Political and Social Research [distributor], 2004.

Jarstad, Anna K., and Timothy D. Sisk, eds. *From War to Democracy: Dilemmas of Peace-building.* New York: Cambridge University Press, 2008.

Knaus, Gerald, and Marcus Cox. 'The "Helsinki Moment" in Southeastern Europe'. *Journal of Democracy* 16, no. 1 (2005): 39–53.

Lemarchand, René. 'Consociationalism and Power Sharing in Africa: Rwanda, Burundi, and the Democratic Republic of Congo'. *African Affairs* 106, no. 422 (2006): 1–20.

Lijphart, Arend. 'Constitutional Design for Divided Societies'. *Journal of Democracy* 15, no. 2 (2004): 96–109.
Lijphart, Arend. *Democracy in Plural Societies: A Comparative Explanation*. New Haven, CT: Yale University Press, 1977.
Lijphart, Arend. 'The Wave of Power-sharing Democracy'. In *The Architecture of Democracy: Constitutional Design, Conflict Management, and Democracy*, ed. Andrew Reynolds, 37–54. Oxford: Oxford University Press, 2002.
Linder, Wolf, and André Bächtiger. 'What Drives Democratization in Asia and Africa?'. *European Journal of Political Research* 44, no. 6 (2005): 861–80.
Manning, Carrie L. 'Elections and Political Change in Post-war Bosnia and Herzegovina'. *Democratization* 11, no. 2 (2004): 60–86.
Manning, Carrie L. *The Politics of Peace in Mozambique: Post-conflict Democratization, 1992–2000*. Westport, CT: Praeger, 2002.
Mansfield, Anna Morawiec. 'Ethnic but Equal: The Quest for a New Democratic Order in Bosnia and Herzegovina'. *Columbia Law Review* 103, no. 8 (2003): 2052–93.
Marshall, Monty, and Keith Jaggers. *Polity IV Project: Dataset Users' Manual*. College Park: Integrated Network for Societal Conflict Research (INSCR) Program, University of Maryland, 2002.
McMahon, Patrice C. 'Rebuilding Bosnia: A Model to Emulate or to Avoid?'. *Political Science Quarterly* 119, no. 4 (2004–2005): 569–93.
Mukherjee, Bumba. 'Why Political Power-sharing Agreements Lead to Enduring Peaceful Resolution of Some Civil Wars, But Not Others?'. *International Studies Quarterly* 50, no. 2 (2006): 479–504.
Norris, Pippa. *Driving Democracy: Do Power-sharing Institutions Work?* New York: Cambridge University Press, 2008.
Ottaway, Marina. 'Promoting Democracy after Conflict: The Difficult Choices'. *International Studies Perspectives* 4, no. 3 (2003): 314–22.
Przeworski, Adam, Michael Alvarez, José Antonio Cheibub, and Fernando Limongi. *Democracy and Development: Political Institutions and Well-being in the World, 1950–1990*. New York: Cambridge University Press, 2000.
Roeder, Philip, and Donald Rothchild, eds. *Sustainable Peace: Power and Democracy after Civil Wars*. Ithaca, NY: Cornell University Press, 2005.
Sambanis, Nicholas. 'What is Civil War? Conceptual and Empirical Complexities of an Operational Definition'. *Journal of Conflict Resolution* 48, no. 6 (2004): 814–58.
Shoup, Paul. 'The Elections in Bosnia and Herzegovina: The End of an Illusion'. *Problems of Post-Communism* 44, no. 1 (1997): 3–15.
Sisk, Timothy D., and Christoph Stefes. 'Power Sharing as an Interim Step in Peace Building: Lessons from South Africa'. In *Sustainable Peace: Democracy and Power after Civil Wars*, ed. Philip Roeder and Donald Rothchild, 293–317. Ithaca, NY: Cornell University Press, 2005.
Spears, Ian S. 'Understanding Inclusive Peace Agreements in Africa: The Problems of Sharing Power'. *Third World Quarterly* 21, no. 1 (2000): 105–18.
Szasz, Paul C. 'The Dayton Accord: The Balkan Peace Agreement'. *Cornell International Law Journal* 30, no. 3 (1997): 759–68.
Tuathail, Gearóid Ó., John O'Loughlin, and Dino Djipa. 'Bosnia-Herzegovina Ten Years after Dayton: Constitutional Change and Public Opinion'. *Eurasian Geography and Economics* 47, no. 1 (2006): 61–75.
Walter, Barbara F. *Committing to Peace: The Successful Settlement of Civil Wars*. Princeton, NJ: Princeton University Press, 2002.
Wantchekon, Leonard. 'The Paradox of "Warlord" Democracy: A Theoretical Investigation'. *American Political Science Review* 98, no. 1 (2004): 17–33.

Watkins, Michael, and Susan Rosegrant. 'Getting to Dayton: Negotiating an End to the War in Bosnia'. Harvard Business School Case 1-800-134. Boston: Harvard Business School Publishing, 1999.

Woodward, Susan L. 'Bosnia and Herzegovina: How Not to End Civil War'. In *Civil Wars, Insecurity, and Intervention*, ed. Barbara Walter and Jack Snyder, 73–115. New York: Columbia University Press, 1999.

Zartman, William I. 'Ripeness: The Hurting Stalemate and Beyond'. In *International Conflict Resolution after the Cold War*, ed. Paul C. Stern and Daniel Druckman, 225–50. Washington, DC: National Academy Press, 2000.

Zürcher, Christoph. 'Building Democracy While Building Peace'. *Journal of Democracy* 22, no. 1 (2011): 81–95.

Two at one blow? The EU and its quest for security and democracy by political conditionality in the Western Balkans

Solveig Richter

Stiftung Wissenschaft und Politik (SWP), Berlin, Germany

The EU is facing a serious conflict of objectives in the Western Balkans, primarily between security interests calling for the rapid integration of these countries and its interest in democratization, which demands a stricter democracy promotion agenda and cautions against a rushed enlargement round including unconsolidated states. I argue that the EU's approach, which enforces both security and democracy through one instrument, namely, political conditionality, has yielded only limited success and has contributed to the emergence of a conflict of objectives for a number of reasons. First, to render its conditionality policy credible and consistent, the EU has been forced to prioritize security at the expense of democracy promotion. Second, compliance patterns in the two areas have differed, resulting in a conditionality dilemma that forces the EU to sanction compliance or reward non-compliance. And third, the use of political conditionality in security issues has generated counterproductive side effects that may impede the consolidation of democracy. The case study of Macedonia empirically supports this argument. The study provides evidence for an argument that contradicts much of the literature on sequencing: democracy promotion should resume playing a significant role in the early stages of post-conflict transition.

Introduction: conflict of objectives between security concerns and democracy promotion

Democracy promotion (DP)[1] has long been considered one of the most effective tools for influencing the political development of other countries[2]: using strategies including cooperation, dialogue, and strict conditionality to the point of creating complex transitional administrations, external actors have intervened in the transformation processes of countries not only for the sake of democratization, but also with the intention of achieving numerous other goals – first and foremost, security and stability. A case in point is the region of the Western Balkans[3] (also referred to in this article as South-Eastern Europe, SEE): The break-up of Yugoslavia and the corresponding state-building processes coincided with the first free elections in some of the new states and with the liberalization of their political systems, but these were more often than not accompanied by violent ethno-political strife. After the end of hostilities, the challenges for European international organizations such as the European Union (EU) and the Organization for Co-operation and Security in Europe (OSCE) were manifold, including assistance for democratic reforms, consolidation of the fragile peace, and reconciliation and strengthening of multi-ethnic states – in short, the establishment of a democratic and secure neighbourhood. However, after the initial period of euphoria, the hybrid regimes and unconsolidated democracies resulting from stagnating transitions created disillusionment. As a result of these languishing democratization processes, the EU now faces a conflict of objectives between its security-based interest in moving ahead with the accession of these countries to the EU and its interest in the further democratization of the countries through strict conditionality, which would result in a much slower integration process. On the one hand, the integration of the SEE countries into the political community of democratic, peaceful states would be the best safeguard against renewed violence. On the other hand, by integrating unconsolidated and still unstable democracies, the EU would inherit their problems but would no longer have any leverage to enforce resolutions after the accession. So the questions which this article seeks to answer are: how and why did this conflict of objectives between security interests and democracy promotion arise? What role did the EU play?

The Western Balkans have long been of strategic relevance for the EU. In addition to the tools of the former Common Foreign and Security Policy (CFSP, for example, police missions, special representatives), with the launch of the Stabilization and Association Process (SAP) in 1999–2000, the key instrument of the EU in the region became political conditionality, with prospective membership as its main incentive. For (potential) candidate countries, a decisive step towards EU membership is compliance with certain criteria formulated by the 1993 European Council in Copenhagen. Essentially, the political criteria require the 'stability of institutions guaranteeing democracy, the rule of law, human rights and respect for and protection of minorities',[4] thus entailing the profound democratization of the SEE countries. Consequently, since 1999–2000, the EU has been intensively engaged in democracy promotion in the region. The Copenhagen political criteria have been further elaborated by the EU institutions, especially the European Commission, although there is 'no single document to clarify the meaning of the criteria'.[5] The Commission's monitoring and progress reports list a wide range of steps and requirements for democratic reforms, which form the centrepiece of the EU's democracy promotion policy. Among these are the democratic functioning of the government, the parliament, the public administration, and the judicial system; an anti-corruption policy; the observance of international human rights laws; and respect for civil, political, economic, and social rights, as well as respect for and protection of minority and cultural rights.[6]

Since the beginning of the 1990s, the Western Balkan region has also been of great interest to the EU in political-security terms, most significantly with regard to political stabilization and peace-building.[7] In addition to democracy promotion, the EU has been pursuing a wide range of security priorities in the region, from post-conflict rehabilitation to state-building, transitional justice, and security sector reforms, to name only the most important issues. Under the umbrella of 'security interests', the EU thus addresses broad and multifaceted processes. In the framework of the SAP, this security dimension has largely been addressed by the EU in the form of additional country-specific criteria – the 'Copenhagen-Plus' criteria – among them, the implementation of peace treaties and cooperation with the International Criminal Tribunal for the former Yugoslavia (ICTY).

Thus, with political conditionality as its main instrument, the EU has been simultaneously attempting to achieve two priorities: democracy and security-building. These two priorities are each linked to a specific set of criteria: democracy-building is linked to the Copenhagen criteria and security-building is linked to the Copenhagen-Plus criteria. While the two types of criteria have different historical backgrounds and motivations, their concrete implementations have overlapped to a certain extent. Usually, in the Copenhagen-Plus criteria, crucial elements of post-conflict rehabilitation (such as refugee return, confidence-building measures, and disarmament) have been complemented by long-term structural changes in the political system and society (for example, decentralization and power-sharing). Although these political reforms were tailored to the particular needs of the peace- and state-building processes in individual countries, they also involved (in addition to the classical Copenhagen criteria) a profound democratization, even when not applied in a comprehensive or systematic fashion. This policy of the EU has been based on the assumption that the advancement of democracy (the Copenhagen criteria) and that of security (the Copenhagen-Plus criteria) go hand-in-hand and can lead to a virtuous circle – in short, that democratization will lead to peace.[8] Academic research has compiled extensive evidence that democracies almost never go to war with one another, instead they cooperate more intensively, and they are able to manage global challenges such as organized crime and terrorism more effectively.[9] Hence, the soft dimension of democracy promotion promises to serve hard security interests.[10] However, while democracy and security are generally positively intertwined, the process of democratization is a double-edged sword. On the one hand, the process is a necessary condition for the global spread of democracy and thus the creation of a more secure world; on the other hand, the process of democratization involves destabilizing effects and facilitates the emergence of violent conflicts, thus itself constituting a security risk.[11] In addition, aggressive or violent policies of democracy enforcement call into question the effects and positive intentions of peace-building.[12] As a consequence, politicians and academics alike have often turned to a more sequential approach in democracy promotion:[13] a minimum of stability together with a sovereign state with a functioning state authority, clear-cut territorial boundaries, and well-defined citizenship are generally said to be the prerequisites for the introduction of a democratic governance system.[14]

This article shows that the EU's approach to, simultaneously, improving security and promoting democracy using one instrument has yielded only partial success. The Western Balkans have shown the limits of the EU's approach[15]: Although the EU has enforced most of the Copenhagen-Plus criteria and has improved security in the region, these efforts have been accompanied by negative side effects in the democratic reform process, such as the strengthening of anti-democratic forces, which in turn have threatened prior achievements in stabilizing and democratizing the countries. Even elements of structural reform included in the security agenda (such as power-sharing) have often proved to be highly problematic in terms of democratization and have inhibited rather than supported the transition. What was meant to create a virtuous circle has resulted in a conflict of objectives for the EU: if Brussels would reward these countries for their efforts in fulfilling the Copenhagen-Plus criteria and integrate them into the EU through a rapid accession, this step would, to be sure, enhance security and consolidate the status quo in the near neighbourhood of the EU, but at the same time entrench the hybrid, semi-democratic character of the states. If Brussels would address the democratic deficits and insist upon the implementation of the Copenhagen criteria, this policy of strict conditionality would give priority to the requirements of the EU's internal procedures, which require a high level of democratic maturity in accession countries. Thus Brussels would address the concerns of some member states, among them Germany, who caution against rushing the next enlargement round in light of the misconduct of Bulgaria and Romania after they joined the Union in 2007. However, inherent in this scenario is the risk of destabilization in the region; as prospects for joining the EU become increasingly uncertain for some SEE countries, there is the danger that inter-ethnic conflict will resurface.

I argue that one of the main causes for the emergence of a conflict of objectives between democracy and security can be found in the functional requirements of the DP instrument of the EU. First, to render its political conditionality consistent and credible, the EU had to assign clear priorities, often prioritizing security and neglecting the DP agenda (*output dimension*). Second, recent studies have revealed that in matters of security (namely, in those criteria touching on the national identity of the recipient state), political conditionality functions differently than in democratic reform projects, often resulting only in partial compliance or in non-compliance (*outcome dimension*). Finally, based on transition literature, I argue that political conditionality in security issues has generated counterproductive unintended consequences in the democratization process (*impact dimension*).

In terms of the special issue, this article focuses on the crucial issue of the emergence of an extrinsic conflict of objectives (specifically, between democracy and security)[16] and the role that external actors (here, the EU) play through their DP instruments. The first part constructs a theoretical argument, revealing how and why the EU's DP policy of political conditionality has contributed to the conflict of objectives, and how this has affected the DP agenda and the democratization process. The second part provides empirical evidence. The Former Yugoslav Republic of Macedonia (hereafter, Macedonia) is a suitable candidate for a case study, as the initial conditions for the EU to achieve both security and democracy were favourable in 2001.[17] While progress in the country was indeed remarkable in political-security terms up to 2006 (that is, the implementation of the Ohrid Framework Agreement), more recently Macedonia's transition process and accession to the EU has ground to a halt. The political situation in the country has even reversed, with increasing intra- and inter-ethnic conflicts and persistent democratic deficits. The conclusion reflects on the lessons Macedonia provides for DP in general and for the instrument of political conditionality in particular.

Theoretical argument: political conditionality and conflicting objectives

EU political conditionality as an incentive-based strategy: conditions of success and effectiveness

In the literature, political conditionality is considered to be one of the most effective EU tools for democracy promotion.[18] Conditionality is an incentive-based strategy that attempts to re-shape the cost-benefit calculations of national actors using carrots and sticks: with the 'conditional promise of membership [the EU] has produced the strongest effect on democratization in Europe's neighbourhood'.[19] Most notably, the countries of Central and Eastern Europe (CEE) have successfully conformed to the EU's standards of democracy and human rights. However, these positive effects of political conditionality only transpire when certain terms are met. In the literature, there is broad consensus on the conditions of success and the causal mechanisms for the effectiveness of the policy,[20] which pertain to the international agency (the EU) and the target countries (here, the Western Balkan states). In order to systematize these conditions in the following and for analytical reasons, I resort to the output, outcome, and impact scheme to analyse political systems; the scheme was originally developed by David Easton but has since been expanded and elaborated by studies on international organizations and conflict management.[21] According to Easton's terminology, the *output* of an international organization refers to its 'products', meaning political programmes, operative decisions, concrete measures, and informal activities.[22] In the context of this article, the output dimension encompasses how the EU shapes its conditionality policy in security issues and democracy promotion. The *outcome* describes the consequences of this output in terms of concrete reactions to the conditionality policy on the part of the target state, which this article does by examining how the Western Balkan states have complied with the EU's criteria. Most of the literature on political conditionality only concentrates on these two sets of functional requirements to measure the effectiveness of a DP instrument;[23] however, this method lacks a perspective of the wider political process in the target country. Studies on the effects of international development aid and post-conflict rehabilitation show that *impact* is a necessary variable to measure the

Table 1. Variables and the emergence of a conflict of objectives.

Dimension	Output	Outcome	Impact
Variable	Credibility and consistency of conditionality	Compliance patterns logic of consequences vs. logic of appropriateness	(Unintended) consequences for the transformation process
Argument	Security first: consistent and credible conditionality in security, inconsistent and incredible conditionality in democracy promotion	Compliance patterns differ; 'conditionality dilemma': rewarding incompliance or sanctioning compliance	Counterproductive side-effects of Copenhagen-Plus conditionality on the democratization process

Source: Author's own compilation.

effectiveness of a certain policy.[24] In contrast to the focus of outcome on goal achievement, the impact dimension examines problem-solving and thus includes the (unintended) effects on the society and the political system over a longer time frame. Since numerous studies have indicated negative side effects this is especially relevant in the case of political conditionality;[25] however, until now this dimension has not been systematically integrated into causal mechanisms. I argue that a third – often forgotten – dimension for the assessment of the effectiveness of political conditionality as an instrument of democracy promotion is a measurement of the wider, often unintended, consequences in the Western Balkan states. In each of these three dimensions, I will explain in the following the reasons why a conflict of objectives between security interests and democracy promotion emerged (see Table 1).

Output: credibility and consistency of conditionality – security first

In the output dimension and thus on the part of the EU, the necessary conditions for political conditionality to effectively induce domestic change are credibility and consistency. *Credibility* means providing a reward in the case of compliance and sanctioning or withholding the reward in the case of non-compliance with a criterion. The other condition, *consistency*, requires that rewards are explicitly and reliably linked to the fulfilment of EU criteria, and that the EU bases its enlargement decisions on the same (democratic) standards. The effectiveness of conditionality increases when rewards are tangible (politically or materially, for example, membership, financial assistance) and sizable enough to balance out the expected domestic adaptation costs for the target government.[26] The credibility of political conditionality in the target countries decreases when insecurity over the promised reward increases, for example, due to internal disagreements in the EU. This has been the case in recent years, where enlargement fatigue and the slow internal reform process of EU structures have nurtured doubts about the EU's willingness and capacity to deliver the promised reward of EU membership.[27]

I argue that the EU's effectiveness in enforcing both democracy and security with one instrument is limited by the fact that when there are two separate strategic interests, the consistency and consequently the credibility of political conditionality are diminished. There is broad consensus in the literature that in the CEE enlargement process the EU linked conditionality to democratic criteria in a consistent and meritocratic way. On the contrary, the EU's democracy promotion policy has fallen short of consistency in non-accession countries (for example, Central Asia and the Mediterranean).[28] There, 'actual policy seems to match rhetoric [of democracy and human rights promotion] only when consistency is "cheap"; otherwise, it is driven by a host of geopolitical, economic and security interests'.[29] In particular, not democratic criteria but strategic interests for stability and security have dominated the EU's foreign relations agenda within the overarching framework of human rights.[30] These double standards in EU democracy promotion have contributed to a 'credibility gap' that undermines the EU's conditionality policy.[31]

The inconsistency argument could under certain circumstances also hold true in the case of the EU's policy in the Western Balkans, at least prior to the start of accession negotiations.[32] First, security issues were of utmost importance for the EU in the SEE countries, as demonstrated by the Copenhagen-Plus criteria. Second, according to the literature, it is only during the actual accession process that compliance with the *acquis communautaire* is at the core of the EU's policy.[33] In the period before the start of accession negotiations, the EU prioritizes its strategic interests (including security). Considering that most of the Western Balkan countries have not yet started accession negotiations,[34] it can be presumed that the EU only inconsistently pursues both objectives through political conditionality and that it, until the start of negotiations, will follow a 'security first' policy at the expense of democracy promotion. This argument is in line with the sequencing argument in the transition literature, by which a minimum of security and stability must be established before (externally induced or supported) democratization should take place.[35]

Outcome: different compliance patterns in democracy promotion and security issues

Even if the EU manages to make its conditionality policy credible and consistent with regard both to security issues and democracy promotion, the outcome – compliance patterns – may differ.

In the literature, the behaviour of the target state's reaction to EU political conditionality has generally been explained by the *external incentives model* or *leverage model*.[36] According to the underlying logic of consequences, governments in the target states behave rationally, calculating the costs and benefits, and reforms are induced by the EU's use of carrots and sticks.[37] Governments comply with the EU's criteria if the political costs of adjustment are not higher than the expected benefits (in this case EU accession is most important). However, if the incentive potential of an external actor does not correspond with the transformation state's sensitivity towards these incentives, conditionality will prove ineffective. According to rational logic, the recipient must subjectively assess if the benefits of a reward or the costs of a sanction are high enough to compensate for the efforts required for change.[38] In general, before rewards such as EU membership can be used as an incentive, 'the decisive change has already taken place. The targets of socialization must be convinced that membership is beneficial to them.'[39] Thus, political conditionality is an incentive-based democracy promotion strategy, in contrast to socialization strategies, which are based upon the logic of appropriateness on the parts of the target states;[40] in such cases, governments comply with the EU's criteria if the EU succeeds in persuading them of the superiority of its rules and if the governments consider these rules to be legitimate.[41]

In the literature, it is widely acknowledged that the EU's outcome in the democratic reform process in CEE – namely successful rule transfer – resulted from the strong incentive provided by the promise of EU membership rather than from its socialization efforts.[42] By offering a reward, the EU was able to lure even uncooperative and generally reform-reluctant governments to comply with its criteria.[43] Since the original Copenhagen criteria are almost identical in the CEE and the SEE, I argue that the compliance patterns of political conditionality in the democracy promotion agenda can be sufficiently explained by rational behaviour on the parts of the SEE countries, that is, by the size of domestic adaptation costs. Thus, if the SEE countries perceive EU membership as beneficial to them and this benefit exceeds the costs of reforms (for example, the risk of loss of political power for the incumbent government) they will comply and pursue democratic reforms.[44]

However, recent studies have raised doubts about whether the compliance of a target state with the EU's criteria in security issues can be adequately explained by the external incentives model. These studies reveal that when the EU's criteria touch sensitive issues of nation-building or the legacy of ethnic conflicts (as is mostly the case in the EU's Copenhagen-Plus criteria such as in reconciliation or transitional justice), governments act as though they were guided not by a logic of consequences, but rather by a logic of appropriateness.[45] Freyburg and Richter have shown that rather than weighing costs and benefits and acting strategically, these governments will stick to what they consider appropriate with regard to their national identity:[46] 'Incentives created by third actors [...] thus have to pass an implicit "identity test" if they are to shape governmental policies in the desired way. [...] [If] national identity runs counter to [...] requirements, this will "block" compliance by framing it as inappropriate action.'[47] Similarly, Noutcheva argues that the legitimacy of the EU's sovereignty related demands (that is, criteria concerning state- and peace-building) have been contested by political leaders in the Western Balkans: 'The Balkan's challenge to the EU's normative influence plays out in the politics of compliance and manifests itself in these countries contesting the appropriateness of the EU's pressure on them to undertake specific statehood-linked changes.'[48] If the EU cannot persuade political leaders – including reform-minded politicians – of the appropriateness of its demands, these leaders will question the EU's authority to set such conditions and will resist them.[49] Thus, even when conditionality is credible, consistent and political adaptation costs are low, a target state might not (or might only partially) comply with the Copenhagen-Plus criteria.

These different compliance patterns may under certain circumstances explain the conflict of objectives for the EU and contribute to an inconsistent and not credible conditionality policy in the output dimension; consequently, the EU may face a 'conditionality dilemma'. As discussed above, a crucial feature of political conditionality is credibility: rewarding in the case of compliance, sanctioning or withholding the reward in the case of non-compliance. In the best-case scenario, compliance patterns would be similar for both the Copenhagen and the Copenhagen-Plus criteria, which would allow the EU to easily determine rewards or sanctions based on the behaviour of the recipient state. However, in a less desirable situation, the outcome will differ; states might comply with the Copenhagen criteria but not comply with the Copenhagen-Plus criteria, or vice versa. The EU would then face the dilemma of either rewarding non-compliance or sanctioning compliance. Although within the framework of EU enlargement policy the EU can resort to a variety of instruments (for example, financial assistance, market access), the decisive benefit is an all-or-nothing indivisible prospect. The crucial leverage of the EU is based on progressive steps in the path towards membership, such as the opening of accession negotiations. Therefore, if compliance patterns differ, the EU is in danger of either making its conditionality policy credible and consistent in security issues at the cost of an inconsistent conditionality policy that lacks credibility in democracy promotion, or vice versa.

Impact: unintended consequences of political conditionality on the democratization process

The third dimension affecting the EU's conflict between security interests and democracy promotion is impact. Most of the studies on the effectiveness or causal mechanisms of political conditionality have focused only on the outcome, especially compliance.[50] As a result, they lack a necessary perspective on the wider transformation process, of unintended consequences, and of how political conditionality contributes to resolution of the 'problem' (that is, the democratization of the countries in SEE). To explain the relationship between the DP instrument, its impact, and the conflict of objectives, this article utilizes transition theory, which describes in detail the course of democratization and patterns of change.[51] I argue that the conditions for success for political conditionality have mostly been met with regard to the Copenhagen political criteria so that compliance with EU requirements has positively contributed to the smooth transformation of the recipient states. In contrast, conditions have often been unfavourable when it comes to the incentive-based strategies prioritizing the Copenhagen-Plus criteria. Even when states comply with these requirements, the unintended consequences of the conditionality policy may negatively affect democratization, which explains the emergence of a conflict of objectives.

For the most part, conditions for the positive impact of political conditionality on the Copenhagen criteria are met after the first, often turbulent, initial changes in the political system have taken place. A widespread consensus for democracy has already been manifested, as is generally reflected in a new or revised constitution. Thus, the implementation of democratic reforms does not necessarily imply a threat to the government's power base.[52] Often the population and the government already share the goal of joining the EU and are convinced that membership would be beneficial.[53] Governments in this situation react to external pressure in a rational and strategic way and they are susceptible to carrots and sticks. Under these conditions, incentive-based strategies may contribute to the democratization process via the elites (*top-down*) or via the population (*bottom-up*).[54] First, although compliance with EU democratic criteria, at the outcome level, only implies behaviour modifications in the government, this may nevertheless change political structures in the long-term, leading to the habitualization of democratic rules and procedures and finally the internalization of democratic norms.[55] Policies of conditionality, which are built on the premise of providing significant rewards and definite punishments, can also keep reform-resistant and uncooperative governments on the right path, shaping their behaviour and coercing them into making the right decisions and installing democratic rules and principles.[56] Second, opposition parties and civil society groups demanding reforms gain credibility and external support by the EU's conditionality policy. By voting accordingly, the citizens are able to affect a change in government and ultimately policy changes.[57]

In the case of the Copenhagen-Plus criteria certain conditions of success for political conditionality are often left unfulfilled, which results in counterproductive side effects for the democratization process. Two aspects are relevant here; the management of reforms and the government's accountability. Pro-democratic governments do not always have the ability to fully implement EU requirements, even when they are willing to reform and have been persuaded that compliance is appropriate. This is especially the case in turbulent or polarized processes of transformation, where national stakeholders might be incapable of action; for example, if they are in a minority government, if they have unstable coalition partners, if there are powerful veto players, or if bureaucracy tries to delay reform.[58] Moreover, conditions, which involve high costs or that demand an action in contravention of national identity, carry a high risk for national governments.[59] Reform-oriented but unassertive elites tend to be caught in the crossfire. For the reform process to continue, they must resolve this dissonance between national values and EU requirements in order to secure both their own re-elections and external support.[60] If they do not succeed in one of these preconditions, they will be rejected by the population or penalized by the withdrawal of EU rewards. Incentive-based strategies, especially in the case of Copenhagen-Plus criteria, with strict criteria may result in systematically overburdened governments that are primarily preoccupied with meeting external requirements. As a result, they lose connection to their own society and neglect the democratic reform process.[61] The opposition can easily profit from such a situation by branding the government a puppet of the international community.[62] In both cases – the challenging management of reforms and the decreasing accountability of the government to the population – political conditionality results in counterproductive side effects for the democratization process. Democratic reforms are delayed and democratic deficits are entrenched, pro-democratic forces are weakened, and support for reform-resistant and perhaps even nationalistic actors grows.[63] Thus, even if the EU succeeds in enforcing the Copenhagen-Plus criteria and enhances security, this may inhibit a smooth transition and burden the democratization in the middle or long term. The gap between progress in security issues and democratic reforms increases, which ultimately creates a conflict of objectives for the EU.

Empirical illustration: the EU's conditionality policy in Macedonia

In the remainder of this article, the argument will be demonstrated empirically. Generally speaking, via the prospect of accession, the EU has indeed been able to induce political change that the SEE states would not have pursued without conditionality.[64] The EU has succeeded partially in forcing these countries to comply with most of the Copenhagen-Plus criteria. To give only a few examples; today, all war-crime suspects indicted by the ICTY have been arrested and are facing trial in The Hague; the separation of Serbia and Montenegro proceeded peacefully; and despite enormous deficits peace treaties still remain the anchor of stability for the multi-ethnic states of Macedonia and Bosnia and Herzegovina. However, as the main democracy promoter in the region, the EU has obviously encountered difficulties in helping these countries to develop into mature democracies. Except for Slovenia, the Western Balkan countries must be considered semi-consolidated democracies, transitional or hybrid regimes, or in the case of Kosovo semi-consolidated authoritarian regimes (according to the definitions and democracy scores in 'Nations in Transit 2011'; see Table 2).[65]

Case selection and overview: Macedonia – from euphoria to disillusion

Macedonia is an appropriate case study to support the theoretical argument and for the empirical study of the emergence of a conflict of objectives between democracy promotion and security interests. If the EU ever had a chance to succeed in simultaneously achieving these two goals with one instrument in SEE, this should have been the case in Macedonia, where the initial conditions were favourable. Thus, if the theoretical argument has explanatory power and accounts for the emergence of a conflict of objectives for the EU in this case, then one could expect to find similar results in other SEE countries, in which the initial conditions for the EU's conditionality policy to achieve both objectives were even worse.

Table 2. State of democracy in the Western Balkans, 2011.

Country	Democracy score	Regime type
Croatia	3.64	Semi-consolidated democracies
Serbia	3.64	
Macedonia	3.82	
Montenegro	3.82	
Albania	4.04	Transitional governments or hybrid regimes
Bosnia and Herzegovina	4.32	
Kosovo	5.18	Semi-consolidated authoritarian regime
Average new EU members in CEE	2.43	All consolidated democracies, except Bulgaria and Romania (semi-consolidated democracies)

Source: Freedom House, 'Nations in Transit 2011', 48, http://www.freedomhouse.org/images/File/nit/2011/NIT-2011-Tables.pdf.
Notes: The ratings are based on a scale of 1–7, with 1 representing the highest level of democratic progress and 7 the lowest. The 2011 ratings reflect the period between 1 January and 31 December 2010. The regime type is clustered as follows: consolidated democracies (1.00–2.99), semi-consolidated democracies (3.00–3.99), transitional governments or hybrid regimes (4.00–4.99), semi-consolidated authoritarian regimes (5.00–5.99), consolidated authoritarian regimes (6.00–7.00).

Compared to the bloody secession conflicts in neighbouring countries, Macedonia had long been considered a prime example of stability and inter-ethnic coexistence.[66] In spring 2001, Macedonia became the first country in SEE to sign a Stabilization and Association Agreement with the EU. By offering the prospect of EU membership, the EU intended to motivate the country's political elites to concentrate on the democratic reform process. However, nearly concurrently with the EU agreement, the dispute between Macedonia's Slavonic majority and Albanian minority escalated into violent unrest, which was largely driven by the National Liberation Army (NLA).[67]

Because the constitution discriminated against them, the Albanian population demanded more rights. In cooperation with the USA, the EU succeeded in mediating the Ohrid Framework Agreement (OFA, 13 August 2001),[68] which substantially elevated the rights of the Albanian minority. The OFA included a revision of the constitution and power-sharing agreements and therefore required a large-scale reconfiguration of the political system.[69] Although democratic reform elements were part of the agreement, 'its main purpose was to maintain the existence of the state, improve the status of ethnic Albanians, stop hostilities between armed groups, and prevent further bloodshed [...]'.[70] However, the drafters of the agreement did not pay enough attention to the complexity of the rifts and the structure of political conflict in Macedonia, the transformation of which proved to be a crucial precondition for democratic consolidation.[71] Indeed, the spirit of the OFA was influenced more by security concerns than by the goal of profound democratization.

Since 2001, the conditionality policy of the EU has primarily been focused on the implementation of the OFA in terms of Copenhagen-Plus criteria; the classic Copenhagen criteria have been of secondary importance. What seemed at first glance to be successful in the long term, in fact ended up being problematic. In December 2005, the EU rewarded the social democratic (SDSM[72]) government of Vlado Bučkovski with EU candidate status because of its efforts in implementing the OFA. However, after 2006 the democratization process has been stagnating, and democratic deficits threaten the peaceful inter-ethnic coexistence in the country. For example, the OFA intensified existing divisions within society by institutionalizing the ethnic conflict through power-sharing agreements. Consequently, elites have resorted to nationalistic rhetoric, and political parties have played 'an especially negative role in interethnic relations'.[73] The EU was facing a trade-off; in light of serious shortcomings in complying with the Copenhagen criteria, the European Commission was initially hesitant to reward the country with the next step towards prospective EU membership, which is the start of actual accession negotiations. However, without the possibility for the government and the population to move forward with integration into the EU, there was a growing risk of destabilization. This complex situation was aggravated by the dispute with Greece over the country's name, which absorbed the government's attention and poisoned the inter-ethnic atmosphere in the country. Greece opposes the constitutional name of 'Macedonia' without any specification (for example, geographically by adding 'northern'), and believes that the name 'Macedonia' implies territorial ambitions towards a region within its own territory, which was historically part of the ancient Macedonia. In 2008, Greece vetoed the accession of Macedonia to the North Atlantic Treaty Organization (NATO). This external dispute has had severe repercussions for the internal political sphere, because Prime Minister Gruevski has used it in a nationalist fashion to strengthen his popularity, which exacerbates tensions between the Albanian minority and the Macedonian majority.[74]

Following efforts by the Gruevski government to fulfil EU demands for political reforms, the Commission finally, in October 2009, recommended opening accession negotiations. However, the European Council has been unable to find consensus for this step, due to the Greek veto. Consequently, after 10 years of political conditionality, the EU has not achieved either of its two objectives. Both security concerns and democracy promotion still dominate the agenda in Macedonia. In the following section, I will explain, in detail and along the three dimensions (*output, outcome,* and *impact*), the effects of the EU's conditionality policy and the emergence of the conflict of objectives.

Output: Ohrid Framework Agreement as top priority

Due to the armed conflict in 2001, the EU adjusted its strategy to serve its own security interests, and with the intention of stabilizing the country and improving the state structure, the EU made the implementation of the OFA as a

Copenhagen-Plus criterion its top priority. The EU aligned its entire Western Balkan 'toolbox', including the SAA and the enlargement process, with this goal.[75] Thanks to its conditionality policy, Brussels, together with its international partners (the USA and OSCE), could consistently and credibly exert pressure on Macedonian politicians. Regardless of the status of the democratic transition, the EU had no choice but to focus all its energy on the mediation and implementation of a peace treaty. Otherwise, the EU risked an escalation that might have forced it to deploy a military mission. While the EU's political conditionality was quite consistent and credible with regard to the Copenhagen-Plus criterion OFA in the years 2001–2005, democracy promotion in terms of the implementation of the Copenhagen criteria was only of secondary importance, and consistent conditionality was only selectively applied. That security issues dominated the conditionality policy of the EU was effectively demonstrated in 2005, where the decision to assign Macedonia the status of candidate state was an explicit reward to Skopje for its efforts to implement the OFA and stabilize the country.[76] Although the European Commission criticized Macedonia in the progress report for its lack of reforms, the European Council took this decision for security reasons. The EU member states were worried that a negative message would have destabilizing and discouraging implications for Macedonia.

After certain crucial laws, prescribed by the OFA, were adopted,[77] the EU has, from 2005, focused its conditionality policy on the fulfilment of the original Copenhagen criteria. The 2006 version of the European Partnership – an instrument of the SAA – set priorities for genuine democratic reform steps, such as amendments to the electoral code and reform of the judiciary.[78] The 2008 version of the European Partnership included additional demands for police reform, de-politicization of the administration, and anti-corruption measures.[79] Thus, in 2005, because of security concerns, the EU showed flexibility; however, from 2005–2009, it adhered much more consistently to its democratic requirements by refraining from approving the next accession step due to the country's serious democratic deficits. It was only in 2009 that the Commission recommended starting the accession negotiations. This decision to reward the country may well be assessed as in line with a consistent and credible conditionality policy, especially as Gruevski had indeed made efforts towards important reform steps between 2008 and 2009. However, after the Greek veto, the Commission repeated its recommendation in the years 2010 and 2011 despite a deteriorating political situation in Macedonia and the region (for example, an unresolved status question in Kosovo and a stagnating state-building process and political crisis in Bosnia and Herzegovina), which suggests that security interests had returned to the fore.

Since 2008 (at the latest), the Commission's consistent conditionality policy in the Copenhagen criteria has been undermined by the European Council, specifically by the Greek veto to start the accession negotiations with Macedonia. In the language of the Commission's progress report the EU's main requirement for Macedonia, to proceed with EU integration, has been 'good neighbourly relations'[80]; this primarily consists of resolving the name dispute with Greece, an EU member state. Political conditionality has, therefore, focused on the resolution of a bilateral dispute, and has neither consistently nor credibly been linked to compliance with Copenhagen or Copenhagen-Plus criteria.

Outcome: Macedonia between rational and appropriate behaviour

Overall, the political conditionality instrument of the EU was successful in bringing the Macedonian government into at least partial compliance with its requirements.[81] However, compliance patterns differed with regard to the Copenhagen and Copenhagen-Plus criteria. From 2002–2006, a coalition of the social democrat SDSM and the Albanian DUI[82] party largely implemented the arrangements prescribed by the OFA. The coalition amended the constitution, adopted crucial legislation, such as decentralization, and began to realize OFA provisions in practice; for example, through equal representation in the administration and judiciary. This compliance pattern can only be explained by the logic of appropriateness, as EU membership was one of the few political goals shared by the two ethnic groups. For the governmental party of the Macedonian majority, the socialist SDSM, national identity issues were of minor importance in comparison to its wish to join the EU. The SDSM implemented large-scale OFA reforms, despite the high power costs it incurred (in terms of an opposition party that campaigned hard against the OFA and was gaining in strength).[83] The EU's demands for OFA enforcement were seen by the government as a legitimate albeit cost-intensive concern. This positive performance in the security dimension stands in contrast to more sobering results regarding compliance with the original Copenhagen criteria in the form of democratic reforms. These different compliance patterns largely mirrored the EU's own policy of prioritizing the OFA, but brought the EU into conflict over its own conditionality policy. The 2005 decision to assign Macedonia the status of candidate state rewarded the country's efforts in fulfilling the Copenhagen-Plus criteria, but was not linked to compliance with the Copenhagen criteria. Here a comment by the British EU-Presidency at the time is striking: 'This was a political gesture to provide the region with stability, but now, as a result, the Commission has to deal with a very challenging and complex case for EU accession.'[84]

In 2006, compliance patterns changed. The new national-conservative government under Prime Minister Nikola Gruevski and his VMRO-DPMNE[85] party has slowed down the implementation of the OFA; however, Gruevski has been susceptible to EU incentives in domestic reforms by showing partial compliance. Between 2002 and 2006 the implementation of the OFA was, due to the short time-frame, unavoidably incomplete and lacking in sustainability, it nevertheless laid a foundation for Gruevski's selective compliance. The new government was 'less concerned about the issue of inter-ethnic relations than previous governments'.[86] It did not ensure equitable representation, implement the law on languages, or oppose cultural exclusion. Moreover, Gruevski's policy for building a strong national Macedonian identity was implicitly against the spirit of the OFA and explicitly against some legal provisions, such as the law on national symbols. Consequently, inter-ethnic relations 'suffered from weak central-government support'.[87] The logic of appropriateness may account for incompliance with the OFA criterion, which is shown by the fact that national identity issues have been of utmost importance for the Gruevski government. Since 2009, Gruevski has followed a '"national renaissance" policy line'.[88] Using projects such as an oversized statue of Alexander the Great and an urban development programme for Skopje, Gruevski has attempted to re-create a strong national identity based on Macedonia's ancient history.[89] In this context, a policy that would enhance minority rights and strengthen the multi-ethnic character of the state was largely considered inappropriate. Political costs cannot sufficiently explain the behaviour of the Gruevski government, since it was not threatened with loss of power by the rather weak and non-nationalist SDSM opposition party.

In contrast, cost-benefit calculations have obviously played a major role in explaining compliance with the Copenhagen criteria since 2006. The Gruevski government's rational and rapid compliance with demands for democratic reforms in the face of rigorous EU conditionality was demonstrated during the so-called endgames – the final phases of negotiations in the run-up to the enlargement decision, during which external pressure rises.[90] For example, after harsh international criticism of the 2008 parliamentary election and heavy pressure by the EU, Gruevski modified the electoral code and ensured orderly presidential and municipal elections in 2009, which overall were in line with international standards.[91] Moreover, the EU incentive to lift visa requirements proved to be an effective carrot for the Macedonian government's compliance with the comprehensive EU benchmarks for reforms in justice and home affairs.[92] However, these efforts were driven only by external incentives; the Gruevski government has neither continuously nor comprehensively invested in democratic reforms. On the contrary, since the EU's conditionality policy was made inconsistent and not credible by the Greek blockade in 2009, the situation regarding the Copenhagen criteria in terms of the independence of the judiciary and media freedom has worsened.[93] To summarize, the advancements that Macedonia has made towards European integration have been based on (partial) compliance with Copenhagen-Plus criteria and security concerns on the part of the EU rather than on substantial progress in democratic reforms which relate to the Copenhagen criteria. In the final section I will describe how these compliance patterns have affected inter-ethnic integration and the political reform process.

Impact: incomplete inter-ethnic integration and the stagnating democratization process

Ethnic discrimination was one important cause of the violent unrest in 2001. On a positive note, the OFA comprehensively changed the country's political system and state structure, where the Albanian minority gained more cultural and minority rights (for example, decentralization and recognition of Albanian as an official language) as well as enhanced political powers (such as double-majority in parliament, power-sharing, equal representation in the administration). Thus, the OFA not only put an end to the violent conflict in 2001 but, more importantly, improved inter-ethnic relations to the point where the majority of the Albanian population has been loyal to the Macedonian state.[94]

Nevertheless, the dynamics of political power and patronage in Macedonia have played a major and often underestimated role.[95] The EU's agenda-setting that focused the government's efforts to implement the OFA proved to be problematic with regard to the management of reforms. By neglecting these transitional problems, the OFA and EU policy even aggravated them in two respects. The institutionalization of power-sharing mechanisms intensified the 'spoiler system', which was already having negative effects on day-to-day political functions. The government in Macedonia only has full decision-making capacity in the parliament when a majority of all representatives and a majority of minority representatives support its policy.[96] Using these new power resources, the Albanian parties have regularly blocked parliamentary functions and the governance system.[97] Cases in point are the decentralization reform, in which the SDSM accused its coalition partner DUI of blackmail, and the parliamentary boycotts by the DPA, the second-largest Albanian party, from 2005–2006 and by the DUI in 2007.[98] Moreover, the OFA strengthened traditional informal networks of clientelism. Because it modified the allocation of scarce resources, old rivalries and patronages were revitalized.[99] A case in point is the requirement of 'equal representation' in the administration and judiciary. Virtually overnight, new positions for Albanian candidates appeared, but the distribution of jobs has since been controlled by the Albanian party in power. These new opportunities reinforced the power struggle between Slavic Macedonian parties and Albanian parties[100] and – even worse – exacerbated the politicization of these institutions. The infiltration of formal institutions by informal networks has given rise to a grave democratic deficit. After the OFA established a comprehensive inter-ethnic power-sharing mechanism, the political decision-making process was parcelled out by the elite into informal processes. For example, the entire decentralization package was arranged between the DUI and the SDSM behind closed doors. Similarly, in 2007 the DUI gave up its boycott of parliamentary work after an unofficial agreement that was even supported by the EU. As a consequence, democratic institutions like the parliament have been reduced to rubber-stamping the decisions of other actors.[101]

Second, the EU's conditionality policy contributed to an accountability deficit. By pushing the SDSM-DUI coalition hard to implement with the OFA a domestically contested issue in a hasty fashion and without any open-ended parliamentary or public debate, the EU's policy paved the way for opposition parties to accuse the government of betrayal. Although the VMRO-DPMNE party had originally supported the constitutional amendments in 2001, it later voted against all related laws and constitutional amendments and campaigned against the OFA by using ethnically charged rhetoric.[102] Unintentionally, the EU's conditionality policy polarized society and party politics; the EU consequently weakened rather than supported the very party, the SDSM, which had intensively worked to satisfy Brussels and to improve inter-ethnic relations. In the highly polarized public sphere, the SDSM, who was (as the party in power) responsible for the implementation of the OFA, was unable to win the support of Slavic Macedonians. The government was primarily occupied with fulfilling restrictive EU criteria, thus it lacked the capacity to undertake other urgent reform projects. The SDSM did not succeed in delivering benefits to its own electorate and ultimately lost the 2006 election to the VRMO-DPMNE, which won after promoting itself as the guardian of national interests. The VRMO-DPMNE has proven to be a problematic partner for the EU and its government has slowed down the pace of reforms and brought democratization to a halt. Their ethno-nationalist policy has terrified the Albanian majority and thereby allowed inter-ethnic tensions to foment.[103]

In summary, since 2001 Macedonia has oscillated between successful state-building and setbacks in democratic consolidation.[104] The stagnating transition has threatened the achievements of the OFA and resulted in growing discontentment on the Albanian side. The EU policy was meant to create a virtuous circle but has resulted in trade-offs: the instrument of political conditionality proved to be effective in the first years but produced counterproductive side effects that have slowed down the pace of transition and ultimately integration into the EU. As the result of Greece hijacking the process, the evanescent prospective membership promised by the EU's incredible and inconsistent political conditionality policy has failed to externally induce a renewed reform dynamic.

Conclusion: bringing democracy promotion back in

The Macedonian case effectively illustrates that even for the EU, which is considered to be one of the most powerful global democracy promoters, not all good things go together; in fact, the EU has contributed to the emerging conflict of objectives with its instrument of political conditionality. I have shown that functional requirements were not met or were only incompletely met in security issues, which resulted in counterproductive side effects for democratization.

On the one hand, the EU's approach to prioritizing security at the expense of the implementation of democratic reforms has proven to be successful in the short to medium term. The EU managed to prevent an escalation of hostilities and maybe even a civil war, and pushed through a constitution that secures peaceful inter-ethnic coexistence in the country. The incentive-based strategy of the EU with the carrot of prospective membership was crucial for the Macedonian government to be able to implement democratic reforms. However, between 2001 and 2005 the EU did not succeed in making its own conditionality policy credible and consistent with regard to the Copenhagen criteria as opposed to the Copenhagen-Plus criteria. As a result, EU democracy promotion proved to be less than effective. The positive picture of the EU's engagement in security issues was also overshadowed by counterproductive side-effects that impeded the consolidation of democracy and negatively impacted the fragile inter-ethnic peace. Today, democratic deficits threaten the achievements of the OFA and the country's integration into the EU.

What can we learn with regard to democracy promotion in post-conflict states in general, and the EU's political conditionality as a DP instrument in the Western Balkan region in particular? First, security issues, among them state-building and conflict management, are closely intertwined with the domestic reform process and cannot be addressed by external actors separately or without any consideration of actual political structures and the dynamics of the transition, especially regarding party and power politics. This brings democracy promotion back in and qualifies the sequencing argument in the transition and state-building literature. While this argument may still hold true in cases of war or violent conflict, it should be adapted in cases of post-conflict democratization. Based on the findings in this article, I argue that a more coherent, parallel policy of security issues and democracy promotion in a stable political context could avoid the counterproductive side effects that a sequencing policy can trigger. However, this conclusion only holds true under the condition that external actors diversify their instruments, which brings me to the second point.

The case of Macedonia has shown, in an exemplary way, that the EU strategy to achieve two priorities – security and democracy – with one instrument was not (fully) successful. We can find similar results in other SEE countries, in which the initial conditions for the EU's conditionality policy to achieve both objectives were worse. Croatia could only concentrate on democratic reforms and fulfil all requirements for EU accession after it complied with the Copenhagen-Plus criteria in 2005. On the other end of the spectrum, Bosnia and Herzegovina and Kosovo must be considered neither stable nor democratic countries. Based on Europeanization literature and transition theory, I have argued that the conditions of success of political conditionality were not met or were only partly met, which resulted in incompliance or partial compliance with EU demands and negative effects on the domestic reform process. Maintaining a credible conditionality policy regarding security issues implied an inconsistent conditionality policy with regard to democracy promotion (*output*). One reason for this can be found in the different compliance patterns, which in the worst case confronted the EU with a dilemma between rewarding and sanctioning (*outcome*).[105] While the logic of consequences accounts for the outcome of political conditionality in domestic reforms, the logic of appropriateness better explains the dynamic for security issues that primarily touched on questions of national identity.[106] Finally, the EU's conditionality policy neglected domestic power relations and party politics,[107] thus weakening pro-democratic forces and strengthening nationalist sentiments and groups (*impact*). To avoid such a negative scenario in the Western Balkans in the future, the EU should diversify its CFSP toolbox and enlargement policies to synchronize processes of stabilization and democratization. The original Copenhagen criteria (that is, democratic reforms) should play an enhanced role at an early stage, even in cases in which the EU has a profound security interest.[108]

Acknowledgements

I am grateful for comments on earlier versions provided by the three editors of this issue, Sonja Grimm, Julia Leininger, and Tina Freyburg, as well as by Jörg Faust, by the participants of the workshop on the special issue in Zürich 2011, and by the two anonymous referees.

Notes

1. In line with this special issue, the term 'democracy promotion' includes all peaceful measures by external actors intended to support or even speed up the political transformation to democracy in a target country. For simplicity, the terms 'democratization (process)', 'transformation (process)', and 'transition' can also be used synonymously as umbrella terms for the process of regime change. A differentiation between these terms would only make sense based on extensive discussion, which is not feasible within the confines of this article.
2. Wolff, 'Theorie des Demokratischen Friedens'; Grävingholt, Leininger, and Schlumberger, 'Demokratieförderung'.
3. The EU coined the term 'Western Balkans'. With the exception of Slovenia, the Western Balkans consist of all of the former Yugoslavian states plus Albania.
4. The Copenhagen criteria for candidate countries additionally demand a functioning market economy with a capacity to cope with competitive pressure and market forces within the Union. Moreover, the respective states are to have the ability to take on the obligations of membership, including adherence to the aims of political, economic, and monetary union. See European Council, 'Copenhagen'.
5. Kochenov, 'Behind the Copenhagen Façade'.
6. Take as an example the 2011 progress reports and the EU's enlargement strategy, which can be found at: http://ec.europa.eu/enlargement/press_corner/key-documents/reports_oct_2011_en.htm (accessed November 15, 2011).
7. Noutcheva, 'Fake, Partial and Imposed Compliance', 1069.
8. See Richter, 'Frieden schaffen', 78.
9. Risse-Kappen, 'Democratic Peace'; Sandschneider, 'Externe Demokratieförderung', 17–18.
10. Carothers, *Aiding Democracy Abroad*, 45.
11. Ohlson and Söderberg, 'From Intrastate-war', 3; Mansfield and Snyder, 'Democratic Transition', 299ff.; Gurr, *People versus State*, 85.
12. Geis and Wagner, 'How Far is it from Königsberg to Kandahar?'; Carothers, 'The Backlash'.
13. Wolff, 'Theorie des Demokratischen Friedens'.
14. Linz and Stepan, *Democratic Transition*, 16; on the sequencing debate, see the articles in the 'Exchange' section of *Journal of Democracy* 18, no. 3 (2007).
15. Börzel argues in a similar way: Börzel, 'When Europeanization Hits Limited Statehood'.
16. On intrinsic and extrinsic conflicts of objectives, see Grimm and Leininger, 'Not All Good Things Go Together'; Spanger and Wolff, 'Universales Ziel'.
17. The constitutional name of the country is 'Republic of Macedonia' (*Republika Makedonija*). Due to an unresolved name dispute with neighbouring Greece, the country is still officially a member of the United Nations under the name 'The Former Yugoslav Republic of Macedonia' (FYROM). In this article, the name Macedonia is used, as it is standard in the academic literature.
18. Cf. Lavenex and Schimmelfennig, 'EU Democracy Promotion'; Kelley, 'International Actors on the Domestic Scene'.

19. Lavenex and Schimmelfennig, 'EU Democracy Promotion', 894.
20. Schimmelfennig, 'EU Political Conditionality After the 2004 Enlargement', 920; see also Börzel, 'When Europeanization Hits Limited Statehood'; Kelley, 'International Actors on the Domestic Scene'; Lavenex and Schimmelfennig, 'EU Democracy Promotion'; Richter 'Fluch oder Segen'; Vachudova, *Europe Undivided*.
21. This scheme is often used in the framework of the result-based management approach for measuring the effectiveness of democracy and governance assistance; cf. Crawford and Kearton, *Evaluating Democracy and Governance Assistance*.
22. Here and in the following: Rittberger and Zangl, 'Internationale Organisationen', 159; Beisheim, Liese, and Ulbert, 'Transnationale öffentlich-private Partnerschaften', 4.
23. Schimmelfennig, 'EU Political Conditionality After the 2004 Enlargement'; Lavenex and Schimmelfennig, 'EU Democracy Promotion'; Kelley, 'International Actors on the Domestic Scene'.
24. For a ground-breaking work see: Anderson, *Do No Harm*; see also Crawford and Kearton, *Evaluating Democracy and Governance Assistance*; Cracknell, *Evaluating Development Aid*; cf. Underdal and Young, 'Research Strategies'.
25. For example, Jacoby, 'The Priest and the Penitent'; Schimmelfennig and Sedelmeier, 'Introduction'; Schimmelfennig and Sedelmeier, 'Conclusion'.
26. Lavenex and Schimmelfennig, 'EU Democracy Promotion', 893–4.
27. Trauner, 'From Membership Conditionality', 774–8.
28. Schimmelfennig, 'Europeanization beyond Europe', 15–8; Warkotsch, 'Non-compliance'.
29. Schimmelfennig, 'Europeanization beyond Europe', 15.
30. Youngs, 'Normative Dynamics', 431.
31. Knodt and Jünemann, 'Introduction', 19.
32. This argumentation stands in contrast to one of the few studies on consistency in the remaining (potential) EU candidate countries, among them the Western Balkans. Schimmelfennig argues that 'the EU's political accession conditionality has been normatively consistent on the whole', that is, that standards remained the same in enlargement decisions; Schimmelfennig, 'EU Political Conditionality After the 2004 Enlargement', 927. However, this conclusion could only have been drawn by the author by subsuming the SAP criteria (such as cooperation with the ICTY) under the overall objective of democracy promotion, thus neglecting the special security dimension of these criteria. Since the outcome of political conditionality in security and in democratization issues must be explained by two different logics of social action (that is, two causal mechanisms), this requires an analytical distinction.
33. Schimmelfennig, 'Europeanization beyond Europe', 9, 16–20.
34. Other than Slovenia, Croatia remained the only SEE country that had started accession negotiations by 2005 (finishing in 2011). By 2009, the European Commission had recommended the opening of negotiations with Macedonia, but the European Council has not yet reached a decision, due to the threat of a Greek veto.
35. Wolff, 'Theorie des Demokratischen Friedens'.
36. Schimmelfennig and Sedelmeier, 'Introduction'; Lavenex and Schimmelfennig, 'EU Democracy Promotion'.
37. Checkel, 'International Institutions', 809; cf. March and Olsen, 'The Institutional Dynamics', 948–54.
38. Schimmelfennig, 'Europäisierung in Osteuropa'.
39. Zürn and Checkel, 'Getting Socialized', 1064.
40. On the logic of consequences and the logic of appropriateness see March and Olsen, 'The Institutional Dynamics', 948–54.

41. Lavenex and Schimmelfennig, 'EU Democracy Promotion', 890. A third model called the 'lessons drawing' model combines the two logics, arguing that governments adopt EU rules if they perceive them as solutions to their problems, either based on instrumental calculations or on the appropriateness of the EU solutions, Schimmelfennig, 'Europeanization beyond Europe', 8.
42. Schimmelfennig and Sedelmeier, 'Conclusion'; for an overview, see Schimmelfennig, 'Europeanization beyond Europe', 9; Trauner, 'From Membership Conditionality', 777; Lavenex and Schimmelfennig, 'EU Democracy Promotion', 894; Kelley, 'International Actors on the Domestic Scene'.
43. Kelley, 'International Actors on the Domestic Scene', 426.
44. Lavenex and Schimmelfennig, 'EU Democracy Promotion', 893–5.
45. For the two logics of action, see March and Olsen, 'The Institutional Dynamics', 948–54. Schimmelfennig follows a different line of reasoning; he argues that 'issues of national identity related to ethnic conflicts potentially cause high political costs to any government'; Schimmelfennig, 'EU Political Conditionality After the 2004 Enlargement', 928.
46. Freyburg and Richter, 'National Identity', 267.
47. Ibid., 263.
48. Noutcheva, 'Fake, Partial, and Imposed Compliance', 1066.
49. Ibid., 1074.
50. For example, Kelley, 'International Actors on the Domestic Scene'; Schimmelfennig, 'Europäisierung in Osteuropa'; Schimmelfennig, 'EU Political Conditionality After the 2004 Enlargement'.
51. Kneuer, 'Der Einfluß externer Faktoren', 242.
52. Cf. Burnell, 'The State of the Discourse', 27; Schimmelfennig, 'Europäisierung in Osteuropa', 324.
53. Zürn and Checkel, 'Getting Socialized', 1064.
54. Schimmelfennig and Sedelmeier, 'Introduction', 11.
55. Checkel, 'International Institutions', 809.
56. Kelley, 'International Actors on the Domestic Scene', 426.
57. Pridham, 'EU Enlargement'; Vachudova, 'The Leverage of International Institutions', 5; Pravda, 'Introduction', 19.
58. Chayes and Chayes, 'On Compliance', 179; Pevehouse, *Democracy from Above*, 29.
59. Ethier, 'Is Democracy Promotion Effective?', 100.
60. Linden, 'Conclusion', 375.
61. Pridham, 'EU Enlargement'.
62. Kelley, 'International Actors – Domestic Effects', 12.
63. Pridham, 'EU Enlargement', 969; Vachudova, 'The Leverage of International Institutions', 24; Vachudova, *Europe Undivided*.
64. An overview of EU policy is provided by Blockmans, *Tough Love*.
65. Semi-consolidated democracies are, by Freedom House's definition, 'electoral democracies that meet relatively high standards for the selection of national leaders but exhibit some weaknesses in their defense of political rights and civil liberties'. Transitional or hybrid regimes are 'typically electoral democracies that meet only minimum standards for the selection of national leaders. Democratic institutions are fragile and substantial challenges to the protection of political rights and civil liberties exist. The potential for sustainable, liberal democracy is unclear.' Semi-consolidated authoritarian regimes 'attempt to mask authoritarianism or rely on external power structures with limited respect for the institutions and practices of democracy. They typically fail to meet even the minimum standards of electoral democracy', Freedom House, 'Nations in Transit 2011 Methodology'.
66. Gromes, 'Between Impositions and Promises', 1, 4.

67. The NLA is also known as the Macedonian UÇK – *Ushtria Çlirimtare Kombëtare*. It was founded at the end of the 1990s by Ali Ahmeti, who in 2001 formed the Albanian political party Democratic Union of Integration, DUI, which can largely be considered the successor to the NLA; Gromes, 'Between Impositions and Promises', 12.
68. The text of the Ohrid Framework Agreement can be found on the homepage of the Venice Commission of the Council of Europe: http://www.venice.coe.int/docs/2001/CDL%282001%29104-e.asp (accessed January 25, 2012).
69. See Willemsen, 'Das politische System Makedoniens'.
70. United Nations Development Programme, 'People-centred Analyses Report 2009', 63.
71. Vetterlein, *Konfliktregulierung*, 238.
72. *Socijaldemokratski Sojuz na Makedonija* (Social Democratic Union of Macedonia).
73. United Nations Development Programme, 'People-centred Analyses Report 2010', 68.
74. In the following analysis, the name dispute is only integrated as far as the EU's conditionality policy is concerned. A detailed explanation and elaboration of its impact on Macedonian society would go beyond the scope of this article; for the name dispute, see ICG, 'Macedonia's Name'.
75. See Vetterlein, 'Bildungspolitik'; Latifi, 'Preventive Engagement', 34.
76. ICG, 'Macedonia's Name'.
77. For example, Constitutional Amendements 2001, Law on Local Self-Government 2002.
78. European Union, *Council Decision of 30 January 2006*.
79. European Union, *Council Decision of 18 February 2008*.
80. European Commission, 'Progress Report 2011'.
81. The leverage of the United States was also crucial; Chivvis, 'The Making of Macedonia', 152f.
82. *Demokratska unija za integracija*, in Albanian: *Bashkimi Demokratik për Integrim* (Democratic Union for Integration).
83. In 2004, the then opposition party VMRO-DPMNE narrowly failed to bring a referendum on the decentralization process that could have brought the entire OFA process to a stalemate. See Reka, 'The Ohrid Agreement', 62.
84. Quote taken from Sebastian, 'The Stabilisation and Association Process', 6.
85. *Vnatrešna Makedonska Revolucionerna Organizacija – Demokratska Partija na Makedonija za Nacionalno Edinstvo* (Internal Macedonian Revolutionary Organization – Democratic Party for Macedonian National Unity).
86. United Nations Development Programme, 'People-centred Analyses Report 2009', 53.
87. ICG, 'Macedonia: Ten Years After the Conflict', i.
88. Ibid.
89. ICG, 'Macedonia: Ten Years After the Conflict'.
90. On endgames see Schimmelfennig, 'EU Political Conditionality After the 2004 Enlargement', 921.
91. OSCE/ODIHR, 'The Former Yugoslav Republic of Macedonia: Presidential and Municipal Elections'; ICG, 'Macedonia: Ten Years After the Conflict'.
92. Trauner, 'From Membership Conditionality'.
93. The situation worsened with regard to the freedom of the press. For example, many lawsuits were filed by politicians against journalists in 2010, and the government's spending on advertising further threatened media independence; Milevska-Kostova, 'Macedonia', 353; ICG, 'Macedonia: Ten Years After the Conflict', 2; Gromes, 'Between Impositions and Promises', 18.

94. Bieber, 'Power-sharing'; Reka, 'The Ohrid Agreement'; Taleski, 'Minderheiten und Mehrheiten', 271.
95. Hensell, 'Typisch Balkan?', 142.
96. Vetterlein, *Konfliktregulierung*, 211.
97. Ibid., 236, 240.
98. Ibid., 204, 209.
99. Hensell, 'Typisch Balkan?', 142.
100. Opfer-Klinger, 'Mazedonien zwischen äußerer Stabilisierung und innerer Krise', 29.
101. Vetterlein, *Konfliktregulierung*, 208–14, 236.
102. Taleski, 'Minderheiten und Mehrheiten', 271; Vetterlein, *Konfliktregulierung*, 205.
103. Latifi, 'Preventive Engagement of the International Community', 33; Reka, 'The Ohrid Agreement', 69.
104. Vetterlein, *Konfliktregulierung*, 239.
105. Cf. Noutcheva, 'Fake, Partial and Imposed Compliance', 1075.
106. In a similar vein, see Zakošek, 'Democratization, State-building and War', 589.
107. On Eastern Europe: Schimmelfennig, 'Europäisierung in Osteuropa'; Pridham, 'EU Enlargement'; Vachudova, *Europe Undivided*.
108. For a similar argument, see Grävingholt, Leininger, and Schlumberger, 'Demokratieförderung: Kein Ende der Geschichte'.

Notes on contributor

Solveig Richter is a senior research associate at the German Institute for International and Security Affairs, Stiftung Wissenschaft und Politik Berlin, research group on EU External Relations. Her research interests are democratization and conflict management by international organizations, especially in Eastern and Southeastern Europe. She is currently working on the impact of political conditionality under difficult conditions.

Bibliography

Anderson, Mary. *Do No Harm: How Aid Can Support Peace – Or War*. Boulder, CO: Lynne Rienner Publishers, 1999.

Beisheim, Marianne, Andrea Liese, and Cornelia Ulbert. 'Transnationale öffentlich-private Partnerschaften in Räumen begrenzter Staatlichkeit – Determinanten der Effektivität ihrer Governance-Leistungen'. Conference Paper, 2007. http://www.politikwissenschaft.tu-darmstadt.de/fileadmin/pg/Sektionstagung_IB/Beisheim_Liese_Ulbert_IB-Sektionstagung_2007.pdf (accessed November 14, 2011).

Bieber, Florian. 'Power-sharing and the Implementation of the Ohrid Framework Agreement'. In *Power Sharing and the Implementation of the Ohrid Framework Agreement*, ed. Friedrich-Ebert-Foundation. Skopje, 2008. http://www.fes.org.mk/pdf/OFA_english.pdf (accessed June 5, 2009).

Blockmans, Steven. *Tough Love: The European Union's Relations with the Western Balkans*. The Hague: TMC Asser Press, 2007.

Börzel, Tanja A. 'When Europeanization Hits Limited Statehood. The Western Balkans as a Test Case for the Transformative Power of Europe'. KFG working paper series no. 30, Kolleg-Forschergruppe (KFG) 'The Transformative Power of Europe', Freie Universität Berlin, September 2011.

Burnell, Peter. 'The State of the Discourse'. In *Democracy Assistance: International Co-operation for Democratisation*, ed. Peter Burnell, 3–33. London; Portland, OR: Cass, 2000.

Carothers, Thomas. *Aiding Democracy Abroad: The Learning Curve*. Washington, DC: Carnegie Endowment for International Peace, 1999.
Carothers, Thomas. 'The Backlash Against Democracy Promotion'. *Foreign Affairs* 85 no. 2 (2006): 55–68.
Chayes, Abram, and Antonia Chayes. 'On Compliance'. *International Organization* 47, no. 2 (1993): 197–205.
Checkel, Jeffrey T. 'International Institutions and Socialization in Europe: Introduction and Framework'. *International Organization* 59, no. 4 (2005): 801–26.
Chivvis, Christopher S. 'The Making of Macedonia'. *Survival* 50, no. 2 (April–May 2008): 141–62.
Cracknell, Basil Edward. *Evaluating Development Aid: Issues, Problems and Solutions*. New Delhi: Sage, 2000.
Crawford, Gordon, and Ian Kearton. *Evaluating Democracy and Governance Assistance*. Leeds: Centre for Development Studies, 2002.
Ethier, Diane. 'Is Democracy Promotion Effective? Comparing Conditionality and Incentives'. *Democratization* 10, no. 1 (2003): 99–120.
European Commission. 'Commission Staff Working Paper: The Former Yugoslav Republic of Macedonia 2011 Progress Report'. Brussels, October 12, 2011. http://ec.europa.eu/enlargement/pdf/key_documents/2011/package/mk_rapport_2011_en.pdf (accessed November 15, 2011).
European Council. 'Copenhagen, Conclusions of the Chairmanship', June 21–22, 1993, http://ue.eu.int/ueDocs/cms_Data/docs/pressData/de/ec/72924.pdf (accessed June 4, 2009).
European Union. *Council Decision of 30 January 2006 on the Principles, Priorities and Conditions Contained in the European Partnership with the Former Yugoslav Republic of Macedonia and Repealing Decision 2004/518/EC*. 2006/57/EC. Brussels, 2006. http://eur-lex.europa.eu/LexUriServ/LexUriServ.do?uri=OJ:L:2006:035:0057:0072:EN:PDF (accessed June 5, 2009).
European Union. *Council Decision of 18 February 2008 on the Principles, Priorities and Conditions Contained in the Accession Partnership with the Former Yugoslav Republic of Macedonia and Repealing Decision 2006/57/EC*. 2008/212/EC. Brussels, 2008. http://www.delmkd.ec.europa.eu/en/bilateral-relations/Accession%20Partnership%20in%20OJEU%20190308.pdf (accessed June 5, 2009).
Freedom House. 'Nations in Transit 2011 Methodology'. http://www.freedomhouse.org/images/File/nit/2011/NIT-2011-Methodology.pdf (accessed November 14, 2011).
Freyburg, Tina, and Solveig Richter. 'National Identity Matters! The Limited Impact of EU Political Conditionality in the Western Balkans'. *Journal of European Public Policy* 17, no. 2 (2010): 263–81.
Geis, Anna, and Wolfgang Wagner. 'How Far is it from Königsberg to Kandahar? Democratic Peace and Democratic Violence in International Relations'. *Review of International Studies* 37, no. 4 (2011): 1555–77.
Grävingholt, Jörn, Julia Leininger, and Oliver Schlumberger. 'Demokratieförderung: Kein Ende der Geschichte'. Analysen und Stellungnahmen Nr. 1/2009. Bonn: Deutsches Institut für Entwicklungspolitik/German Development Institute, 2009.
Grimm, Sonja, and Julia Leininger, 'Not All Good Things Go Together: Conflicting Objectives in Democracy Promotion'. *Democratization* 19, no. 3 (2012): 391–414.
Gromes, Thorsten. 'Between Impositions and Promises: Democracy in Macedonia'. PRIF-Reports No. 91. Frankfurt/M.: PFIF/HSFK, 2009.
Gurr, Ted Robert. *People versus State: Minorities at Risk in the New Century*. New York: United States Institute of Peace, 2000.
Hensell, Stephan. 'Typisch Balkan? Patronagenetzwerke, ethnische Zugehörigkeit und Gewaltdynamik in Mazedonien'. *Internationale Politik und Gesellschaft*, no. 4 (2003): 131–46.

International Crisis Group (ICG). 'Macedonia's Name: Breaking the Deadlock'. Europe Briefing Nr. 52. Pristina/Brüssel: ICG, 2009, http://www.crisisgroup.org/library/documents/europe/balkans/b52_macedonias_name___breaking_the_deadlock.pdf (accessed June 5, 2009).

International Crisis Group (ICG). 'Macedonia: Ten Years After the Conflict'. Europe Report No. 212. Skopje; Istanbul; Brussels, ICG: 2011, http://www.crisisgroup.org/~/media/Files/europe/balkans/macedonia/212%20Macedonia%20-%20Ten%20Years%20after%20the%20Conflict.pdf (accessed September 30, 2009).

Jacoby, Wade. 'The Priest and the Penitent: The European Union as a Force in the Domestic Politics of Eastern Europe'. *East European Constitutional Review* 8, no. 1 (1999): 62–7.

Kelley, Judith. 'International Actors – Domestic Effects: Explaining Ethnic Politics in Europe'. Working Paper Series SAN03-01. Durham, NC: Sanford Institute of Public Policy, 2003.

Kelley, Judith. 'International Actors on the Domestic Scene: Membership Conditionality and Socialization by International Institutions'. *International Organization* 58, no. 3 (2004): 425–57.

Kneuer, Marianne. 'Der Einfluß externer Faktoren: Die politische Strategie der EU bei demokratischen Transformationen am Beispiel der Slowakei als defekter Demokratie'. In *Zwischen Demokratie und Diktatur – Zur Konzeption und Empirie demokratischer Grauzonen*, ed. Petra Bendel, Aurel Croissant, and Friedbert W. Rüb, 237–55. Opladen: Leske & Budrich, 2002.

Knodt, Michèle, and Annette Jünemann. 'Introduction: Theorizing EU External Democracy Promotion'. In *Externe Demokratieförderung durch die Europäische Union/European External Democracy Promotion*, ed. Annette Jünemann and Michèle Knodt, 9–29. Baden-Baden: Nomos, 2005.

Kochenov, Dimitry. 'Behind the Copenhagen Façade: The Meaning and Structure of the Copenhagen Political Criterion of Democracy and the Rule of Law'. *European Integration Online Papers* (EIoP) 8, no. 10 (2004), http://eiop.or.at/eiop/texte/2004-010a.htm (accessed August 16, 2009).

Latifi, Veton. 'Preventive Engagement of the International Community: The Model Case of Macedonia?'. *Foreign Policy in Dialogue: A Quarterly Newsletter on German and European Foreign Policy* 8, no. 23 (November 2007): 32–8.

Lavenex, Sandra, and Frank Schimmelfennig. 'EU Democracy Promotion in the Neighbourhood: From Leverage to Governance?'. *Democratization* 18, no. 4 (2011): 885–909.

Linden, Ronald H. 'Conclusion: International Organizations and East Europe – Bringing Parallel Tracks Together'. In *Norms and Nannies: The Impact of International Organizations on the Central and East European States*, ed. Ronald H. Linden, 369–82. Lanham, MD: Rowman and Littlefield, 2002.

Linz, Juan J., and Alfred Stepan. *Problems of Democratic Transition and Consolidation: Southern Europe, South America and Post-Communist Europe*. Baltimore, MD; London: Johns Hopkins University Press, 1996.

Mansfield, Edward D., and Jack Snyder. 'Democratic Transition, Institutional Strength, and War'. *International Organization* 56, no. 2 (2002): 297–337.

March, James G., and Johan P. Olsen. 'The Institutional Dynamics of International Political Orders'. *International Organization* 52, no. 4 (1998): 943–69.

Milevska-Kostova, Neda. 'Macedonia'. In *Nations in Transit 2011*, ed. Freedom House, http://www.freedomhouse.org/images/File/nit/2011/NIT-2011-Macedonia.pdf (accessed September 27, 2011).

Noutcheva, Gergana. 'Fake, Partial and Imposed Compliance: The Limits of the EU's Normative Power in the Western Balkans'. *Journal of European Public Policy* 16, no. 7 (2009): 1065–84.

Ohlson, Thomas, and Mimmi Söderberg. 'From Intrastate-war to Democratic Peace in Weak States'. Uppsala Peace Research Papers No. 5. Uppsala: Uppsala Peace, 2002.
Opfer-Klinger, Björn. 'Mazedonien zwischen äußerer Stabilisierung und innerer Krise'. *Aus Politik und Zeitgeschichte* no. 32 (2008): 25–33.
Organization for Security and Co-operation in Europe/Office for Democratic Institutions and Human Rights (OSCE/ODIHR). 'The Former Yugoslav Republic of Macedonia. Presidential and Municipal Elections. Statement of Preliminary Findings and Conclusions'. Skopje, March 23, 2009, http://www.osce.org/documents/odihr/2009/03/36921_en.pdf (accessed June 5, 2009).
Pevehouse, Jon C. *Democracy from Above: Regional Organizations and Democratization*. Cambridge: Cambridge University Press, 2005.
Pravda, Alex. 'Introduction'. In *International and Transnational Factors*, ed. Jan Zielonka, 1–27. Vol. 2 of *Democratic Consolidation in Eastern Europe*. Oxford: Oxford University Press, 2000.
Pridham, Geoffrey. 'EU Enlargement and Consolidating Democracy in Post-Communist States: Formality and Reality'. *Journal of Common Market Studies* 40, no. 3 (2002): 953–73.
Reka, Armend. 'The Ohrid Agreement: The Travails of Inter-ethnic Relations in Macedonia'. *Human Rights Review* 9, no. 1 (2008): 55–69.
Richter, Solveig. 'Fluch oder Segen? Wirkungsmechanismen politischer Konditionalität in den Demokratisierungsprozessen Osteuropas'. In *Externe Faktoren der Demokratisierung*, ed. Gero Erdmann and Marianne Kneuer, 147–68. Baden-Baden: Nomos, 2009.
Richter, Solveig. 'Frieden schaffen mit den Waffen der Demokratie? Theorie und Praxis von Demokratisierung als Friedensstrategie'. *Zeitschrift für Internationale Beziehungen (ZIB)* 12, no. 1 (2005): 77–116.
Risse-Kappen, Thomas. 'Democratic Peace – Warlike Democracies? A Social Constructivist Interpretation of the Liberal Argument'. *European Journal of International Relations* 14, no. 4 (1995): 491–517.
Rittberger, Volker, and Bernhard Zangl. *Internationale Organisationen. Politik und Geschichte*, 3rd ed. Wiesbaden: VS-Verlag für Sozialwissenschaften, 2005.
Sandschneider, Eberhard. 'Externe Demokratieförderung – Theoretische und praktische Aspekte der Außenunterstützung von Transformationsprozessen'. Working paper, Centrum für Angewandte Politikforschung (CAP), Munich, 2003.
Schimmelfennig, Frank. 'EU Political Conditionality After the 2004 Enlargement: Consistency and Effectiveness'. *Journal of European Public Policy* 15, no. 6 (2008): 918–37.
Schimmelfennig, Frank. 'Europäisierung in Osteuropa: Reaktionen auf die demokratische Konditionalität'. *Osterreichische Zeitschrift für Politikwissenschaft* 32, no. 3 (2003): 321–37.
Schimmelfennig, Frank. 'Europeanization Beyond Europe'. *Living Reviews in European Governance* 4, no. 3 (2009). http://europeangovernance.livingreviews.org/Articles/lreg-2009-3/ (accessed September 30, 2011).
Schimmelfennig, Frank, and Ulrich Sedelmeier. 'Conclusion: The Impact of the EU on the Accession Countries'. In *The Europeanization of Central and Eastern Europe*, ed. Frank Schimmelfennig and Ulrich Sedelmeier, 210–28. Ithaca, NY; London: Cornell University Press, 2005.
Schimmelfennig, Frank, and Ulrich Sedelmeier. 'Introduction: Conceptualizing the Europeanization of Central and Eastern Europe'. In *The Europeanization of Central and Eastern Europe*, ed. Frank Schimmelfennig and Ulrich Sedelmeier, 1–28. Ithaca, NY; London: Cornell University Press, 2005.

Sebastian, Sofia. 'The Stabilisation and Association Process: Are EU Inducements Failing in the Western Balkans?'. Working Paper Nr. 53. Madrid: Fundación para las Relaciones Internacionales y el Diálogo Exterior, 2008.

Spanger, Hans-Joachim, and Jonas Wolff. 'Universales Ziel – partikulare Wege? Externe Demokratieförderung zwischen einheitlicher Rhetorik und vielfältiger Praxis'. In *Schattenseiten des Demokratischen Friedens. Zur Kritik einer Theorie liberaler Aussen- und Sicherheitspolitik*, ed. Anna Geis, Harald Müller, and Wolfgang Wagner, 261–84. Frankfurt: Campus, 2007.

Taleski, Dane. 'Minderheiten und Mehrheiten in Makedonien: Sichtweisen und Auffassungen der Bevölkerung'. In *Inklusion und Exklusion auf dem Westlichen Balkan*, ed. Ulf Brunnbauer and Christian Voss, 263–80. Munich: Südosteuropa-Jahrbuch 33, 2008.

Trauner, Florian. 'From Membership Conditionality to Policy Conditionality: EU External Governance in South Eastern Europe'. *Journal of European Public Policy* 16, no. 5 (2009): 774–90.

Underdal, Arild, and Oran R. Young. 'Research Strategies for the Future: Where We Go From Here?'. In *Regime Consequences – Methodological Challenges and Research Strategies*, ed. Arild Underdal, and Oran R. Young, 361–80. Dordrecht: Kluwer Academic, 2004.

United Nations Development Programme (UNDP). 'People-centred Analyses, Regional Development, Local Governance and the Quality of Life'. Report, March 2009, http://undp.org.mk/content/Publications/PCA%202009%20ENG%20new%20final.pdf (accessed November 14, 2011).

United Nations Development Programme (UNDP). 'People-centred Analyses: Quality of Social Services'. Report, April 2010, http://undp.org.mk/content/Publications/People-centered%20Analyses%20ENG%20web.pdf (accessed November 14, 2011).

Vachudova, Milada Anna. *Europe Undivided: Democracy, Leverage, and Integration after Communism*. Oxford: Oxford University Press, 2005.

Vachudova, Milada Anna. 'The Leverage of International Institutions on Democratizing States: Eastern Europe and the European Union'. European University Institute (EUI), Working Papers RSC No. 2001/33. Florence: EUI, 2001.

Vetterlein, Merle. 'Bildungspolitik als Schlüssel zur Konfliktlösung in Makedonien'. Bonn: Friedrich-Ebert-Stiftung, Internationale Politikanalyse, February 2007, http://library.fes.de/pdf-files/id/04270.pdf (accessed June 5, 2009).

Vetterlein, Merle. *Konfliktregulierung durch Power-Sharing-Modelle: das Fallbeispiel der Republik Makedonien*. Baden-Baden: Nomos, 2010.

Warkotsch, Alexander. 'Non-compliance and Instrumental Variation in EU Democracy Promotion'. *Journal of European Public Policy* 15, no. 2 (2008): 227–45.

Willemsen, Heinz. 'Das politische System Makedoniens'. In *Die politischen Systeme Osteuropas*, 3rd ed., ed. Wolfgang Ismayr, 769–804. Opladen: Leske+Budrich 2004.

Wolff, Jonas. 'Theorie des Demokratischen Friedens – Politik der internationalen Demokratieförderung. Eine Skizze des Aufschwungs und der Fusion zweier Paradigmen'. In *Frieden durch Demokratie? Genese, Wirkung und Kritik eines Deutungsmusters*, ed. Jost Dülffer and Gottfried Niedhart, 272–42. Essen: Klartext, 2011.

Youngs, Richard. 'Normative Dynamics and Strategic Interests in the EU's External Identity'. *Journal of Common Market Studies* 42, no. 2 (2004): 415–35.

Zakošek, Nenad. 'Democratization, State-building and War: The Cases of Serbia and Croatia'. *Democratization* 15, no. 3 (2008): 588–610.

Zürn, Michael, and Jeffrey T. Checkel. 'Getting Socialized to Build Bridges: Constructivism and Rationalism, Europe and the Nation-State'. *International Organization* 59, no. 4 (2005): 1045–79.

Inconsistent interventionism in Palestine: objectives, narratives, and domestic policy-making

Sandra Pogodda

School of International Relations, University of St Andrews, UK

> In recent years, the liberal state-building agenda, in which foreign policy objectives such as democratization, state-building, and national security are regarded as mutually reinforcing elements of a broader peace-building strategy, has come under criticism for its internal contradictions, its epistemology, and its unintended consequences on the ground. In the case of Palestine, these three objectives of Western foreign policies have never gone hand in hand. Rather, the history of state-building and democratization in Palestine reads like a drama in three acts: a period of authoritarian state-building, followed by democratization during a period of state demolition, and finally the current phase of competing undemocratic institution-building in the West Bank and the Gaza Strip. This contribution examines whether those policy objectives have indeed been incompatible in Palestine and how Palestine's major donors have dealt with perceived trade-offs. The subsequent analysis explores to what extent external and internal actors' policy shifts have shaped and partially undermined the project of democratic state-building in Palestine.

Introduction

In the spring of 2011, when a wave of popular uprisings swept through North Africa and the Middle East, Palestine remained strangely quiet. However, there was a brief period during which events in the occupied territories seemed to echo the revolutionary fervour of the region: In March, a youth movement ('March 15') emerged and began to organize mass protests demanding the resumption of unity talks between Salam Fayyad's Fatah government in the West Bank and Ismael Haniyeh's Hamas administration in the Gaza Strip, in order to pave the way for new elections. Talks resumed and a unity platform was signed on 11 May 2011 promising elections in the autumn.[1] However, in stark contrast to the Egyptian protesters who remained in Tahir Square for months after Hosni

Mubarak's resignation, the March 15 movement fell apart even before the unity plan did, and to date no successor organization has taken up its cause.

In large part, domestic resistance is tempered by Palestinians' recognition that they face fundamentally different obstacles to democratization than their neighbouring countries do. Although neither Salam Fayyad's government in the West Bank, nor Ismael Haniyeh's Hamas-led administration in Gaza have valid democratic mandates,[2] their citizens are not subjugated by dictators who cling to power until their final breath.[3] In the case of Palestine, rather, international donors have used the power of their purses to select and reject Palestinian political elites in an attempt to control Palestinian politics.[4]

This article examines possible tensions between Western donors' foreign policy objectives as well as their impact on Palestinian policy formation. The subsequent analysis focuses on the institution-building process that began in 1993 with the establishment of a Palestinian National Authority (PA) in the Declaration of Principles. For this period, the article identifies democratization, national security, and state-building as potentially competing policy goals. According to Grimm and Leininger a genuine conflict of objectives implies a trade-off between policy goals, rather than mere prioritization of two objectives over a third.[5] Hence, this article examines whether perceived conflicts between foreign policy objectives have obstructed democratization and state-building in Palestine, to what extent this has affected domestic politics, and whether the assumed trade-offs between policy objectives were genuine or exaggerated.[6]

This contribution demonstrates how shifting donor preferences have stunted Palestinian state-building in both its democratic set-up and its institutional scope and strength, while certain security objectives have been pursued throughout. Moreover, the article investigates possible tensions between the policy objectives, arguing that such conflicts are a matter of perception and thus subject to manipulation. Consequently, state-building, democratization, and security policies represent different levels of a power game between domestic stakeholders, in which international donors serve as referees to the competing narratives.

Exploring the constraints of liberal state-building in Palestine has clear policy relevance with regard to the current re-thinking of the peace process: With the legitimacy and viability of a future Palestinian state constituting the difference between positive and negative peace in the Israeli-Palestinian conflict, external actors must be aware of the socio-economic legacy of their interventions. The more external actors engage in liberal state-building assistance, the more they need to understand the difference between conflicting policy objectives and competing narratives, which manipulate external actors into believing in a trade-off between policy objectives. This contribution may thus feed into wider academic debates on external involvement in state-building projects.[7]

The article starts by drawing an analytical distinction between the concepts of democratization, state-building, and security. The history of (un-)democratic state-building in Palestine will then be divided into three time periods in which distinct priorities may be observed in EU and American foreign policy agendas. Here the contribution investigates to what extent democratization, state-building, and national security have been pursued on the ground. Have major sponsors' policies significantly affected the PA's shifting prioritization of those objectives? Was the alleged conflict between policy goals responsible for the asymmetric and varying pursuit of individual objectives? The final section of the contribution elaborates on whether the perceived trade-offs between the three objectives were genuine or exaggerated.

Democratization, security, state-building, and their narratives

Policy-making at the national and international level is based on sets of assumptions about the causes and effects of political and economic phenomena, human behaviour, societal change, and the influence of institutions on these processes. However, the empirical foundation of these assumptions might be unsound or too limited to allow for adequately sophisticated and robust conclusions. Uncertainty caused by conflicting empirical evidence on the one hand and the need to explain political decisions to the electorate on the other draw policy-makers to narratives. These narratives integrate a set of complementary assumptions into a conclusive storyline, while reducing the complexity of socio-economic phenomena.

International relations is the marketplace for competing national and local narratives, a venue in which conflict parties can attempt to persuade external actors to intervene on their behalf or to dissuade other governments from interference altogether. Once committed to a narrative, external actors can use conditionality, political leverage, and other incentive regimes to shape national or local policies, which, in turn, have to be adjusted to the local narrative. In the case examined here, there are three narrative-based policy objectives: state-building, security, and democratization.

State-building implies institutional capacity-building at the state level, either by improving existing public institutions or establishing new ones. This can be done through an expansion of the functions of the state (its 'scope') or of public institutions' capacity to project their authority across the territory ('strength').[8] In order to attract external state-building assistance, however, an aspiring nation such as Palestine requires a narrative of oppression, conflict, and marginalization that explains why its people can only thrive in their own state. The narrative of the Palestine Liberation Organization (PLO) refers to the 'brutality of aggression and racial discrimination', 'ethnic cleansing', and the 'apartheid policy' imposed by the Israeli occupation against a 'defenceless people'.[9] International law has failed to protect the Palestinians against human rights violations due to a lack of enforcement.[10] Moreover, the Palestinian narrative warrants urgency because of the daily territorial assault of settlements on the viability of a future Palestinian state.[11]

This narrative competes with the accounts of consecutive Israeli governments, which have warned of the danger involved with Palestinian statehood. While the intensity of Israeli concerns regarding a Palestinian state has varied over time, the official Israeli narrative has remained largely unchanged since the beginning of the Oslo Process: Palestinian sovereignty jeopardizes Israel's security as long as paramilitary movements are operating in the West Bank and Gaza.[12]

Security in the Israeli-Palestinian conflict is best understood as: the 'pursuit of freedom from threat and the ability of states and societies to maintain their independent identity and their functional integrity against forces of change, which they see as hostile'.[13] Of particular importance here is the focus on subjectivity: threats and hostility as the reasons (or justifications) for security measures are a matter of perception.[14] Thus, even if threat perceptions are so deeply engrained that they provide the texture to unify an otherwise disjointed society, these fears could be unfounded. Security measures are thus rooted in a narrative about the threats to and the survival of a society and its state apparatus in a hostile environment.

In the Palestinian case, internal and external threat perceptions are interwoven. Opinion polls suggest that two-thirds of all Palestinians regard the Israeli Defence Forces (IDF) as a threat to their lives, land, or property.[15] Responses often encountered in recent fieldwork[16] suggest that many Palestinians consider all types of resistance against this threat as justifiable, even though some of them have proven counterproductive and thus undesirable. The Fatah leadership, in contrast, focuses on feasibility rather than justice, and consequently ties Israeli to Palestinian threat perceptions in its security narrative. Given the power asymmetry between the demilitarized Palestinian Authority (PA) and the highly militarized US-backed IDF, the PA finds itself unable to respond directly to the occupation-related threat. Accordingly, the PA can only reduce the likelihood of IDF incursions by mitigating Israeli threat perceptions. This means that the PA's security policy is determined by Israeli security interests; namely, combating paramilitary groups in the occupied territories.[17] Deviation from this security strategy is costly for Palestine, since Israel pursues the policy of punishing the wider Palestinian society for the actions of paramilitary groups.[18] The discrepancy between the security needs of Palestine's population and the security strategy of its elites has raised popular suspicions that the PA has subcontracted the Israeli occupation.[19]

External actors such as the EU or the US can affect the power balance between Israel and Palestine by buying into one of the two competing security narratives and intervening on its behalf. This intervention can come either in the form of state-building or security policy, which intersect when it comes to the reform of the security apparatus. Capacity-building in security institutions will be viewed here as state-building, as it allows the state to obtain a monopoly of force.[20] The actual use of these capabilities (for example to enforce law and order or as anti-resistance forces), in contrast, will be regarded here as security policy.

Democratization implies the transition from a (semi-)authoritarian regime to a polity in which free and fair elections allow for non-violent regime change, and in which the separation of powers, political freedoms, and civil liberties prevail. Given the diversity of democracy promotion strategies, ranging from political to developmental approaches,[21] democracy assistance and the promotion of state-building can overlap in the field of governance and institutional reform. The term *democracy promotion* will be used here in the narrow political sense of supporting civil liberties, political rights, the separation of powers, and elections.[22] State-building, in contrast, entails the improvement of public infrastructure and thus the expansion of the authority's capacity to guarantee public goods such as education, health, and economic growth. Simply put, this article understands democratization as polity reforms that advance liberal political principles, whereas state-building endeavours to advance the effectiveness and reach of state institutions.

Democracy promotion follows its own narratives, varying between different sponsors but broadly following international trends. The collapse of the Soviet Union boosted the narrative that the accountability of democratic regimes generates an efficient allocation of resources, turning democratization into a prerequisite for development policies. Moreover, liberal peace theorists allege that democratization facilitates conflict resolution.[23] In the aftermath of 9/11, many policy-makers bought into the narrative that the lack of civil and political freedoms fuels radicalization. Needless to say, there are counter-narratives refuting all of these hypotheses. Significantly, however, the above narratives characterize democratization as a means to an end – a way to foster economic growth, conflict resolution, or security – but not, as an end in itself. The tensions between these objectives will be analysed in the following section.

The case of Palestine

The Oslo era (1993–2002):[24] authoritarian state-building

In contrast to the objectives of state-building and external security, the democratization of the emerging Palestinian administration fell by the wayside during the Oslo phase. The EU and the US as the main sponsors of the peace process subscribed to Arafat's narrative that power must be centralized in order to crush opposition to the peace process. As a result, the major donors to the PA accepted the argument that the dual priorities of state-building and external security required temporary concessions on democratization.

The Oslo era represents the most active period of state-building in recent Palestinian history, but it started off with only a weak legal basis for Palestine's sovereignty. To soothe Israeli fears the 1993 Declaration of Principles established the PA as a transitional institution. However, Palestinian statehood was the presumed outcome of final status negotiations after a period of Israeli-Palestinian confidence-building.[25] The PA's political structure was initially laid out in the Israeli-Palestinian Interim Agreement of 28 September 1995. It was modelled after Western-style presidential democracies, with the PA as an executive branch headed by the president, the Palestinian Legislative Council (PLC) constituting its parliament, and an independent judiciary. Under the chairmanship of Yasser Arafat, the newly established Palestinian leadership took over the previously Israeli-controlled civil service in the West Bank and Gaza, doubling the PA's workforce between 1994 and 1996 by hiring PLO personnel and former Palestinian guerrillas.[26] Massive recruitment drives allowed the new government to co-opt local elites, professional associations, and Palestinian refugees.[27]

Financially, international donors played a crucial role in bankrolling the institution-building process. Politically, however, the donors interfered little with President Yasser Arafat's state-building project.[28] Aid was granted largely unconditionally with two major exceptions: first, the World Bank's use of conditionality to leverage financial transparency after Arafat's secret bank accounts came to light in 1997; and second, the Oslo Accords' 'land for peace' formula, which tied state-building assistance to the PLO's commitment to crack down on paramilitary resistance. Democratization, however, was not among the aid priorities warranting conditionality during this period.

In terms of security, Arafat submitted to the 'land for peace' formula and thus modelled the PA's security narrative on the Israeli narrative,[29] prioritizing the crackdown on resistance movements for the sake of Israel's security over the enforcement of law and order beneficial to the Palestinian population. This manifested itself in Arafat's establishment of nine security agencies with overlapping competencies, shady human rights track records, and exclusive accountability to Arafat rather than the law.[30] Palestinian civilians had no protection against crimes committed by Israeli settlers, the IDF, or even criminal elements in the PA security forces.[31] Controlling the security sector and cracking down on resistance movements made Arafat indispensable to the US, which had internalized the Israeli security narrative and consequently pushed for the elimination of Palestinian paramilitary groups.[32]

As the 'father of the nation' and Palestine's strongman, Arafat received European and American aid despite the increasingly authoritarian tendencies of the PA. Arafat centralized executive decision-making in the presidential office while marginalizing the ministries and the cabinet in order to prevent alternative power centres from arising.[33] He secured a de facto veto position in the legislative process through decrees and the strategic non-promulgation of laws.[34] Furthermore, he interfered with the judiciary by appointing judges based on their loyalty rather than their qualifications and by establishing 'state security courts' with sole accountability to the president.[35] Arafat additionally undermined Palestinian democracy by depositing up to 40% of Palestine's tax revenue in undisclosed bank accounts abroad, thus eroding the budgetary authority of the PLC.[36]

By the end of the Oslo era, the 'land for peace'-formula had lost its credibility. Despite the PA's strategy of catering to Israeli security interests, Palestine remained a patchwork of territories without clear borders fragmented by growing settlements. Most of its public institutions remained devoid of state authority. An economic peace dividend was equally lacking, since the Israeli closure policy had suffocated economic activities, contributing to the doubling of the Palestinian unemployment rate.[37] The 'paradox of Palestinian state-building'[38] – being forced to renounce sovereignty in exchange for institution-building – had thus failed to pave the way to meaningful self-determination. In the aftermath of the unsuccessful Camp David negotiations in 2000, widespread frustration with the oppressive occupation, fuelled by the belief that the negotiation track had left the Palestinian people worse off than before, erupted in the violence of the al-Aqsa Intifada.

Consequently, under Arafat, the democratic state-building project in Palestine came under attack from both sides: Arafat's leadership emptied the institutions of their democratic content, while the Israeli occupation obstructed the empowerment of the PA outside the areas of education, culture, health, welfare, and tourism.

The Roadmap phase (2002–2006): democratization without a state

After 9/11, Western and Israeli threat perceptions converged, providing an international environment in which the violence of the al-Aqsa Intifada widely discredited Palestinian resistance as terrorism. Changes in the predominant Western security narrative during the Roadmap phase shifted foreign policy priorities towards democratization and away from state-building.

The Roadmap phase was marked by the securitization of Western foreign policies after 9/11 and the heightened violence of the al-Aqsa Intifada. Combating 'terrorism' became the security priority of both the US and the EU, although the prevailing Western analysis of terrorism's root causes remained overly simplistic. The European Security Strategy of 2003 and American President George W. Bush's 'Forward Strategy to Freedom' identified authoritarian rule as a root cause of radicalization.[39] With regard to Palestine, Bush linked the unprecedented levels of violence to corruption within the PA, and called on the Palestinian population to elect a new leadership in his Rose Garden speech in June 2002.[40]

Given the international alliance against 'terrorism', Israel's Prime Minister Ariel Sharon had sufficient leeway to dismantle the Palestinian state-building project in retaliation for paramilitary violence. Following a suicide bombing at a Passover dinner in March 2002, the IDF launched its largest military operation since the 1967 war, Operation Defensive Shield. Within a few weeks, the IDF eradicated the Palestinian police infrastructure,[41] attacked government buildings, disrupted the public infrastructure through closures and curfews, and destroyed the port and airport in Gaza, all while reoccupying every major West Bank town except Jericho and Hebron.[42] Palestine was now – more than ever – reduced to a political construct devoid of any attributes of statehood.

The willingness of the EU and the US to stand idly by while Sharon destroyed the Palestinian infrastructure that they had sponsored reveals that Palestinian state-building was merely a sideshow compared to the security objective of containing paramilitary groups.[43] State-building was justified as long as it enabled a political elite to enforce the Oslo Accords. Once the donors had internalized Sharon's narrative that Israel had 'no partner for peace',[44] they came to regard Arafat's control over public institutions as dangerous and view Operation Defensive Shield as self-defence.[45]

It therefore came as no surprise when, a few months later, the Middle East Quartet (the US, Russia, the UN, and the EU) announced a new initiative aimed at curbing the powers of the Palestinian president, the Roadmap to Peace in the Middle East.[46] Democratization was intended to limit Arafat's influence in the political system by reinforcing the separation of powers and by cutting him off from his main sources of influence. First, the Roadmap required the creation of an 'empowered prime minister' position to counterbalance presidential authority in the executive branch.[47] Second, the proposed reform of the security apparatus sought to increase transparency and accountability in the security forces and to transfer authority over the security agencies to the Ministry of the Interior.[48] Third, the Roadmap required that all external funding had to be channelled through the Single Treasury Account.[49]

Under the combined pressure of the EU, the US, the World Bank, and his own parliament, Arafat allowed limited reforms, including a cabinet reshuffling, finance reforms, and the consolidation of the nine security agencies into an internal branch (the civil police), a national branch (foremost among them the 'preventive security forces' for counterterrorism operations), and an intelligence service.[50]

Attempts to further curb presidential powers, however, remained an intra-Palestinian power struggle until the end of Yasser Arafat's presidency.[51] He drove any internal competitor who tried to limit his authority out of office.[52] By using their financial leverage to push for democratization and security sector reforms the Western donors tried to weaken Arafat's position in this struggle. Despite the rhetorical support for a two-state solution,[53] this phase marks a low point in Palestinian state-building.

Phase of inner-Palestinian division (since 2006)

In the aftermath of Hamas's sweeping election victory in 2006, Western donors fundamentally changed their policy narratives again: Suddenly, democratization transformed from a security strategy into a risk.[54] European sponsorship for the rebuilding of the civil police, moreover, suggests that Western security strategies for Palestine were expanding from combating insurgency to maintaining law and order. Domestic political leaders meanwhile turned state-building into a strategy of party competition between Hamas and Fatah.

After Arafat's death and the end of the Intifada, a new moderate PA leadership facilitated constructive re-engagement. Arafat's successor Mahmoud Abbas had reassured Israel and international donors of his trustworthiness by adopting Israel's security narrative in 2003 when he briefly served as prime minister.[55] However, meaningful reforms were postponed as a consequence of the election of a new PLC in January 2006.

Concerns over Israel's security after the landslide victory of Hamas's political branch (the Reform and Change Party) in the legislative elections in January 2006 prompted Western donors not only to drop democracy promotion, but to actively undermine the outcome of the free and fair election. The US halted its funding of the PA in January 2006. Even the European Council followed suit in April 2006, despite its traditionally inclusive approach to resistance groups.[56] Because almost half of the previous PA budget had been financed by donors,[57] the international aid boycott meant that the Hamas-led government was primed for failure and prevented from entering a coalition with more moderate Palestinian parties.[58]

Since democratization has produced undesirable results from US President Bush's point of view American pressure prompted President Abbas to reverse the democratic reforms initiated under the Roadmap.[59] In order to contain Ismael Haniyeh's government, the US pressed Abbas to establish presidential bank accounts and to override decisions made in Hamas-led ministries.[60] Acting on the Israeli fear that a Hamas government could deploy PA security forces against Israel, Washington urged Abbas to assume control over the security forces. Moreover, the Bush administration expanded the mandate of Lt. Gen. Keith Dayton's training mission in Jericho to include training of Abbas's Presidential Guard and sponsored a new Fatah militia under the command of National Security Adviser Muhammad Dahlan to take on Hamas's al-Qassam Brigades.[61]

Western intervention on behalf of Israel's security eventually backfired by eroding political stability and security in Palestine, resulting in an unprecedented disintegration of the Palestinian state-building project. Mounting pressure on Hamas's political leadership eventually strengthened the radical elements within the movement. Restrained by Abbas's power grab, financially squeezed by the necessity to keep the public sector afloat without international aid or tax revenues and militarily threatened by the IDF as the build-up of Fatah militias, Hamas's political branch gave in to the al Qassam Brigade's pressure for military action.[62] In June 2007 Hamas took over Fatah's security installations and government institutions in Gaza, thereby splitting Palestine into Hamas-governed Gaza and the Fatah-ruled West Bank.

This split turned Fatah and Hamas into competitors in the area of institution-building, ironically at the expense of creating an inclusionary state entity for all Palestinians. Western donors helped Salam Fayyad's caretaker government in the West Bank to rebuild the Palestinian security sector after the IDF's destruction of its pre-Intifada infrastructure. In 2007, the EU began to reform the civil police, marking a security strategy that for the first time responded to Palestinian needs for law and order. Since the Palestinian security forces were 'inefficient, unaccountable to legislative or judicial oversight, and popularly viewed as corrupt', the personnel had to be retrained and refocused.[63] The EU Coordinating Office for Palestinian Police Support (EUPOL COPPS) in Ramallah trained thousands of police officers, refurbished police stations throughout the West Bank, restocked their vehicle fleet, and branched off into justice, rule of law, and detention reform.[64] Additionally, Prime Minister Salam Fayyad's Two-Year Plan envisioned the creation of the institutional, administrative, and physical framework for viable statehood in the West Bank by the autumn of 2011.[65]

By comparison the Haniyeh government in Gaza, expanded Hamas's military branch, the al-Qassam Brigades, through large recruitment drives, tapping new sources of state revenues (such as taxes on smuggler tunnels) to raise the required funding. Cleansing the state apparatus of potential political opponents also became a strategy of party competition.[66] Hamas reportedly replaced all civil servants – even hospital and teaching staff – with party loyalists, in violation of civil service laws.[67]

However, many Palestinians have become frustrated with the competing state-building projects of the two administrations. Hamas's confrontation with Israel has inflicted dramatic losses on the population of Gaza (especially as a result of the 2009–2010 war). Fayyad's unilateral state-building plan, in contrast, has simply exhausted itself. Institutions have been reformed (rather than created) but lack sovereignty,[68] since the strength and scope of Palestine's public institutions remain constrained by Israeli demands. The promised large-scale infrastructure projects in Israeli-controlled areas of the West Bank were never realized, thwarting hopes of reclaiming Palestinian territory in this way. Economic development continues to be stunted by the occupation. Moreover, both governments appear to be rife with patronage.[69]

Neither Palestinian political elites nor external actors have helped to create a viable state entity, allowed democratization, or mitigated Palestinian fears of IDF and settler violence. Many Palestinians now speak of Western aid as financing a façade. By supporting Salam Fayyad's government, donors are seen as sponsoring his subcontracted occupation.[70] There is widespread alienation with European and American interference on behalf of Israeli security interests. Western actors have yet to use their leverage to pressure Israel into implementing its obligations to Palestinian security and state-building detailed in UN Security Council Resolutions, the Roadmap, and the Oslo Accords.[71]

Democratization, security, state-building, and narratives revisited

The above analysis shows that in the Palestinian case, security, democratization, and state-building were not simultaneously realized during any of the time periods discussed, as summarized in Table 1. The PA's strategy during the Oslo phase (1993–2002) was marked by autocratic state-building and an anti-insurgency policy. During the Roadmap phase (2002–2006), the PA pursued the same security strategy, but was externally forced into democratic reforms. The PA's public infrastructure was meanwhile demolished by Israel. In the current phase of internal Palestinian division (since 2006), the Fatah government has received external assistance for institution-building and security sector reforms, at the expense of democratization.

However, does the neglect of one objective in each phase necessarily indicate a conflict between objectives? Conflicting objectives as defined by Grimm and Leininger in the introduction of this volume imply a genuine trade-off between policy goals, rather than mere prioritization of two objectives over the third.[72] Thus, the question is: have measures initiated in pursuit of democratization,

Table 1. Implementation of objectives.

	State-building	Security	Democratization
Oslo phase (1993–2002)	(+) Creation of the PA, judiciary, PLC	(+) Crackdown on paramilitary resistance	(−) Presidential power accumulation and interventions in legislature/judiciary
Roadmap phase (2002–2006)	(−) No reconstruction of physical/service infrastructure	(+) Strengthening of 'anti-terrorism' capabilities	(+) Curbing of presidential powers, promulgation of Basic Law
Internal division (2006–2010)	(+) Reconstruction of infrastructure; Fayyad's Two-Year Plan	(+) Reform of civil police; strengthening of 'anti-terrorism' capabilities	(−) Unelected caretaker government governs WB; Hamas's unconstitutional take-over of Gaza; elections overdue

Source: Author's own compilation.

security provision, and state-building been mutually exclusive during any of the time periods analysed above?

Analysts have observed that security objectives and state-building are likely to clash with democratization in post-conflict environments.[73] To end civil strife, political leaders are likely to centralize the means of coercion in a strong executive branch. The degree of coercion as well as the extent of power centralization, however, may violate democratic principles. The need for 'illiberal transitions' has been widely accepted as one approach to peace-building.[74] Accordingly, Arafat's authoritarian governance style and his regime's systematic abuse of Palestinians' human rights, political liberties, and the rule of law could be regarded as a necessary sacrifice in order to establish a monopoly of violence and enforce external security.[75] This would imply a temporary trade-off between democratization and security.

However, most of Arafat's autocratic interventions in the Palestinian political system neither served the purpose of state-building, nor helped to mitigate Israeli threat perceptions. His appointment of judges, use of secret bank accounts, and vetoes of ministerial decisions cemented his power through networks of patronage, but did not help to combat paramilitary groups. Over time, even the state security courts were gradually hijacked by Arafat's own interests. Set up to prosecute violent opposition to the peace process, the state security courts increasingly tried regular crimes with no bearing on external security.[76]

Moreover, Arafat's security strategy fundamentally failed to advance the Palestinian state-building agenda: the PA neither achieved a monopoly of force nor a clear definition of Palestine's territory or population. Despite the PA's repression of paramilitary movements, Israel did not compromise on Palestinian sovereignty. Consequently, Arafat's hard-line security strategy and his authoritarian style of governance eventually eroded domestic support for the PA and thus undermined the Palestinian state-building project. Prior to the outbreak of the al-Aqsa Intifada, the PA was as unpopular as Arafat.[77] In sum, the Oslo phase does not constitute an example of a genuine trade-off between democratization and security.

During the Roadmap phase, Western donors' focus on combating paramilitary movements and promoting Palestinian democratization came at the expense of state-building. Here, the argument was that Arafat's resumed backing of armed resistance groups required the weakening of his position and the state institutions under his control for the sake of Israel's security. Ironically, the decision to discontinue state-building assistance in order to promote external security may have helped Hamas to garner support among the population. Bent on eradicating armed resistance at all costs, the occupation depressed the Palestinian economy[78] and, thus, increased the need for public services, which the PA was increasingly unable to provide. This gave Hamas an opportunity to shine: the stark contrast between Fatah's mismanagement and Hamas's efficient charities and its well-run municipalities made the political branch of the Islamist resistance movement a promising alternative to the incumbent regime in the 2005 and 2006 elections. Thus, it can be argued that the Western neglect of Palestinian state-building in the Roadmap phase had unintended negative consequences that far outweighed the benefits of the securitization approach.

Since Hamas's victory in the 2006 elections, donors have increasingly viewed democratization as a threat to Israel's security. With democratically elected Hamas in control of the security sector and public finances, Western governments feared that the PA's resources could be used for attacks against Israel. However, was this conflict between democratization and Israeli security genuine and inevitable? Recent literature on counter-insurgency and political Islam suggests that violent movements can be moderated through democratic accountability or could lose their appeal by failing once in office.[79] Public disenchantment with Hamas's governance in the Gaza Strip seems to confirm this latter hypothesis;[80] Ismael Haniyeh's government has failed where many Hamas-led municipalities have succeeded: in representing a clean and effective alternative to the corrupt Fatah. Political favouritism, not only in public service employment but also in health care and the crushing of political dissent has estranged many Palestinians from Hamas.

In terms of moderation, there was a clear indication that the paramilitary movement was ready to engage in non-violent politics even prior to the 2006 elections. For six months before and 10 months after the elections, Hamas implemented a unilateral ceasefire, which it maintained despite increased Israeli attacks. Caged in by its own anti-terrorism laws, however, the Middle East Quartet missed this opportunity to engage with the group, instead insisting on its three conditions while ignoring Hamas's concessions. The unilateral *hudna* imposed by Hamas on militant resistance groups in the Gaza Strip since Operation Cast Lead again attests to the moderating effect of politics.[81] Unfortunately, it seems that Western donors and Israel will miss the new window of opportunity for engagement set out in the unity agreement of 2 May 2011.

Conclusion

As this article demonstrates, security, democratization, and state-building have not been pursued simultaneously during any phase in the PA's history. This contribution has attempted to challenge the assumptions, which justify the neglect of certain policy objectives as trade-offs with others. The article shows that the crucial conflict was not between the *policy objectives*, but between the interpretations of developments (the *narratives*), which shaped policy strategies. By reinterpreting Palestine's history since 1993 as a counter-narrative of the negative side effects of recent foreign policies, wasted opportunities, and simple neglect of Palestinian needs, it has been shown that policy-guiding narratives are by nature simplifications and may be misleading. Given divergent interpretations of political and socio-economic events, this article urges governments to be aware that perceived conflicts between policy goals might be based on politically motivated narratives. Every narrative – including those reflected here – reduces the complexity of socio-economic or political phenomena and thus may be manipulative rather than reflect a thorough interpretation of their causes and effects.

Notes

1. For more information, see ICG, 'Palestinian Reconciliation: Plus Ca Change'.
2. Hamas's electoral mandate ended in 2010; its takeover of the Gaza Strip was unconstitutional to begin with. The West Bank's caretaker government lacks parliamentary approval.
3. For example, Mahmoud Abbas, the current Palestinian president, has attempted to resign several times, but has always been cajoled back into office by external actors.
4. Turner, 'Creating Partners for Peace'.
5. See introduction to this special issue: Grimm and Leininger, 'Not All Good Things Go Together'.
6. This contribution thus addresses questions 1, 3, and 4 from the introduction to this special issue, Ibid., 396.
7. See, for example, Chandler, *International State-building*; Paris and Sisk, *The Dilemmas of State-building*; Richmond and Franks, *Liberal Peace Transitions*; Chesterman, *You, the People*.
8. Terminology developed by Fukuyama, *State-building*, ix.
9. Abbas, 'Statement before UN General Assembly', 2–5.
10. In particular, UN Security Council Resolutions 242 and 338, the Oslo Accords, and the Roadmap constitute legal obligations for Israel to end its occupation of Palestinian territory.
11. Abbas, 'Statement before UN General Assembly', 2.
12. For the latest evidence, see Benjamin Netanyahu's remarks to the UN General Assembly on 23 September 2011 (see *Journal of Palestine Studies*, 41, no. 2 (2012): 216). The narrative of the Netanyahu administration differs from previous governments, in that Netanyahu openly admits that Israel intends to continue its occupation even after the potential implementation of a two-state solution.
13. Buzan, 'New Patterns of Global Security in the Twenty-first Century', 432–3.

14. Wendt, 'Anarchy is What States Make of It'.
15. PSR's September 2011 poll suggests that 72.7% of all Palestinians are (very) worried that Israel could hurt them or their families, confiscate their land, or demolish their houses. See http://www.pcpsr.org/survey/polls/2011/p41efull.html.
16. In my most recent fieldwork in Palestine – in July 2011 – I conducted 18 interviews (14 in English, four in Arabic) on the state-building process, unarmed grassroots resistance, and inner-Palestinian unity. This trip was sponsored by the research project ADJUST ('Advancing Justice and Reconciliation for Long-Term Peace-building in the Middle East').
17. On the Israeli security narrative: see Kimmerling, *Clash of Identities*, 154–78.
18. For details on human rights violations resulting from IDF incursions, see Palestinian Centre for Human Rights, *Annual Report 2010*.
19. Roy, *Failing Peace*, 236.
20. Weber, *From Max Weber: Essays in Sociology*, 78.
21. For details, see Carothers, 'Democracy Assistance'.
22. Ibid., 6–7.
23. For an overview of liberal thought and the links between liberal institutions and peace see Richmond, *Peace in International Relations*, 21–39.
24. The Oslo phase started with the Declaration of Principles in 1993 and technically ended in September 2000 with the outbreak of the al-Aqsa Intifada. However, since an alternative strategy for peace- and state-building was only initiated in 2002, this article considers the Oslo era as lingering on until then.
25. Brynen, 'Palestine', 219.
26. Frisch and Hofnung, 'State Formation and International Aid', 1249.
27. Brynen, 'Palestine', 220.
28. Miller, *The Too Much Promised Land*, 249.
29. Carothers, 'Democracy Assistance', 6–7.
30. Riley and Jones, 'Law and Order'.
31. Ibid., 160.
32. US Middle East advisor Dennis Ross regards America's unconditional commitment to Israel's security as a yardstick for the credibility of US foreign policy. Ross and Markowsky, *Myths*, 271.
33. Shu'aybi and Shikaki, 'A Window', 90–1.
34. Jamal, 'State-building, Institutionalization and Democracy'; Abu Amr, 'The Palestinian Legislative Council'.
35. Rubenberg, *The Palestinians*, 250.
36. Abu Issa, 'Arafat's Swiss Bank Accounts'.
37. For details, see RAND Corporation, 'Terrorism and Development', 29.
38. Butenschoen, 'The Paradox of Palestinian Self-determination', 75.
39. See Council of the European Union, *A Secure Europe in a Better World*; President Bush's speech at the 20th Anniversary of the National Endowment for Democracy, US Chamber of Commerce, Washington, DC, November 6, 2003.
40. See President Bush's Rose Garden speech, June 24, 2002: http://archives.cnn.com/2002/ALLPOLITICS/06/24/bush.mideast.speech/index.html.
41. The IDF even targeted security forces that had stayed out of the resistance; see Hammami, 'Interregnum'.
42. Ibid.
43. In his Rose Garden speech, President Bush stated that the US would not support the establishment of a Palestinian state until its leaders engaged in anti-terrorism measures.
44. Shlaim, *Israel and Palestine*, 292.
45. Bush, Rose Garden speech.

46. 'The Roadmap: Full Text', *BBC News Online*, April 30, 2003: http://news.bbc.co.uk/2/hi/2989783.stm.
47. Paragraph 13, Roadmap.
48. Paragraphs 4, 7, and 8, Roadmap.
49. Paragraph 11, Roadmap. This Roadmap requirement echoed the complaints of the PLC, which had been unsuccessfully pushing for financial transparency since 1997; Shu'aybi and Schikaki, 'A Window', 92.
50. For security sector reforms, see ICG, 'Squaring the Circle', 1–3. For other reforms and their limits, see Esposito, 'Quarterly Update on Conflict and Diplomacy: 16 May–15 August 2002', 134.
51. Seitz, 'Appointing Abu Mazen'.
52. Interior Minister Abdel Razak Al-Yahya and Prime Minister Mamoud Abbas resigned in 2002 and 2003, respectively, for this reason.
53. In November 2001, President Bush explicitly endorsed a two-state solution for the first time in a speech before the UN (Mandel, 'Try, Try, Try Again').
54. Dennis Ross characterized this fundamental policy change as the 'pendulum effect, swinging to the opposite end of the most recent policy' (Ross and Markowsky, *Myths*, 291).
55. He committed his government to combat the lawlessness of Arafat's security forces and identified the unauthorized possession of weapons as the biggest threat to the Palestinian people; see his speech at the PLC, 29 April 2003, in Laqueur and Rubin, *The Israel-Arab Reader*, 588.
56. The EU supported the PLO's inclusion in peace talks in the 1980s, when the organization was considered a terrorist movement, and established diplomatic channels to Hamas during the al-Aqsa Intifada and after Hamas's impressive showing in the municipal elections of 2005.
57. Brynen, 'Palestine', 2008.
58. Sayigh, 'Inducing a Failed State in Palestine'.
59. Esposito, 'February–May 2006', 102–13.
60. Esposito, 'February–May 2006', 103–5.
61. Dahlan was Washington's trusted ally, having previously overseen violent crackdowns on Hamas; see Esposito, 'Quarterly Update on Conflict and Diplomacy, 16 May–15 August 2007', 144.
62. Ibid., 144–5.
63. Riley and Jones, 'Law and Order', 160.
64. See ICG, 'Squaring the Circle', 1–3.
65. Fayyad, 'Why I'm Building Palestine'.
66. Fatah has only cleansed its security forces of Hamas members, not its entire civil service (Esposito, 'Quarterly Update on Conflict and Diplomacy, 16 May–15 August 2007', 158).
67. ICG, 'Ruling Palestine', 12–5.
68. Brown, 'Are Palestinians Building a State?'.
69. According to many interviewees, party affiliation and personal contacts are still the pivotal factors in recruitment decisions in both administrations. A coordinator of a refugee camp in the West Bank stated in an interview with me on 4 July 2011 that to get a job in Fatah's security forces, one is required 'to make 1,000 phone calls and to get references from the right people'.
70. In contrast to previous fieldwork, this argument came up in many of my interviews in July 2011.
71. The US remains Israel's largest provider of military aid, while the EU is its most important trading partner and continues to initiate new policies in which Israel seeks to participate. Since the Roadmap was published, the EU has included Israel

in the European Neighbourhood Policy, expanded EU-Israeli trade relations, and signed a memorandum of understanding allowing Israel to take part in the European Enterprise and Industry Program. However, none of these agreements were conditional upon implementation of the Roadmap.
72. Grimm and Leininger, 'Not All Good Things Go Together'.
73. See Brynen, *A Very Political Economy*, 30–1; Fukuyama, 'Liberalism Versus Statebuilding'; Carothers, 'Misunderstanding Gradualism'.
74. Paris, *At War's End*, 188.
75. For the violation of Palestinian human rights in state security courts, see 'Courts and Judgements'; for human rights abuses by the security agencies, see Rubenberg, *The Palestinians*, 263–77.
76. See the list of charges in the State Security Court, online at http://www.phrmg.org/phrmg%20documents/Courts/security%20court/Tables/state%20security%20court%20english.htm.
77. Rubenberg, *The Palestinians*.
78. In particular, the IDF's destruction of large development projects including the Gazan harbour and airport has hampered trade, as have its checkpoints and closures. Moreover, Israel's eradication of Palestinian police stations accelerated the region's descent into lawlessness and thus undermined any potential investment or development projects. In 2005, the Palestinian economy had shrunk by 30% in comparison to 1999 levels.
79. Byman, *The Five Front War*; Hamzawi, 'The Key to Arab Reform'; Fuller, *The Future of Political Islam*.
80. See PSR's September 2011 poll.
81. ICG, 'Radical Islam in Gaza'.

Notes on contributor

Sandra Pogodda is a Research Fellow at the University of St Andrews. She received her PhD in International Relations from the University of Cambridge before starting a postdoctoral fellowship in the School of Advanced International Relations at Johns Hopkins University and the United States Institute of Peace. Her current work focuses on foreign policy interventions, political mobilization and reform processes in the Middle East and North Africa. She was granted a Marie Curie Fellowship, a TAPIR Fellowship, and the Duncan Black Award.

Bibliography

Abbas, Mahmoud. 'Statement before UN General Assembly'. 36th Session, September 23, 2011.
Abu Amr, Ziad. 'The Palestinian Legislative Council: A Critical Assessment'. *Journal of Palestine Studies* 26, no. 4 (Summer 1997): 90–7.
Abu Issa, Issam. 'Arafat's Swiss Bank Accounts'. *Middle East Quarterly* (Fall 2004): 15–23.
Brown, Nathan. 'Are Palestinians Building a State?'. Carnegie Commentary, June 2010. http://www.carnegieendowment.org/files/palestinian_state1.pdf (accessed March 28, 2012).
Brynen, Rex. 'Palestine: Building Neither Peace Nor a State'. In *Building States to Build Peace*, ed. Charles T. Call, 217–48. Boulder, CO: Lynne Rienner Publishers, 2008.
Brynen, Rex. *A Very Political Economy*. Washington, DC: USIP, 2000.
Butenschoen, Nils. 'The Paradox of Palestinian Self-determination'. In *Where Now for Palestine? The Demise of the Two-state Solution*, ed. Jamil Hilal, 75–98. New York: Zed Books, 2007.

Buzan, Barry. 'New Patterns of Global Security in the Twenty-first Century'. *International Affairs* 67, no. 3 (1991): 431–51.
Byman, Daniel. *The Five Front War: The Better Way to Fight Global Jihad.* Hoboken, NJ: John Wiley & Sons, 2008.
Carothers, Thomas. 'Democracy Assistance: Political vs. Developmental?'. *Journal of Democracy* 20, no. 1 (2009): 5–19.
Carothers, Thomas. 'Misunderstanding Gradualism'. *Journal of Democracy* 18, no. 3 (2007): 18–22.
Chandler, David. *International State-building: The Rise of Post-Liberal Governance.* London: Routledge, 2010.
Chesterman, Simon. *You, the People: The United Nations, Transitional Administration, and State-Building.* Oxford; New York: Oxford University Press, 2004.
Council of the European Union. *A Secure Europe in a Better World – The European Security Strategy.* Brussels: Council of the European Union, December 12, 2003.
'Courts and Judgements'. *The Jurist.* http://jurist.law.pitt.edu/world/palest.htm (accessed March 8, 2012).
Esposito, Michele K. 'Quarterly Update on Conflict and Diplomacy: 16 February–15 May 2006'. *Journal of Palestine Studies* 35, no. 4 (2006): 101–30.
Esposito, Michele K. 'Quarterly Update on Conflict and Diplomacy: 16 May–15 August 2002'. *Journal of Palestine Studies* 32, no. 1 (2002): 120–45.
Esposito, Michele K. 'Quarterly Update on Conflict and Diplomacy: 16 May–15 August 2007'. *Journal of Palestine Studies* 37, no. 1 (2007): 142–72.
Fayyad, Salam. 'Why I'm Building Palestine'. *Foreign Policy* (December 2010), http://www.foreignpolicy.com/articles/2010/11/29/why_im_building_palestine (accessed March 30, 2012).
Frisch, Hillel, and Menachem Hofnung. 'State Formation and International Aid: The Emergence of the Palestinian Authority'. *World Development* 25, no. 8 (August 1997): 1243–55.
Fukuyama, Francis. 'Liberalism Versus State-building'. *Journal of Democracy* 18, no. 3 (2007): 10–13.
Fukuyama, Francis. *State-building: Governance and World Order in the Twenty-First Century.* London: Cornell University Press, 2004.
Fuller, Graham E. *The Future of Political Islam.* New York: Palgrave Macmillan, 2003.
Grimm, Sonja, and Julia Leininger. 'Not All Good Things Go Together: Conflicting Objectives in Democracy Promotion'. *Democratization* 19, no. 3 (2012): 391–414.
Hammami, Rema. 'Interregnum: Palestine After Operation Defensive Shield'. *Middle East Report* 223 (Summer 2002): 18–27.
Hamzawi, Amr. 'The Key to Arab Reform: Moderate Islamists'. Policy Brief 40. Carnegie Endowment for International Peace, Washington, DC, August 2005.
International Crisis Group (ICG). 'Palestinian Reconciliation: Plus Ca Change'. Middle East Report 110. ICG, Ramallah/Gaza/Jerusalem/Washington/Brussels, July 20, 2011.
International Crisis Group (ICG). 'Radical Islam in Gaza'. Middle East Report 104. ICG, Gaza City/Ramallah/Jerusalem/Brussels, March 29, 2011.
International Crisis Group (ICG). 'Ruling Palestine I: Gaza Under Hamas'. Middle East Report 73. ICG, Gaza/Jerusalem/Brussels, March 19, 2008.
International Crisis Group (ICG). 'Squaring the Circle: Palestinian Security Sector Reform'. Middle East Report 98. ICG, Ramallah/Jerusalem/Brussels, September 7, 2010.
Jamal, Amal. 'State-building, Institutionalization and Democracy: The Palestinian Experience'. *Mediterranean Politics* 6, no. 3 (Fall 2001): 1–30.
Kimmerling, Baruch. *Clash of Identities: Explorations in Israeli and Palestinian Societies.* New York: Columbia University Press, 2010.
Laqueur, Walter, and Barry Rubin. *The Israel-Arab Reader.* London: Penguin, 2008.

Mandel, Daniel. 'Try, Try, Try Again: Bush's Peace Plans'. *Middle East Quarterly* 11, no. 3 (Summer 2004): 27–36.
Miller, Aaron David. *The Too Much Promised Land*. New York: Bantam Books, 2008.
Palestinian Centre for Human Rights. *Annual Report 2010*. Ramallah: West Bank Office, 2011.
Paris, Roland. *At War's End*. Cambridge: Cambridge University Press, 2008.
Paris, Roland, and Timothy D. Sisk, eds. *The Dilemmas of State-building: Confronting the Contradictions of Postwar Peace Operations*. London: Routledge, 2009.
RAND Corporation. 'Terrorism and Development: Using Social and Economic Development to Inhibit a Resurgence of Terrorism'. 2003. http://www.rand.org/pubs/monograph_reports/2005/MR1630.pdf (accessed December 10, 2011).
Richmond, Oliver. *Peace in International Relations*. New York: Routledge, 2008.
Richmond, Oliver, and Jason Franks. *Liberal Peace Transitions: Between State-building and Peace-building*. Edinburgh: Edinburgh University Press, 2009.
Riley, Keith Jack, and Seth Jones. 'Law and Order in Palestine'. *Survival* 46, no. 4 (Winter 2004–2005): 157–78.
Ross, Dennis, and David Markowsky. *Myths, Illusions and Peace*. London: Viking, 2009.
Roy, Sara. *Failing Peace: Gaza and the Palestinian-Israeli Conflict*. London: Pluto Press, 2007.
Rubenberg, Cheryl A. *The Palestinians: In Search of a Just Peace*. London: Lynne Rienner Publishers, 2003.
Sayigh, Yezid. 'Inducing a Failed State in Palestine'. *Survival* 49, no. 3 (2007): 7–39.
Seitz, Charmaine. 'Appointing Abu Mazen: A Drama with Two Enactments'. Middle East Report, 2003. http://merip.org/mero//mero050103.html (accessed December 10, 2011).
Shlaim, Avi. *Israel and Palestine: Reappraisals, Revisions, Refutations*. London: Verso, 2009.
Shu'aybi, Azmi, and Khalil Shikaki. 'A Window on the Workings of the PA: An Inside View'. *Journal of Palestine Studies* 30, no.1 (2000): 88–97.
Turner, Mandy. 'Creating Partners for Peace'. *Journal of Intervention and State-building* 5, no. 1 (2011): 1–21.
Weber, Max. *From Max Weber: Essays in Sociology*. Ed. H.H. Gerth and C. Wright Mills. London: Routledge, 1991.
Wendt, Alexander. 'Anarchy is What States Make of It: The Social Construction of Power Politics'. *International Organization* 46, no. 2 (1992): 391–425.

Peace-building and democracy promotion in Afghanistan: the Afghanistan Peace and Reintegration Programme and reconciliation with the Taliban

Marissa Quie

Faculty of Politics, Psychology, Sociology, and International Studies, University of Cambridge, UK

Democracy and peace are commonly promoted as concomitant objectives in war-torn societies; however, the underlying assumption of the convergence of these two goals often proves problematic in practice, leading to conflict and ineffective intervention. This contribution focuses on the connections between democracy and peace-building in Afghanistan, through the lens of the Afghanistan Peace and Reintegration Programme (APRP). It finds that in this case, the two aims have not always complemented one another, resulting instead in multiple trade-offs and disputes. The article demonstrates how a better understanding of the connections between democracy and peace can help improve the efficacy and legitimacy of interventions of this type. Some elements of the APRP strategy are context-appropriate and *do* enhance the potential for more substantive democracy and peace: for example, the National Community Recovery plan, centrepiece of the third stage of the process, which aims to enfranchise former insurgents and their communities through mechanisms of local government, emphasizing consultation and enhancing participation. However, the argument here is that the complexity of the insurgency, the lack of coherent communication within and between international and local actors, the ambiguity surrounding the meaning of democracy, and the failure to pursue genuine reconciliation have all served to undermine the dual objectives of the APRP initiative.

Introduction

Democracy promotion has been a fundamental component of international initiatives to achieve peace in war-torn societies since the late 1980s. Democracy and peace have been promoted as concomitant goals. However, the implicit assumption of the consonance of the two objectives is often problematic in practice: they do not always progress in parallel. Practitioners are confronted with a significant paradox, whereby the pursuit of democracy can undermine efforts to secure peace, and efforts to secure peace can undermine the quality of democracy.

This contribution seeks to enhance the understanding of the intricate connections between democracy promotion and peace-building, shedding light on the complementarities and conflicts between the two foreign policy objectives. International strategies to promote democracy in order to foster peace are increasingly being called into question.[1] This analysis focuses on the Afghanistan Peace and Re-integration Programme (APRP), launched in 2010, providing insights into the legitimacy and effectiveness of the APRP strategy in accomplishing the dual objectives of democracy promotion and peace-building. The case of Afghanistan is especially relevant to an analysis of the linkages between democracy promotion and peace-building, because it represents a particularly difficult example of enforced regime change, democratization, and the promotion of democracy within a society experiencing intense ongoing conflict.

Democracy assistance measures, whether in the form of the establishment of democratic institutions, judicial reform, or assistance to civil society, have been extensively implemented in Afghanistan. In the aftermath of the terrorist attacks on the USA on 11 September 2001, there have been more reform initiatives led by international actors in Afghanistan than at any other point in the country's history (other than the period under Communist rule between 1978 and 1992). An international meeting in Bonn in 2001 set the framework for Afghanistan's political transition. Paradoxically, Afghans were invited only to the final stage of negotiations, and the Taliban excluded entirely. Excluding the Taliban meant that a key piece of the puzzle with respect to promoting representative democracy was missing.

This framework reflects the original motives of the US-led intervention, which sought to install a stable, cooperative regime and eradicate an environment conducive to terrorism as part of the 'war on terror'. Despite the Bush administration's initial unwillingness to engage in 'nation-building', regime change soon found its place within the wider framework of democratization in the Bonn process.

Bonn set the pattern for extreme dependence on international financing and the military and logistical support necessary to sustain democracy in Afghanistan, leading to what Krasner has labelled a situation of 'shared sovereignty',[2] which has inevitably undermined the legitimacy and effectiveness of Afghan democracy. In addition, enormous domestic challenges confront democracy promoters, including poverty, social fragmentation, a complex regional environment, deeply entrenched corruption, and continued hostilities.

In the years following the 2001 intervention, Afghanistan did not undergo transition from war and the authoritarianism of the Taliban government to peace or democracy. This article argues that Western governments must clarify their objectives and re-focus intervention on *appropriate* forms of democracy promotion and peace-building, rather than the achievement of 'mere' military success. Against this backdrop, the underlying assumption of the designers of the APRP was that peace-building and democracy promotion are harmonious objectives, and that the pursuit of this dual agenda reinforces the potential for a positive outcome of both goals. The implication is that such external actors view democracy promotion and peace-building as compatible. The argument of this article is that this perspective is open to question, as evidenced by empirical analysis of the APRP.

The APRP's rationale is based on the mainstream assumptions which often determine international interventions. The aim of democratic intervention through military operations in war-torn countries is to attempt to build institutions of state and security, creating a central monopoly of force and a functioning bureaucratic administration. However, the ultimate goal of democracy promotion is to democratize political institutions and the behaviour of political elites and civil society.[3] This entails transforming norms of violence to those of compromise and dialogue, characterized by peace. Although political conflicts are unlikely to be fully resolved, democracy provides a framework within which they can be managed by peaceful means. In order to give this framework substance, fundamental conditions for the peaceful resolution of grievances must be in place.

This clarifies a crucial dimension of the connection between democracy and peace-building. If the conditions for conflict resolution are created by a peace programme, opportunities for democracy promotion are increased. If peace negotiations end without a widely accepted agreement, prospects for both peace- and democracy-building might be compromised.[4]

In accordance with the introduction to this special issue, I argue that democracy promotion through external force is confronted with a range of conflicting objectives.[5] Two principal types of contradictions are examined here: *intrinsic* contradictions within democracy promotion in the APRP, and *extrinsic* contradictions between democracy promotion and peace-building in the programme. This contribution therefore focuses on conflicting objectives in democracy promotion, through an examination of the *inclusion/exclusion* contradictions inherent in the APRP. These centre on the ramifications of the decision to re-integrate the Taliban. The article explores the background of these conflicts to demonstrate clashes within the normative conceptualization of democracy promotion, and the inherent weaknesses of the democracy promotion and peace-building strategies that have emerged as a consequence. Implementation of these strategies results in significant trade-offs, undermining the quality and form of democracy in Afghanistan.

The article explores three hypotheses related to the prospects for democracy promotion and peace-building. These objectives are hindered when: (a) politically relevant factions are included while others are excluded; (b) there is a disparity between the interests of internal and external actors; (c) there are divergent conceptualizations of the meaning or even the acceptance of democracy; and (d) the peace-building programme fails to contribute to reconciliation among internal actors.

This contribution therefore addresses two research questions that relate to this special issue's theme: (1) What were the conflicting objectives in democracy promotion in Afghanistan since the intervention in 2001, and which of these conflicts still exist? (2) Under what conditions did these conflicts emerge in the APRP since its inception in 2010?

The analysis reinforces the argument of Grimm and Leininger that international actors overload their democracy promotion agendas and expect too much in terms of what can be achieved.[6] Afghanistan has been placed in a position whereby it must accelerate its political development (via the democracy promotion and peace-building measures of the APRP) before the planned withdrawal of coalition forces in 2014. This article describes the resultant clash between locally- and externally-driven democracy promotion. Finally, it aims to illustrate how a better understanding of the connections and impact of democracy promotion and peace-building within a specific context can improve the effectiveness and legitimacy of interventions of this type.

The article is structured as follows: Section two, the research design, focuses on how democracy promotion and peace-building are defined in the context of the APRP, and the meaning of inclusion/exclusion contradictions within the wider framework of the Counter-Insurgency (COIN) Campaign. Section three explores the connections between peace-building and democracy promotion within the initiative. Section four provides an empirical exploration of the four hypotheses under discussion, and their impact on the two key research questions. Which politically relevant factions are included and which are not has a profound effect on democracy promotion and peace-building; disparities between internal and external actors on the question of inclusion undermine the effectiveness and legitimacy of the APRP. Inclusion is further complicated by divergence between various actors regarding what democracy actually *means*. The section concludes by examining how the programme has been undermined by the lack of genuine reconciliation amongst key players in the process.

Section five summarizes the extrinsic contradictions posed by inclusion of the Taliban, and Section six presents conclusions regarding the four hypotheses. The final section offers recommendations on how combining democracy promotion and peace-building in Afghanistan can prove more effective in the future.

Research design for analysing conflicting objectives in democracy promotion in Afghanistan

Definition of democracy promotion in the context of the APRP

While there is a substantive body of literature on how war-torn societies move from conflict to peace, comparatively little research has been devoted to an examination of the connections between peace-building and democracy promotion.[7] Grävingholt, Leininger, and Schlumberger characterize *democracy promotion* as 'all non-military means of (re-) establishing and strengthening a democratic political order'. They acknowledge that a distinction is often made in the literature between *democracy assistance* (direct, positive, and peaceful measures) and *democracy promotion* (which may also include military and/or economic incentives or coercion).[8] The term is employed here in a form that incorporates military means. In 2001, international intervention in Afghanistan triggered by force a putative transformation to democracy. The central protagonists of this militarily enforced regime change were external actors, namely, the United States-led 'coalition of the willing'. Powerful domestic actors interested in democracy promotion have been scarce; internal anti-democratic forces strong.

The APRP should be viewed in the context of forced democratic intervention.[9] It is an integral component of the COIN, which embraces both civilian and military strategies to achieve peace and democracy. Moreover, Grimm and Leininger further distinguish between *direct* and *indirect* democracy promotion.[10] Both the strengthening of core institutions and capacity-building (direct promotion) and the creation of favourable conditions for democracy (indirect promotion) are included within the APRP.

Peace-building and democracy

The term *peace-building* covers a range of strategies that support the political, institutional, and socio-economic transformation necessary to bring about lasting peace.[11] Its central task is to create a 'stable social equilibrium in which the surfacing of new disputes does not escalate into violence and war'.[12]

In practice, combining this vision of peace with a liberal form of democracy may be too much to expect of Afghanistan. The heterogeneity and complexity of both its society and the conflict itself may mean that some form of compromise that undermines the essential meaning of democracy is all that can be achieved at this point. The outcome of both the APRP and the COIN may therefore be a hybrid state, dictated by the international community's directives and interpreted by the local elite.[13] Internal and external actors privately acknowledge this.[14] Nevertheless, the liberal narrative of peace and democracy continues to inform APRP rhetoric.

Peace-building initiatives such as the APRP attempt to resolve the core problems that underlie the conflict and change the patterns of interaction of those involved. The goal here is to create cooperation and dialogue among community members, thus gradually displacing the culture of violence. The architects of the APRP were mindful of the failures of democracy promotion and peace-building in Iraq and other cases. Minister Mohammed Stanekzai, Chief Executive Officer of the APRP, contends that the 'institutional prerequisites of democracy promotion are bankrupt without the corollary establishment of a culture of peace'.[15]

This is what is missing in Afghanistan. The legitimacy and effectiveness of democratic institutions depend upon their constituent parts: namely, individual Afghans and the population as a whole. First, the institutions must be representative of the population: hence the initiative to include the Taliban in the political process. Second, they must 'foster a culture of peace and dialogue'. As Wolpe and McDonald argue,

> The principal challenge in building peace and democracy, in all divided societies, lies not in abstract sector-specific 'fixes', but rather in bringing key leaders together in a

long-term process designed to resolve the tensions and mistrust that are the inevitable by-product of conflict and war, and to build (or re-build) their capacity to work effectively together across all of the country's lines of ethnic and political division. Failing that, institutional transformation will have little substance and no sustainability.[16]

Contradictions between inclusion and exclusion of relevant actors

The *intrinsic* inclusion/exclusion contradiction refers to the issue of which parties are included and which are excluded in negotiations concerning peace and a more representative form of democracy. This has significant implications for sustainable peace and democracy promotion. A viable peace programme cannot be achieved without involvement by leaders of the warring factions.[17] Sustainable peace presupposes a system of governance in which disparate interests and grievances are accommodated.[18] However, for the sake of democracy, the exclusion of those involved in violence seems warranted, as their inclusion might undermine democratic legitimacy and long-term stability. The conundrum regarding inclusion of the Taliban is an inherently irreconcilable dilemma; however, the negative ramifications of their potential inclusion in the democratic system can be mitigated by genuine inclusion of civil society in the peace process, as well as in a power-sharing government. Half of all peace agreements fail because too few people support them. Only a broad, multi-tiered, sequential process will enable the country to build a national consensus on the way forward and therefore deepen democracy in Afghanistan.[19]

The APRP places the quest for peace at the forefront of its agenda. Paris and Sisk and Barnett and Zürcher agree that peace-builders essentially prioritize stability over the reforms required to produce the form of liberal democracy they desire.[20] In terms of the *extrinsic* inclusion/exclusion contradiction, this means that the potential costs of including the Taliban within the democratic framework are deemed lower than the benefits offered by peace. In other words, peace-building ultimately trumps democracy promotion in the Afghan case.

Methodology and data collection

This article aims to provide a context-based, qualitative analysis of the APRP through participatory observation and analysis of secondary sources. My participation as a member of the APRP design and implementation teams through the Joint Secretariat (JS) and the United Nations Development Programme (UNDP) provided the opportunity for an inside view of the development of the programme, but inevitably generated certain biases. The design and implementation of the APRP entailed constant interaction with government officials and key ministry representatives. My brief focused on Afghanistan's Ministry of Rural Rehabilitation and Development, Ministry of Agriculture, and Ministry of Labour. The APRP unit at the JS worked together with International Security Assistance Force (ISAF) advisers and principal international donors.

My remit involved consultation with Afghan women, human rights groups, and representatives of civil society.[21] I also participated in joint consultations with the Taliban, along with JS and ISAF staff responsible for other dimensions of the programme. As part of the implementation phase, I organized specialized development programmes for former insurgents and plans for de-radicalization centres.

Although there is a risk of bias in this study, it is outweighed by access to highly sensitive sources. Information was gathered using a variety of these, including data from reports on the emerging re-integration and reconciliation strategy, semi-structured interviews with Afghan and international stakeholders, primary documents connected to the APRP, media reports, recorded and unofficial conversations (held in Kabul between 7 April and 12 November 2010), and correspondence with Afghan leaders (from November 2010–October 2011).

Given the highly sensitive nature of the material, many of those interviewed are not named, and often requested that their views be disassociated from their institutions. Every effort was made to substantiate views articulated in the interviews, particularly in the case of Taliban spokesmen. Finally, it is important to note that the APRP is being implemented in environments experiencing high levels of conflict. Consequently, there is a large degree of fluidity in terms of adaptations to specific circumstances, and discrepancies sometimes develop between the design rubric and practical applications as lessons are learnt and applied.

The APRP: peace-building and democracy promotion

How does the APRP address both the objectives of peace-building and democracy promotion? International forces plan to withdraw in 2014 in accordance with the COIN,[22] which calls for an '80/20' balance in which emphasis is placed on the political or civilian dimension. The expectation underlying the APRP was that the US-led military surge in 2010 would undercut the momentum of the insurgency. Between 2011 and 2014, the plan is for Afghanistan to take responsibility for its own security as part of a 'responsible' transition. The APRP faces a particular challenge because it was initiated before any potential peace agreement with the Taliban insurgency had been achieved. The civilian surge tripled the number of international development advisers on the ground to 1100. Coupled with the socio-economic and educational incentives embodied in the APRP, it was hoped that this expansion would draw the Taliban into participation within the emerging democratic system. The third dimension, the diplomatic surge, is designed to support an Afghan-led process of reconciliation within Afghanistan and engage Pakistan and other significant regional neighbours, including India, Russia, Iran, and China, in the peace process.[23]

The APRP was given the imprimatur of democratic legitimacy by the Consultative Peace *Jirga* (CPJ) of June 2010. It is founded upon the principle of 'inclusive governance', seeking to rectify some of the failures of Bonn in terms of exclusion of insurgents and create a framework within which Afghans can explore their differences and utilize consultative mechanisms to resolve grievances. The objective is to identify ways to bring those who have been disenfranchised into the fabric of democracy, offering them full recognition of their rights as Afghan citizens.

A key component of democracy promotion lies in the strengthening of the 'institutions of governance to more closely connect with the interests of the people of Afghanistan'.[24] Institutional capacity-building is planned at all levels of government. The High Peace Council (HPC) brings Taliban representatives into the political process at the top echelon of government. It also engages in high-level dialogue with the insurgency. Provincial government structures are to be strengthened, and there is a concerted emphasis on local government, consultation, and decentralization through the National Community Recovery Programme.[25]

This programme is led and implemented by the JS, which receives direction from the HPC, a 70-member body established in 2010; one of its primary goals is to support the main ministries involved in the APRP. Provincial and district governors are given a pivotal role in organizing the support and inclusion of political, tribal, and religious leaders from outside Kabul. The HPC also engages in regional and international efforts to build consensus in the support of peace and democracy in Afghanistan: examples including delegation visits to Islamabad, Istanbul, and Saudi Arabia.

The operational dimension of the programme targets local peace processes through inclusion of the foot soldiers and local leaders who constitute the bulk of the insurgency. It concentrates on addressing grievances to gain support for peace and conflict resolution *through the democratic system*, intertwining peace-building with democracy promotion. The principal mechanisms for this are the Community Development Councils (CDCs), which serve as a bridge between communities and government, encouraging participation at grassroots level.

In the first stage of the APRP, community, district, and provincial leaders reach out to insurgents to understand their grievances and encourage them to re-join their communities. In the second phase, de-mobilization aims to transform insurgents into citizens who participate within democracy. It includes vetting and biometric data collection, preventing future exchange of identities. Assessment involves gathering data on individuals and their communities, followed by weapons management. Community security is addressed through the 'Afghanistan Public Protection Force', made up of trained former fighters. In the third phase, transition assistance to meet basic needs is provided through the National Community Recovery programme. This final stage is viewed as the centrepiece of the programme by both domestic and international actors. Community participation represents one of the most successful aspects of the intervention.[26] The rationale is that if insurgents can be incorporated at this level, democratic enfranchisement and legitimacy will be reinforced. Cooperation within the political framework should also enhance the potential for peace.

The APRP is designed to unfold over a five-year horizon. In some 'priority provinces' experiencing high levels of conflict, the first two stages have already been implemented, and are continually monitored so that the programme can be refined according to their specific requirements.[27]

Inclusion/exclusion contradictions

The Bonn Agreement excluded the Taliban and *Hizb-e-Islami*,[28] and marginalized much of the Pashtun population: exacerbating the Pashtun hegemonic crisis and setting the stage for future problems. The participating delegations at Bonn represented the Northern Alliance and the various factions within it (primarily Tajik); the supporters of the former king, Zahir Shah (The Rome Group), and two smaller delegations (The Cyprus and the Peshawar Groups). They did not convene to reach a peace settlement: the Taliban were considered defeated and, in the view of the US, beyond the pale, in consequence of their association with Osama Bin Laden. Instead, their intention was to agree a road map consisting of various stages, culminating in general elections in 2004. Bonn largely reflected US policy interests, and focused on a 'light footprint approach' which would establish a stable, pro-Western government, able to prevent international terrorists from making use of Afghan territory. These objectives conflicted with the demands of democratic development and left the inclusion/exclusion contradiction unresolved.[29]

This article contends that the chances for democracy promotion are hindered by the inclusion/exclusion contradiction, together with three other factors: (1) the disparity in the interests of internal and external actors; (2) the divergent conceptualizations of the meaning or acceptance of democracy between local and international actors; and (3) the failure to achieve reconciliation between internal actors. These are discussed in detail below.

Inclusion of politically relevant factions and the exclusion of others

Addressing the failures of Bonn necessitates a role for the Taliban in the democratic process, from which they were excluded in 2001. This is conceptualized by external actors as a measure for 'deepening democracy'.[30] Inclusion is complicated by the risk of increased violence in the short-term, the prospect of exacerbating ethnic/tribal cleavages, potential fragmentation within the movement, and the fact that the Taliban transcend international borders. The inclusion/exclusion contradiction is at the core of the APRP. Inclusion of the Taliban might help transfer the conflict from the battlefield into the democratic political arena. The APRP aims to create the conditions for this transition, thus pre-empting a wider war.

The architects of the APRP recognized that inclusion was likely to hinder the quality of democracy, should the programme realize its aims. The case for exclusion to protect the democratic process is recognized by Afghan law.[31] However, this option was trumped by calls for 'inclusive government' to enfranchise those who had been marginalized at Bonn. As a result, it was hoped that former insurgents would be gradually included in the democratic process at all levels of government.

The unfolding of the programme has revealed that inclusion results in an over-burdening of weak institutions, especially at provincial level. For instance, provincial governors, whose cooperation is critical to the success of the programme, have been unable or unwilling to provide robust support.[32] Moreover, significant non-Pashtun elites view the APRP as the final stage in Pashtun dominance of the political sphere.[33] This perspective is reinforced by the ongoing violence perpetrated by Taliban factions.[34]

Inclusion is further complicated by fragmentation. The insurgency consists of seven armed structures, the core of which is the Taliban movement.[35] Its principal networks are in south-eastern Afghanistan, but it has now spread throughout the country. There are also three other insurgent organizations: *Hizb-e Islami*, the *Haqqani* network, and *mujahidin* groups, who have taken on the modus operandi of the Taliban. Other than the *mujahidin* groups, all these networks recognize the *amir ul-mo'menin* (Taliban's head), Mullah Mohammad Omar, as their spiritual guide. The Taliban movement is effectively of a dual nature: its vertical organization, in the form of a centralized 'shadow state', reflects its Islamist ideology; whereas its horizontal military structures connect it to tribal divisions.[36] At local level, Taliban fronts are strongly based in tribes or smaller subgroups. This became clear as the APRP developed, notably in the problems encountered in developing a pilot programme for Shindand in 2010. Efforts to meet fighters' needs ultimately failed, largely because of conflict between the *Barakzai* and *Alakozai* tribes.[37] The complex fragmentation of the Taliban, including tribal divisions, means that democracy promotion cannot be a uniform strategy and must be sensitive to differences in local context.

The assassination of Burhanuddin Rabbani, head of the HPC, in 2011 underlines the significance of these divisions. Rabbani was a former *mujahidin*, a leader of the Northern Alliance, and later, president of Afghanistan. His killing complicates the question of inclusion. As a Tajik, a central part of his role in the APRP was to gain the support of what former Intelligence Director Amrullah Saleh terms the 'anti-Taliban constituency': Afghans disturbed by the prospect of old enemies returning to power. Without their support, the APRP has little chance of success.

Inclusion is also hampered by the fact that the Taliban are not constrained by international borders. Chains of command invariably connect Afghan and Pakistani groups, and the Pakistan Inter-Services Intelligence (ISI) has a particularly strong influence. This means that an initiative designed to address the needs of the 'Afghan Taliban' effectively relies on artificial divisions. This has been overtly recognized by local actors involved in the programme,[38] and tacitly by a number of international ones. The reluctance of the *Haqqani* network to be engaged in the APRP process and detrimental role of the ISI underscore this point. The latter often works independently of the Taliban; specialized negotiations may be required to bring it into the peace process.

External actors are generally reluctant to address the problem in a more holistic way because of the increased time and financial commitment that would be necessary. In other words, the inclusion/exclusion contradiction will remain virulent, as long as inclusion of the insurgency is only partial. In such a scenario, goals of peace-building and democracy promotion are unlikely to be accomplished, and both inter- and intra-state peace will continue to be undermined.

Disparities between internal and external actors

The second hypothesis focuses on how inclusion is complicated by disparities between internal and external actors. International intervention is necessary to promote democracy and secure peace; however, the visible presence of external actors in the funding and implementation of APRP undermines its potential to generate trust and, by extension, possibilities for democracy promotion.

The Afghan government and the international community frame APRP as an 'Afghan-owned', 'Afghan-led' process, but this is contradicted by its being entirely financed by foreign donors, at a total cost of over US$700 million, and consequently, has been strongly influenced by them in the normative phase. The parallel pursuit of war together with a peace programme linked with democracy promotion has led to a confused international agenda for the Kabul government to follow. The decision in 2009 to escalate the number of troops further exposed the divergence of roles among key international forces: between the ISAF mandate to support the government in Kabul, the US operation to defeat the insurgency, and the political mandate of the UN. This strengthened the perception of many Afghans that the US is effectively making *all* the important choices; and that the Afghan government has little influence on overall strategy.

Grimm and Leininger highlight the ways in which conflicts emerge in the interactions between international and local actors when they are confronted by a clash of interests, lack of coordination, and lack of ownership.[39] At the core of this clash in Afghanistan is disagreement over democracy promotion. For factions of the Taliban that accept either full democracy or some version of it, local ownership on all levels is paramount. In contrast, the US and other international donors have chosen to pursue a path of exogenous enforcement of democratic standards.

Disparities in strategy

The COIN prescribes an 80/20 balance between political and military strategy, but the continuation of war undermines the long-term objectives of democracy promotion and peace-building. Seamless cooperation between political and military sectors has proven difficult to achieve, as illustrated by the fundamental disagreements over the concept and implementation of 're-integration' in the APRP.

As the principal external actor, the US administration conceptualizes the insurgency in terms of a 'moderate/radical dichotomy'. This is consistent with the original discourse employed by US officials in descriptions of the 'war on terror.' Afghan actors focus instead on the hierarchical differentiation of the insurgency. This disparity in perspectives permeated JS meetings; internal and external actors found it difficult to reach consensus on the key questions, such as: what do the Taliban want? And how are re-integration, reconciliation, and democracy promotion best achieved?

International donors and ISAF want a robust 'de-radicalization' component to help transform insurgents into citizens of a democratic polity. Afghan officials largely reject this, arguing that radicalization within the Taliban is not a 'disease to be cured'.[40] Instead, they advocate re-integration with 'dignity' and honour', via 'independent mediators' through 'civic education', although there is a marked lack of clarity about what this actually means.

External and internal actors have resolved their differences in the strategy-building phase, through what Grimm and Leininger term 'compromise'.[41] They agree that de-radicalization will be used in some cases, civic education in others. However, this inconsistency will inevitably undermine the effectiveness of the APRP in both peace-building and democracy promotion. In fact, evaluation reports on the APRP reveal the 'interim' period between the second and third phases of demobilization and 'consolidation of peace' (designed to deepen democratic participation), to be particularly problematic: the strategy linking these two stages is unclear.[42]

In terms of the operational dimension of the APRP, the Afghan government's lack of capacity to fully implement the programme means that ISAF, using Provincial Reconstruction Teams (PRTs), has stepped in to fill the gaps. The government's shortcomings are exacerbated by the unwillingness of important actors in key ministries to provide genuine support. ISAF and the UN have attempted to redress this through additional support (for example, via quick impact community development projects and transitional assistance grants), but the problem has only been compounded; and legitimacy weakened as a result.

External actors and the Taliban

Events since 2001 have demonstrated that the military mandate has frequently been unclear, meaning that international objectives are inconsistent and often at odds with democracy promotion and peace-building through inclusion of the Taliban. There are reports that the governments of the USA and Afghanistan are close to an agreement that will keep approximately 25,000 troops (bolstered by the construction of 'super bases') in Afghanistan until at least 2024.[43] In November 2011, Hamid Karzai called a *Loya Jirga*, the traditional grand council of tribal elders and leaders, in an attempt to gain support for a long-term military presence in Afghanistan.[44] Potential agreement on this would undermine the HPC's legitimacy as a sovereign, democratic body. The Taliban have capitalized: arguing that the Afghan government is not the interlocutor in negotiations regarding the APRP, but merely a puppet for US interests.[45] The schism between local and international actors reinforces Taliban critiques of Afghan democracy, undermining the legitimacy and effectiveness of the APRP in promoting democracy and peace-building.

Divergent conceptions of the meaning and acceptance of democracy

My third hypothesis focuses on the manner in which divergent interpretations of the meaning of democracy or what constitutes acceptance of democracy renders inclusion problematic. The Taliban portray the conflict as an 'illegitimate war'; they offer neither a coherent alternative to democracy, nor a unified vision of what form of government would be acceptable.[46] International actors lack consensus on the meaning of democracy promotion in Afghanistan, further complicating the prospects for democracy and peace-building.

Mullah Nazimi, former spokesman for Mullah Omar, has spoken of a practical willingness to find a peaceful solution: 'The Taliban want to participate in government', though this would entail 'changes to the Constitution'.[47] These changes are centred on the position of women and interpretations of equality and individual rights. The 2004 Constitution contains a number of provisions formally consistent with democracy, including in its preamble the intention to 'establish an order based on the people's will and democracy'.[48] It commits the country to universal rights, guarantees equal rights to citizens, and establishes the Afghanistan Independent Human Rights Commission (AIHRC).[49]

Taliban representatives argue that the Constitution contains a range of ambiguities. Articles 1–3, for example, establish Islam as the foundation for a republic.[50] This leaves open the possibility for conflict between articles referring to Islam and those based on international human rights instruments. There is no precise mechanism for the interpretation or resolution of ambiguities between Islamic and international perspectives. Women's groups and female representatives to the HPC have expressed strong reservations about potential interpretations of and changes to the Constitution, citing the Taliban's past record as evidence of deep-seated intolerance to women's rights and to human rights in general,[51] concerns echoed by Afghan civil society groups and the AIHRC.[52]

For women's groups, guarantees regarding 'co-existence culture' are dubious. International donors insisted on consultation with these groups in the normative phase of the programme and on their representation on the HPC; however, women hold only nine seats on the 70-member Council. Women's groups and female members of the HPC also believe that genuine dialogue was impossible in the normative phase, complaining that an extensive list of recommendations to the CPJ was ignored in the APRP rubric.[53]

In the normative phase of the APRP, external actors framed democracy promotion as a 'stabilizer' against possible upheaval generated by inclusion of the Taliban.[54] At this stage, plans for broad consultation across civil society were suggested, demonstrating that external actors have preferences regarding the form of democracy that evolves out of the APRP. The emphasis is on broad representation, pluralism, and tolerance; however, in both strategic and implementation phases, there has been a marked lack of follow-through on these points.

The issue here is whether external actors agree to tolerate deviation from their perspectives on the shape democracy should take and how the conflict will be played out. Normative disagreements with internal actors have resulted in a 'compromise' in strategy. In practice, 'consultation' with civil society, human rights groups, and women's groups was limited, taking the form of contact rather than dialogue. The process was not closely monitored by external actors. The liberal democratic narrative of 'gender mainstreaming' and 'public outreach' continues to permeate the APRP as it unfolds, but real implementation remains problematic. This indicates a lack of consensus among international actors on democracy promotion.

Significant internal actors, for example, Aziz Rafiee, Director of the Afghan Civil Society Forum, argue that inclusion of the Taliban may be too high a price to pay for peace. Rafiee notes: 'If the Afghan people were consulted, they might say the Taliban should not be in government.' Rafiee suggests that inclusion of civil society is the best strategy to militate against the negative effects of integration of the insurgency. Donors required meetings with civil society groups in the normative phase of APRP; Rafiee complained that this exercise lacked substance and highlighted the ways democracy was eroded.[55] The CPJ, for instance, was criticized for being unrepresentative and lacking transparency.[56] Ramazan Bashardost, a 2009 Presidential candidate, underscored this: 'Members of the HPC have better experience of war than peace and this undermines trust in the APRP'.[57] An analysis of the HPC indeed confirms that many of these leaders have committed war crimes and serious human rights abuses.

The Taliban themselves are divided on the question of inclusion within a democratic framework. Nazimi believes the Western conception of democracy to be inappropriate for Afghanistan, contrasting it with an Islamic Emirate from which foreign forces have withdrawn.[58] For Nazimi and other representatives of what might be referred to as the 'Omar faction', withdrawal of coalition forces represents a key condition for achieving genuine peace, which he insists the APRP cannot deliver. In contrast, Mullah Hotak, a member of the HPC and former Taliban minister, believes that 'withdrawal of foreign forces would result in a return to the violent civil war of the *mujahidin* period' and would undermine efforts to achieve peace. Hotak believes that 'democracy and Islam are in no way incompatible' and that 'men and women are equal but different'.[59]

These perspectives illustrate the fragmentation of the Taliban and the difficulties in determining what they want. This hinders the potential for an agreement that would satisfy the interests of all factions and therefore be durable. The aversion of civil war protagonists to democracy promotion and peace-building poses severe obstacles to the attainment of these goals.[60] Some segments of the Taliban accept democracy, while others view it as irreconcilable with their aims. Those who accept it have a variety of outlooks on the shape it should take, and whether their participation in politics will require changes to the Constitution.

The peace-building programme fails to contribute to reconciliation between actors

The central linkage between democracy promotion and peace-building in the APRP is in the creation of a framework through which tensions and mistrust between the Taliban and other segments of Afghan society can be addressed, leading to collaboration in the democratic system. The initiative therefore has a strong focus on reconciliation, the issue at the centre of this contribution's fourth hypothesis.

The objectives of democracy promotion and peace-building have a greater chance of success if there is a clear understanding regarding key concepts from the outset. Unfortunately, there remains a profound lack of clarity in Washington and Kabul on the meaning of 'reconciliation' and how it should be realized. Precisely what reconciliation means in terms of accountability for abuses committed during the conflict is ambiguous. Key international actors suggest reconciliation will mean different things to different people, depending upon their experiences of the conflict and their positions within the political spectrum. The APRP works closely to involve grassroots community-level groups in reconciliation (*musaleha*). Baca, an adviser at ISAF, has described what might emerge as a 'series of natural organic processes which would be context-dependent and different within different communities'.[61]

External actors have framed the 'natural, organic' approach to reconciliation as recognition of the complexity of the idea in Afghan society: a bow to local ownership, recognizing that Afghanistan has different types of customary law, traditional societal structures, and authorities.[62] Afghans at the vanguard of human rights issues are profoundly disturbed by this[63]; and express concerns that the diverse interests of non-Taliban sections of society are inadequately catered to in the discussions concerning reconciliation.

The AIHRC 'Call for Justice' found that 69% of the population claim either that they themselves had been directly subjected to violence or human rights abuse, or a member of their family had experienced this during the last three decades of the conflict.[64] Bashardost has emphasized the significance of public acknowledgement of such abuse. He believes it essential that the perpetrators publicly admit what they have done and commit themselves to reparations.[65]

Extensive advice was received during the normative phase of the APRP on the issue of transitional justice. These norms should form a substantive part of the reconciliation process, setting out clear parameters and mechanisms for grievance resolution. The 'natural, organic' alternative does not provide a framework that generates the levels of trust necessary for the attainment of genuine reconciliation.[66]

Extrinsic contradictions

Inclusion of the Taliban is an inherently risky venture. By granting warring parties a stake in democratic government, violence is effectively rewarded, violating a fundamental principle of democracy. The APRP clearly gives precedence to peace-building over democracy promotion. This connects to the broader wishes of the Afghan population, who generally approve of democracy promotion measures when the corollary involves a reduction in violence.[67]

Interestingly, external actors, particularly the US, are willing to accept potential electoral gains for the Taliban.[68] For decades, US foreign policy has been inhibited by the 'Islamist dilemma': how can the US promote democracy in Muslim countries without running the risk of Islamists coming to power? The question, then, is whether the Taliban's rather fundamentalist approach can co-exist with respect for human rights, equality, democracy, and pluralism. In terms of *realpolitik*, Western fears revolve around what kind of foreign policy a government incorporating the Taliban might pursue, and how this form of inclusion may further destabilize an already volatile region ripe for the expansion of terrorism. It now appears that the choices have been narrowed by demands of the domestic electorates that comprise the coalition, and the relatively short-term nature of the governments they support.

Conclusion

The APRP is founded on a tripartite rationale, targeting first the strengthening of security and civilian institutions of governance to create a framework through wider inclusion, which should be conducive to peace. This leads to conditions in which, second, peace and democracy can lay down deep roots. The third component involves the enhancement of national, regional, and international support to foster peace. As hypothesized in the introduction, these objectives are hindered by the four dimensions of the inclusion contradiction, discussed further below.

Inclusion of politically relevant factions and exclusion of others

The intricacy of inclusion is complicated by fragmentation of the Taliban, the movement's expansion across international borders, and the heterogeneity of Afghan society. Fragmentation means it is difficult to determine what the Taliban want and meet their demands within the rubric of the APRP. Some factions of the Taliban seem willing to participate in the APRP: which entails both re-integration and ultimate participation in the democratic system. Others, like the *Haqqani* network, seek to undermine the process and to continue the conflict. This makes it difficult for both international and domestic actors to pursue consistent strategies for peace-building and democracy promotion. Partial inclusion will ensure that the conflict remains potent. 'Anti-Taliban' factions are highly heterogeneous and have gained strength as a consequence of continuing violence. Inclusion may exacerbate ethnic/tribal tensions, leading to extensive re-arming and a widening of the conflict: weakening prospects for the realization of the two objectives.

Disparities between internal and external actors

As Grimm and Leininger suggest,[69] conflicts have emerged in the interactions between international and local actors; as is especially evident with respect to the inclusion/exclusion contradiction (hypothesis (b)). The APRP is wholly funded by external donors, and therefore relies upon the support of international actors. Its foremost national body, the HPC, has been damaged by the dilemma over withdrawal timetables and potential presence of US troops until 2024. The Taliban pierces the core of this dilemma, arguing that the rhetoric of local ownership cannot conceal the Afghan government's impotence. This trade-off demonstrates the limits of self-determination for democracy promotion through the APRP.

In the strategic phase, international actors were prepared for trade-offs, resulting in compromise on re-integration. External actors pushed for the de-radicalization of ex-combatants, while Afghan actors opted for 'moderate Islamic mentoring and civic education'; yet details of both processes remain unclear. In practice, some former fighters are undergoing de-radicalization, while others are not. This inconsistency has undercut the effectiveness of the programme in the first stages of its implementation.[70]

Divergent conceptions of the meaning or acceptance of democracy

In terms of hypothesis (c), the Taliban advisers to the APRP did not offer a coherent alternative to democracy; in fact, they expressed a willingness to participate in the democratic political arena, provided that certain conditions were met. Participation will almost certainly entail changes to the 2004 Constitution and result in an 'Islamicized' version of democracy. Inclusion of the Taliban will lead to a marginalization of moderate actors, particularly women and civil society groups. As research indicates that widespread participation enhances the potential for peace,[71] this means that prospects for peace-building in Afghanistan will be reduced. Not unnaturally, anti-Taliban groups remain unconvinced by an initiative that provides democratic legitimacy for their opponents.

Afghanistan has a vibrant civil society, but its integration into the APRP has been inadequate. The requisite levels of secrecy for sensitive negotiations hamper consultation; however, without more complete integration of civil society, the APRP will only achieve what Rafiee calls 'transient peace at the expense of genuine democracy'.[72]

International actors have played a significant role in determining the normative outlines of the APRP, where a liberal vision of democracy is evident. They insisted on 'consultation' with civil society, human rights groups, and women's groups. In practice, however, this took the form of contact rather than authentic dialogue. This amounted to a compromise, indicative of the fact that external APRP actors prioritize peace over democracy promotion, and recognize that the liberal democratic ideals of international actors and the groups they support will not be fully realized. The result, should the APRP be 'successful', will be a hybrid political arrangement in which pluralism and tolerance are difficult to achieve. This is an imperfect resolution, but some external actors argue that it is 'as good as it gets'.

The peace-building agreement fails to contribute to reconciliation among actors

The connection between democracy promotion and peace-building in the APRP centres on the creation of a framework in which tensions and mistrust are reduced, so that dialogue is possible. However, there has been an ongoing lack of consensus on the key concepts of re-integration and reconciliation (hypothesis (d)). Afghan actors who embrace the liberal narrative of democracy contend that building trust is impossible if there is no accountability for past actions. The 'organic' compromise to local ownership made by international actors will undermine genuine reconciliation, which will remain difficult to accomplish in the absence of transitional justice mechanisms.

Can all good things go together?

An examination of the APRP shows that in the case of Afghanistan, all good things do *not* go together. Inclusion of the Taliban has resulted in a destabilizing, violent process, which has yet to realize the goals of some form of peace or democracy. Even if comprehensive levels of timely assistance are forthcoming, it is uncertain whether either objective will be realized. The consequences of the APRP may ultimately produce a backlash: resulting in the election of Islamist factions of the Taliban, which would have the effect of reducing democratic initiatives. Thus, the goal to deepen democracy through inclusion may be undercut by expansion of the conflict.

Are there ways in which the combination of peace-building and democracy promotion could be productive? The conclusions of the study lead to a number of recommendations. Democracy promotion objectives of initiatives such as the APRP must be more clearly detailed and organized to harmonize with the goal of peace-building. A clear understanding on the part of external actors is required regarding what 'democracy promotion' actually entails. The APRP's failure to provide support for women, civil society, and human rights groups only illustrates this point.

The APRP has enjoyed 're-integration successes', which have had a positive impact on peace-building and have exposed former combatants to the promises of democracy. These gains could still be undermined by re-population of the insurgency from across Afghanistan's porous border; this singles out the third pillar (regional and international cooperation) as one of the weakest dimensions of the programme. Lack of institutional capacity challenges the APRP's ability to deliver. Lack of cooperation from key ministries and provincial actors weakens the initiative. However, the emphasis on 'National Community Recovery' suggests a movement towards a more decentralized form of democracy, which, if successful, will strengthen participation and democratic legitimacy in the rural periphery, something the post-Bonn process has failed to achieve.

If the APRP and wider COIN strategies fail and the Karzai government disintegrates, Afghanistan could fall back into the anarchy and civil warfare of the 1990s. Such a state would have strong parallels with the one originally taken over by the Taliban. It is still unclear where the peace-building and democracy promotion process may be heading; there are too many inflection points and uncertainties. The best hope for avoiding failure lies in strong leadership, supported by consistent international allies with a commitment to democracy promotion.

Notes

1. Burnell and Youngs, *New Challenges to Democratization*; Goldsmith, 'Making the World Safe for Partial Democracy?'
2. Krasner, 'Building Democracy After Conflict'.
3. Paris, 'International Peacebuilding'; Newman and Rich, *The UN Role in Promoting Democracy*.
4. Grimm and Merkel, 'War and Democratization'.
5. Grimm and Leininger, 'Not All Good Things Go Together'.
6. Ibid.
7. Jarstad and Sisk, *From War to Democracy*, 17–36.
8. Grävingholt, Leininger, and Schlumberger, *The Three Cs*.
9. Grimm and Merkel, 'War and Democratization'.
10. Grimm and Leininger, 'Not All Good Things Go Together'.
11. Bertram, 'Re-inventing Governments'.
12. Haugerudbraaten Intern, 'Peacebuilding'.
13. Hill, 'International Actors and Democratisation', 160.
14. Interviews with ISAF and Afghan government officials, April–November 2010.
15. Joint Secretariat (JS) internal meeting, July 3, 2010.
16. Wolpe and McDonald, 'Democracy and Peace-building', 138.
17. Sisk, 'Democracy and Conflict Management'.
18. Licklider, 'Comparative Studies of Long Wars'.
19. USIP, 'Designing a Comprehensive Peace Process for Afghanistan'.
20. Paris and Sisk, *The Dilemmas of State Building*; Barnett, Fang, and Zürcher, 'The Peacebuilder's Contract'.
21. This entailed meetings with female politicians and representatives to the CPJ (Consultative Peace *Jirga*) and HPC (High Peace Council). The JS held discussions with women's groups, including the Afghan Women's Network (AFN), Ministry of Women's Affairs, Afghanistan Independent Human Rights Commission and Afghanistan Civil Society Forum.
22. Petraeus and Mattis, *Counterinsurgency*.
23. Clinton, 'Remarks'.
24. APRP, *Afghanistan Peace and Reintegration Programme*.
25. Ibid.
26. Interview with Scott Guggenheim, June 2010.
27. UNDP, *APRP-UNDP Support Second Quarter Progress Report 2011*; UNDP, *APRP-UNDP Support Third Quarter Progress Report 2011*.
28. *Hizb-e-Islami*, meaning Islamic Party, was founded by Gulbuddin Hekmatyar, and established in Pakistan in 1975. It is Afghanistan's second largest insurgency group.
29. Suhrke, Harpviken, and Strand, 'Conflictual Peacebuilding'.
30. Von Mettenheim and Malloy, *Deepening Democracy in Latin America*.
31. CMI, *Constitution of Afghanistan*, Preamble: particularly point 8.
32. UNDP, *APRP-UNDP Support Second Quarter Progress Report 2011*, 20; UNDP, *APRP-UNDP Support Third Quarter Progress Report 2011*, 29.
33. Porter, 'Did the Rabbani Hit Really Kill the Peace Talks?'

34. Tarzi, 'Recalibrating the Afghan Reconciliation Program'; Rondeaux, 'Reconsidering Reconciliation in Afghanistan'.
35. It is important to note that the Taliban movement is fluid, and in a state of constant flux.
36. Ruttig, 'How Tribal are the Taliban?'
37. Shindand, one of 13 districts in the province of Herat, has a confirmed shadow Taliban government. As a consequence of long-standing internal conflicts between the *Barakzai* and *Alakozi* tribes (both Pashtun 'sub-tribes'), it is highly unstable. The JS held meetings with insurgent groups, and determined that they were unwilling to work together: to the point where they were unable even to share the same physical space.
38. A point made by JS staff and Minister Stanekzai.
39. Grimm and Leininger, 'Not All Good Things Go Together'.
40. JS meeting, June 2010.
41. Grimm and Leininger, 'Not All Good Things Go Together'.
42. UNDP, *APRP-UNDP Support Second Quarter Progress Report 2011*.
43. Farmer, 'US Troops May Stay in Afghanistan'.
44. Partlow and Salahuddin, 'Karzai to Convene *loya jirga*'.
45. Interviews with the author, April–November 2010.
46. Ibid.; Nixon, 'Achieving Durable Peace'.
47. Interviews with the author, June–November 2010.
48. CMI, *Constitution of Afghanistan*, Preamble and Chapter 1, Article 6.
49. Ibid., Article 58.
50. Ibid., Article 3.
51. Interviews with the author, April–November 2010.
52. Ibid., July 2010.
53. No comment was made by the donors regarding this complaint.
54. JS Meeting, June 2010.
55. Interview with the author, November 2010.
56. Sajjad, 'Peace at all Costs?'
57. Interview with the author, October 2010.
58. Ibid., June 2010.
59. Ibid., November 2010.
60. Jarstad and Sisk, *From War to Democracy*, 6.
61. Internal meeting, July 6, 2010.
62. JS Meetings and discussions with international donors to the APRP, June–July 2010.
63. Discussions with the Afghan Civil Society Forum and Afghanistan Independent Human Rights Commission, April 2010–December 2011.
64. AIHRC, *A Call for Justice*.
65. Interview with the author, November 2010.
66. Scharf, 'The Letter of the Law'.
67. Theors and Kaldor, 'Building Afghan Peace from the Ground Up'.
68. Interviews with international embassy, APRP, JS, and ISAF staff, April 2010–November 2011.
69. Grimm and Leininger, 'Not All Good Things Go Together'.
70. UNDP, *APRP-UNDP Support Second Quarter Progress Report 2011*.
71. Hunt Alternatives Fund, *The Institute for Inclusive Security*.
72. Interview with the author, November 2010.

Notes on contributor

Marissa Quie is an Affiliated Lecturer in PPSIS at the University of Cambridge, and Director of the Cambridge Afghanistan Support Programme.

Bibliography

AIHRC. *A Call for Justice*, http://www.aihrc.org.af/Rep_29_Eng/rep29_1_05call4justice.pdf (accessed January 10, 2012).

APRP. *Afghanistan Peace and Reintegration Programme*. Kabul: D & R Commission, July 2010, https://ronna-afghan.harmonieweb.org/FRIC/APRP%20Policy%20Documents%20Structures%20and%20SOPs/APRP%20Program%20Document%20English.pdf (accessed April 9, 2012).

Barnett, Michael, Songying Fang, and Christoph Zürcher. 'The Peacebuilder's Contract: How External Statebuilding Reinforces Weak Statehood'. Paper presented at the annual meeting of the ISA's 49th Annual Convention, San Francisco, USA, March 26, 2008, http://www.allacademic.com/meta/p250944_index.html (accessed January 10, 2012).

Bertram, Eva. 'Re-inventing Governments: The Promise and Perils of United Nations Peacebuilding'. *Journal of Conflict Resolution* 39, no. 5 (1995): 387–418

Burnell, Peter, and Richard Youngs, eds. *New Challenges to Democratization*. London: Routledge, 2010

Clinton, Hillary R. 'Remarks at the Launch of the Asia Society's Series of Richard C. Holbrooke Memorial Addresses'. New York, February 18, 2011, http://www.state.gov/secretary/rm/2011/02/156815.htm (accessed April 9, 2012).

CMI. *The Constitution of Afghanistan*. Unofficial translation, 2004, http://www.cmi.no/afghanistan/background/docs/DraftConstitution.pdf (accessed April 9, 2012).

Farmer, Ben. 'US Troops May Stay in Afghanistan until 2024'. *The Daily Telegraph*, August 19, 2011, http://www.telegraph.co.uk/news/worldnews/asia/afghanistan/8712701/US-troops-may-stay-in-Afghanistan-until-2024.html (accessed April 9, 2012).

Goldsmith, A.A. 'Making the World Safe for Partial Democracy? Questioning the Premises of Democracy Promotion'. *International Security* 33, no. 2 (2008): 120–47

Grävingholt, Jorn, Julia Leininger, and Oliver Schlumberger. *The Three Cs of Democracy Promotion Policy: Context, Consistency and Credibility*. Bonn: German Development Institute, 2009, http://www.die-gdi.de/CMS-Homepage/openwebcms3.nsf/%28ynDK_contentByKey%29/ANES-7QAH6E/$FILE/BP%201.2009.pdf (accessed January 10, 2012).

Grimm, Sonja, and Julia Leininger. 'Not All Good Things Go Together: Conflicting Objectives in Democracy Promotion'. *Democratization* 19, no. 3 (2012): 391–414.

Grimm, Sonja, and Wolfgang Merkel. 'War and Democratization: Legality, Legitimacy and Effectiveness'. *Democratization* 15, no. 3 (2008): 457–71

Haugerudbraaten Intern, Henning. 'Peacebuilding: Six Dimensions and Two Concepts'. *African Security Review* 7, no. 6 (1998), http://www.iss.co.za/pubs/ASR/7No6/Peacebuilding.html (accessed April 9, 2012).

Hill, Matthew A. 'International Actors and Democratisation: Can USAID Deliver a Democratic Culture to Afghanistan?' *Journal of International Relations* 24, no. 2 (2010): 155–74

Hunt Alternatives Fund. *The Institute for Inclusive Security*, http://www.huntalternatives.org/pages/7_the_institute_for_inclusive_security.cfm (accessed April 9, 2012).

Jarstad, Anna K., and Timothy D. Sisk, eds. *From War to Democracy*. Cambridge: Cambridge University Press, 2008

Krasner, Stephen D. 'Building Democracy After Conflict: The Case for Shared Sovereignty'. *Journal of Democracy* 16, no. 1 (2005): 69–83

Licklider, Roy. 'Comparative Studies of Long Wars'. In *Grasping the Nettle: Analysing Cases of Intractable Conflict*, ed. C.A. Crocker, F.O. Hampson, and P. Aall, 33–46. Washington, DC: USIP, 2005

Newman, Edward, and Roland Rich, eds. *The UN Role in Promoting Democracy: Between Ideals and Reality*. Tokyo: United Nations University Press, 2004

Nixon, Hamish. 'Achieving Durable Peace: Afghan Perspectives on a Peace Process'. Oslo: Peace Research Institute, 2011, http://www.humansecuritygateway.com/documents/USIPPRIO_AchievingDurablePeace.pdf (accessed April 9, 2012).

Paris, Roland. 'International Peacebuilding and the "Mission Civilisatrice"'. *Review of International Studies* 28 (2002): 637–56

Paris, Roland, and Timothy D. Sisk. *The Dilemmas of State Building: Confronting the Contradictions of Post War Operations*. London: Routledge, 2009

Partlow, Joshua, and Sayed Salahuddin. 'Karzai to Convene *loya jirga*, a Meeting of Afghans, on U.S. Relationship'. *The Washington Post*, November 13, 2011, http://www.washingtonpost.com/world/middle_east/karzai-to-convene-meeting-of-more-than-2000-afghans-to-debate-us-relationship/2011/11/13/gIQAHteHIN_story.html (accessed April 9, 2012).

Petraeus, David H., and James N. Mattis. *Counterinsurgency*. December 15, 2006, http://www.fas.org/irp/doddir/army/fm3-24fd.pdf (accessed April 9, 2012).

Porter, Gareth. 'Did the Rabbani Hit Really Kill Peace Talks?' *Al-Jazeera*, September 26, 2011, http://english.aljazeera.net/indepth/opinion/2011/09/20119257325871362.html (accessed April 9, 2012).

Rondeaux, Candace. 'Reconsidering Reconciliation in Afghanistan'. *Foreign Policy*, September 21, 2011, http://afpak.foreignpolicy.com/posts/2011/09/21/reconsidering_reconciliation_in_afghanistan (accessed April 9, 2012).

Ruttig, Thomas. 'How Tribal are the Taliban?'. April 2010, http://aan-afghanistan.com/uploads/20100624-TR-ExecSumHowTribalAreTheTaleban.pdf (accessed April 9, 2012).

Sajjad, Tazreena. 'Peace at all Costs? Reintegration and Reconciliation in Afghanistan'. Afghanistan Research and Evaluation Unit, June 2010, http://www.mtnforum.org/sites/default/files/pub/7144.pdf (accessed April 9, 2012).

Scharf, Michael P. 'The Letter of the Law: The Scope of the International Legal Obligation to Prosecute Human Rights Crimes'. *Law and Contemporary Problems* 59 (1996): 41–61.

Sisk, Timothy D. 'Democracy and Conflict Management'. August 2003, http://www.beyondintractability.org/essay/democ_con_manag/?nid=1353 (accessed April 9, 2012).

Suhrke, Astri, Kristian B. Harpviken, and Arne Strand. 'Conflictual Peacebuilding: Afghanistan Two Years After Bonn'. CMI, 2004, http://bora.cmi.no/dspace/bitstream/10202/141/1/Report%20R%202004-4.pdf (accessed January 10, 2012).

Tarzi, Amin. 'Recalibrating the Afghan Reconciliation Program'. *Prism* 1, no. 4 (2010), http://www.ndu.edu/press/lib/images/prism1-4/Prism_67-78_Tarzi.pdf (accessed April 9, 2012).

Theors, Marika, and Mary Kaldor. 'Building Afghan Peace from the Ground Up'. The Century Foundation, 2011, http://tcf.org/publications/2011/2/building-afghan-peace-from-the-ground-up/pdf (accessed April 9, 2012).

UNDP. *APRP-UNDP Support Second Quarter Progress Report 2011*, http://www.undp.org.af/Projects/Report2011/APRP/2011-07-25-%20Second%20Quarter%20Progress%20Report%20of%20APRP.pdf (accessed January 10, 2012).

UNDP. *APRP-UNDP Support Third Quarter Progress Report 2011*, http://www.undp.org.af/Projects/Report2011/APRP/3rdQ/APRP_00076674_QPR_Q3_2011.pdf (accessed April 9, 2012).

USIP. 'Designing a Comprehensive Peace Process for Afghanistan'. *Peaceworks* 75 (2011), http://www.usip.org/files/resources/Designing_a_Comprehensive_Peace_Process_for_Afghanistan.pdf (accessed April 9, 2012).

Von Mettenheim, Kurt, and James M. Malloy, eds. *Deepening Democracy in Latin America*. Pittsburgh, PA: University of Pittsburgh Press, 1998

Wolpe, Howard, and Steve McDonald. 'Democracy and Peace-building: Re-thinking the Conventional Wisdom'. *The Round Table* 97, no. 394 (2008): 137–45

The two sides of functional cooperation with authoritarian regimes: a multi-level perspective on the conflict of objectives between political stability and democratic change

Tina Freyburg[a,b]

[a]Swiss Federal Institute of Technology (ETH) Zurich, Switzerland; [b]European University Institute (EUI) Florence, Italy

> Development cooperation exemplifies the conflict of foreign policy objectives between short-term political stability and long-term democratic change that international actors face in their relations with authoritarian regimes. Previous studies have found empirical evidence for two seemingly contradictory effects of functional cooperation: democratization and the stabilization of authoritarian regimes. Taking EU–Morocco cooperation on water management as an example, this article demonstrates that the effect of functional cooperation depends on the level of policy-making examined. Although cooperation may stabilize an authoritarian regime at the macro-level of the overall polity by contributing to the effective handling of economic and social grievances (output legitimacy), it can also introduce democratic governance at the level of state administration (input legitimacy). Methodologically, the article applies both multivariate regression analyses and qualitative comparative case studies in order to explore data from diverse sources including an original survey of Moroccan state officials, interviews with governmental and non-governmental representatives, and legal texts. The article points to the complexity of the effects that external activities can have on governance in recipient countries, and highlights the importance of improving our knowledge of the more indirect effects of functional cooperation at levels below the overall polity.

Introduction

These days, democracy promotion features high among the policy objectives of international actors. Along with direct strategies in support of democracy (most prominently, political conditionality and assistance of pro-democratic, domestic opponents), the democracy promotion toolbox of international actors also includes more indirect means for transmitting the precepts of democratic governance via functional cooperation.[1] However, conventional wisdom suggests that concerns other than democratic change have greater influence on the use of development cooperation: 'The interest is in short-term stability and predictability; longer-term political reform is supported only insofar as it can be made consistent with such objectives.'[2]

The article analyses the conflict of objectives between democratization and stability inherent in the foreign policies of democracies in relation to authoritarian regimes. This conflict of objectives qualifies as extrinsic conflict, since the goal of democracy promotion (namely, democratization) interferes with another objective of development cooperation: political stability and predictability.[3] On the one hand, democratic countries seek to encourage processes of democratization among their neighbours and in the global community. In line with the democratic peace proposition, they consider well-governed democratic states to be guarantors of long-term political stability, peaceful relations, and economic prosperity.[4] From this perspective, functional cooperation is seen as assisting the modernization of the recipient country, which will prepare the ground for improved economic growth and consequently increase the demand for democratic government.[5] On the other hand, international actors are interested in preventing conflict and maintaining political stability and security, in particular when the regime in question is of geo-political interest, whether because of its geographical proximity, its strategically important location, or its natural resources (such as oil).[6] In the short-run, the path to democracy can be a conflict-ridden process.[7] International actors are thus often unwilling to sacrifice good cooperative relations with agents of (regional) stability for potentially turbulent periods of transformation and the unpredictable results of any subsequent elections. Following this reasoning, functional cooperation can be used to provide a regime with effective solutions for grievances, thus preventing social unrest that might challenge the regime's stability. Reinforcement of the current political status quo contributes to the stabilization rather than the democratization of authoritarian regimes.

This article argues that development cooperation serves both objectives – stability and democratization – at the same time. Scholars and practitioners have asserted a wide variety of views on the effects of functional assistance on a collaborating authoritarian regime.[8] Some see development cooperation as stabilizing authoritarian regimes by providing effective responses to social problems, which generates output legitimacy.[9] Others praise cooperation as contributing to democratic change by implanting democratic procedures in domestic laws and popular attitudes, thereby empowering reform-oriented agents and supporting their calls for increased input legitimacy.[10] This article demonstrates that these two perspectives are not mutually exclusive. Rather, I show that while development cooperation can stabilize authoritarian regimes at the macro-level of the overall polity, it also qualifies as a means of indirect support for democracy if we consider the meso-level of administrative governance or the micro-level of individual state officials. In doing so, I concentrate on short-term effects and, correspondingly, the primary mechanisms that directly link a specific feature of functional cooperation to its effect on policy-making at the respective level. Secondary mechanisms triggered by primary mechanisms are beyond the focus of this study. In brief, this article provides a more comprehensive picture of the consequences of functional cooperation that takes into account effects and trends at multiple levels.

In theoretical terms, I examine three lines of reasoning drawn from different branches of research: the literature on external governance, on foreign aid, and on socialization in international institutions. Each branch suggests an alternative evaluation of functional cooperation as a means of external support of democracy. These views can be empirically illustrated using the example of the European Union's functional cooperation in the field of water management in Morocco. Morocco is widely referred to as a 'liberalized autocracy'[11]; its mixture of 'guided pluralism, controlled elections, and selective repression'[12] has led to a particularly durable and resilient authoritarian regime whose institutions, rules, and logic defy any linear model of democratization, as was evident in the comparatively moderate political protests in Morocco in 2011. Water management is a field that is particularly salient in arid countries like Morocco. Water management is crucial for the preservation of the incumbent regime's authority, as the provision of good quality, because fresh water 'is a basic human need, the foundation of livelihoods, the lifeblood of critical ecosystems, a cultural symbol, and a marketable commodity'.[13] For the same reasons, the field of water management also attracts a multitude of external donors. The European Union (EU) and its water framework directives have played a particularly important role in the modernization of water management in the Mediterranean countries of North Africa and the Middle East.[14] Given the field's high degree of institutionalization and relevance, cooperation on water issues can be expected to influence policy-making at all three levels of state institutions: polity, administration, and the attitudes of individual state officials.

This article first outlines various theoretical perspectives, identifying mechanisms and deriving expectations with regard to the effect of functional cooperation on policy-making in authoritarian regimes at multiple levels. The second section describes the methodological approach, which is based on a qualitative case study of functional cooperation in the field of water management in Morocco, drawing upon document analysis, semi-structured interviews with European Commission officials and non-governmental and governmental actors (specialists in the field of water management), and original data from a survey of the attitudes of Moroccan state officials towards democratic governance.[15] Empirical evidence for the arguments is provided in the third section. The concluding section reflects on possible dynamics in which the effects of functional cooperation may ultimately contribute to regime change, and explains the limitations of the study.

Functional cooperation and the legitimacy of political regimes: the theoretical argument

The two trends in the political development of regimes examined in this article, democratization and stabilization, are ultimately determined by whether and on what basis the political regime and public policy-making is accepted by the citizens of a nation. Public policy-making is most commonly defined as the making of binding decisions and actions for a society, notably laws and decrees.[16] Binding rules can be made either by exercising coercion or through governance. According to Max Weber, power – which he narrowly defines as coercion[17] – means 'every chance within a social relationship to assert one's will even against opposition'.[18] In contrast, governance presumes a legitimacy that exists when the governed people accept the governing regime and are willing to voluntarily adhere to its decisions, even if these are against their original interests. Political regimes that consider the use of coercion and costly state repression as inadequate means of enforcing and maintaining order rely on legitimate governance.

Legitimacy can be generated from a number of sources, including religion, charismatic leadership, tribal traditions, democratic procedures, and the guarantee of general welfare and protection to the governed.[19] Fritz Scharpf suggests that this wide variety of sources can be categorized by the heuristic device of input and output legitimation.[20] *Output legitimacy* refers to 'governance for the people' (to paraphrase Abraham Lincoln) and thus to the substantive performance of the regime with regard to problem-solving or effectiveness in governing. Political decisions are seen as legitimate if they effectively promote the common well-being (predominantly in terms of the provision of welfare and material goods) and personal security.[21] In contrast, *input legitimacy* ('governance by the people') is derived from the participatory nature of the decision-making process. In established democracies, input legitimacy refers to the involvement of a plurality of non-state actors and the consideration of their views in policy-making, even when these views challenge the regime's preferred policy.[22] It further implies that political decisions can be traced back to public consent. However, public participation in authoritarian regimes is generally either 'ceremonial'[23] or limited to some consultative measures at the local level.[24] As such, consultations are subordinate to authoritarian rulings; they are *per definition* deficient, even when they involve the existence of political parties or the possibility of 'competitive' institutions at the sub-national level.

Input and output legitimacy are both seen as preconditions for political stability, not only for advanced capitalist democracies but also for authoritarian regimes.[25] Hence, by contributing to the legitimacy of political regimes, development cooperation may reinforce rather than alter the political institutions of non-democratic states ('amplification effect').[26] However, this observation neglects the more indirect and subtle effects yielded at levels below the overall polity. Implementation of an approach that disentangles mechanisms and effects at different levels of policy-making allows me to demonstrate that the impact of development cooperation on political institutions in authoritarian regimes is more ambiguous, encompassing both democratization and stabilization. This approach is in line with recent calls for more comprehensive evaluation of projects in development cooperation.[27] Table 1 juxtaposes the impact of functional cooperation on the legitimacy of policy-making in authoritarian regimes from the perspective of three different branches of research: international socialization, external governance, and foreign aid. In focusing on different levels and identifying different mechanisms that link cooperation and policy-making in authoritarian regimes, researchers in these three fields have developed alternative theories regarding the effects of functional cooperation.

The ultimate target *level* of the promotion of external democracy is the polity: that is, the political institutions in which the 'binding decisions for society' are made and their legitimation through democratic procedures.[28] However, the processes of transformation that take place at lower levels of the political system are also important in order to facilitate fruitful and sustainable democratic reforms at the polity level. For instance, political transformation requires administrative staff familiar with democratic modes of governance. Otherwise, processes of democratization run the risk of resulting in an 'enlightened dictatorship' that circumvents rather than allows effective democratic control by the citizens; in such circumstances, specific classes or oligarchies control political power and sustain ineffective, corrupt regimes.[29] Drawing on this reasoning, I apply a broad understanding of democracy promotion that encompasses subtle processes of democratic change, notably processes at the meso-level of administrative governance and at the micro-level of individual attitudes toward democratic governance. To this end, I measure the effect of functional cooperation on political regime development at these different levels. At the macro-level of the polity, functional cooperation can influence how the system is managed to maintain political order and stability. At the meso-level of administrative governance, functional cooperation might leave imprints in domestic law codes and administrative practices. Finally, at the micro-level of individuals, it might shape the opinions of administrative staff involved in cooperation activities.

Table 1. Theoretical approaches regarding the effect of functional cooperation on authoritarian regimes.

	International socialization	External governance	Foreign aid
Level	Micro-level of individual state officials' attitudes	Meso-level of administrative governance	Macro-level of regime performance
Mechanism	Socialization	Legislation	Problem–solution
Effect	Attitude change toward democratic decision-making	Adoption and application of democratic governance	Stabilization of authoritarian rule

Depending on the target level, functional cooperation can trigger different *mechanisms*. If one is interested in effects at the micro-level of attitudes, the proposed mechanism is socialization. In this article, socialization is understood as a change in attitude toward favouring democratic governance as a consequence of participation in activities of cooperation. Legislation refers to the formal adoption of the international actors' legal standards of administrative governance by the recipient country and ultimately their application in day-to-day practice. The third mechanism, problem–solution, is about the provision of effective responses to social and economic grievances that are perceived as threats to the regime's stability. Cooperation can thus unleash the potential for subtle processes capable of altering political institutions that are initially quite autonomous from regime-level changes.

The most basic distinction regarding the *effect* of functional cooperation on the political development of a regime is the democratization versus the stabilization of the authoritarian regime. Functional cooperation contributes to the stability of authoritarian rule if it enables the incumbent political elite to effectively deal with social and economic grievances. In contrast, cooperation contributes to democratization if it fosters the spread of democratic norms and practices, thus challenging the prevailing authoritarian rule. However, it is perfectly conceivable that functional cooperation could actually produce the reverse of what is indicated in Table 1. As an example, the provision of solutions to policy problems from the outside may de-stabilize a regime if it is perceived that the incumbent political elite are dependent on external support in order to produce effective responses to current challenges. Furthermore, if state officials socialized in democratic governance actually begin applying participatory principles in day-to-day administrative governance, citizens may be satisfied with these sub-level opportunities to shape policy and thus abstain from demanding overall regime change. These examples illustrate the distinction between short- and long-term effects and the probability of subsequent effects at other levels.

Theoretical approaches to the effect of functional cooperation on authoritarian regimes

The three theoretical approaches examined – socialization, external governance, and foreign aid – each provide interesting insights into the potential effects functional cooperation can have on the legitimacy of policy-making in authoritarian regimes. While the external governance approach is based on the EU's relations with its neighbours, it is closely linked to the broader literature on (the diffusion of) regulatory governance and legalization in world politics.[30] Thus, in principle, all three approaches are applicable to a wide range of state actors and international organizations, including the EU. In general, studies on the promotion of democracy evaluate external attempts to promote democratic change in terms of their effectiveness in supporting processes of democratization at the macro-level of the polity. Consequently, this section starts with a presentation of the macro-level argument, citing studies on foreign aid and the resilience of authoritarianism, and then extends the analysis to the meso- and micro-levels.

Foreign aid, problem-solution, and regime stabilization at the macro-level

Given the durability of authoritarian rule, in particular in East Asia and the Middle East, scholars have started to explore the determinants of 'authoritarian consolidation'.[31] The capacity to maintain authoritarian rule without resorting to coercion and with a certain degree of responsiveness to domestic problems is considered key to the survival of non-democratic regimes. Functional cooperation is expected to affect the political development of such regimes by improving regime performance, which is understood as the ability to create effective solutions to challenges. This is based on the observation that authoritarian rulers are particularly interested in addressing social and economic grievances, as these are perceived as potential threats to the regime's stability. In addition, the provision of effective policy solutions and assistance in their implementation generates fiscal latitude for the incumbent government; this surplus could then be used for the purposes of strengthening the existing regime, by financing patronage-based networks or increasing the military budget, for example ('fungibility problem').[32] Problem-specific functional cooperation is thus considered to contribute to the stabilization of authoritarian regimes, as it helps the ruling political elite to remain in power by generating output legitimacy and preserving regime stability.[33]

External governance, legal approximation, and democratic governance at the meso-level

In light of the perceived shortcomings of straightforward strategies for the promotion of democracy in the stable (semi-)authoritarian regimes among the EU's neighbours, scholars have developed a new model that complements traditional policies based on conditionality ('leverage') and civil society support ('linkage').[34] This new governance model draws on the EU's policy goal of third-country approximation to the EU *acquis*. The model takes into account that in addition to its substantial body of rules for regulating public policy, the *acquis* incorporates procedural rules on democratic governance that are also transferred to associated third states. This transfer can be imagined as a two-step process, starting with the formal adoption of legislation and followed by application in administrative practices.[35] In this respect, cooperation is not only about acquiring policy solutions and enacting legal requirements, but also involves the introduction of new patterns of governance. Significantly, in this instance, the promotion of democratic governance does not target institutions and processes at the level of the polity (for example, in terms of free and fair elections and parliamentary checks on government authority), but instead refers to processes of public participation at the sectoral level of state administration.[36] Democratic modes of governance entail changes in the culture and the rules and practices of administrative offices in authoritarian regimes; they call for the involvement of the public in the process of making binding decisions, with the aim of ensuring that citizens' interests and concerns will be taken into consideration.[37] In this vein, functional cooperation might yield successful processes of democratization at the meso-level of sectoral policy-making by introducing the principle of input legitimacy in national legislation and providing bureaucratic support for its actual implementation in practice.

International socialization, trans-governmental networks, and democratic attitudes at the micro-level

The third approach endorses the idea that an international institution can constitute a 'site of socialization' in which participating actors internalize transnational norms and values as a consequence of social interaction and cooperation.[38] Trans-governmental networks that implement functional cooperation represent a site of socialization, as they bring together specialists from the administrations of both democratic donor countries and non-democratic recipient countries to implement policy solutions and codify legal requirements that approximate the legal and administrative standards in the recipient countries to those of the donor countries. Since the external specialists have been professionally socialized in a democratic polity, they apply and impart democratic governance when serving as experts abroad. As part of their advisory services they might also address issues suppressed in domestic discourse, such as the participation of non-state actors in administrative decision-making and the availability of information to the public. In this way, their counterparts could possibly become familiarized with practices of administrative governance in democracies and be introduced to democratic principles of governance unknown under authoritarian rule. The information made available through trans-governmental networks can allow recipient country administrators to compare democratic modes of governance with domestic authoritarian rule. While participating in the activities of these networks, state officials employed in a non-democratic polity may thus become socialized into democratic principles of decision-making.[39] Consequently, functional cooperation is expected to anchor the principle of input legitimacy in the minds of state officials employed in authoritarian regimes.

Assessing the effect of functional cooperation at multiple levels: methodological approaches

The three different theoretical perspectives presented above call for three different methodological approaches. I have therefore opted for a multi-method design that allows data collection and analysis to be tailored to a specific theoretical focus and analytical level. Although there have been previous studies on the connection between effective water management in arid regions and the political stability of the respective regimes,[40] the effects of functional cooperation at the meso-level of administrative decision-making and the micro-level of individual state officials have so far been neglected in the literature on democracy support. This article presents recent research on the subject, embedding it in the broader context of the effects of functional cooperation on an authoritarian regime's chances of survival. Since the analyses of effects at the meso- and micro-levels are based on original data, the methodological approaches implemented are outlined in more detail.

Functional cooperation and administrative governance

The analysis of the effect of functional cooperation on policy-making at the meso-level is based on a qualitative case study that combines a comparative analysis of EU and Moroccan law codes with information obtained in interviews. The promotion of democratic environmental governance ranks high in the EU's priorities regarding relations with its neighbours,[41] and this is emphasized in all finished Action Plans. With regard to the EU environmental *acquis*, the principles of democratic governance are described in Directive 2003/4/EC (concerning access to environmental information), Directive 2003/35/EC (providing for public participation in certain cases, amending the Environmental Impact Assessment Directive 1985/337/EEC, the IPPC Directive concerning integrated pollution prevention, and control 1996/61/EC), and Regulation (EC) 1367/2006 (applying norms of democratic environmental governance to the EU's institutions and bodies), among other directives. Together with the Water Framework Directive 2000/60/EC which similarly includes provisions of participatory governance, these directives serve as points of reference in professional exchanges on water governance between European experts and their Moroccan counterparts.[42] To investigate the effects of functional cooperation in the field of water management at the meso-level, semi-structured interviews conducted in 2007 and 2008 with European Commission officials and non-governmental and governmental actors in Brussels and Rabat (specialists in the field of water management) served two purposes. First, in order to learn whether the existence of elements of democratic governance can be traced back to EU functional cooperation, I interviewed 22 Commission officials and Moroccan bureaucrats who had been involved in the modification of the Moroccan water laws. Second, in order to measure the actual use of democratic methods, I asked rule addressees – specifically, environmental activists, journalists, and scientists – to what extent the provisions of democratic governance are applied in practice.

Functional cooperation and the attitudes of individual state officials

Data for the micro-level analysis came from an original survey I conducted of 58 state officials in Morocco in the summer of 2008. For the survey, I constructed a closed-ended questionnaire on administrative rules and practices in public administration. The respondents were selected by a theoretically controlled cluster sampling, with equal representation from two groups of officials. The first group consisted of officials who had participated in a specific EU policy project on the environment, namely the Twinning Project 'Coordinated Management of the Environment and the Harmonization of National Environmental Legislation' (MA04/AA/EN03), which was conducted from December 2005 to November 2007 by the Italian Ministry for the Environment, Land and Sea, together with the Austrian Environment Agency ($N = 32$). The second group included officials who were employed in a thematically related department in ministries not targeted by a Twinning project ($N = 26$). Twinning projects as facilitators of inter-administrative cooperation seek to make the administrative expertise and technical know-how of practitioners from EU member states available to public administrations in third countries, usually with a focus on a specific policy issue. Initially created for the countries of Eastern Europe during the EU 2004 enlargement, twinning has been offered to the EU's neighbours to the south since 2004. Twinning projects involve the secondment of European experts to partner countries for up to 33 months; not only does this long-term exposure help to build relationships based on trust and mutual understanding, but it can also be expected to familiarize state officials with democratic administrative practices.

Personal on-site distribution of the questionnaire encouraged a response rate of approximately 96%. Due to the persuasive approach and because respondents were given the opportunity to leave inconvenient questions blank, outright refusal to participate was almost non-existent; biases stemming from the complete refusal to respond by specific groups of officials can thus be discounted. Guarantees of anonymity and strict confidentiality in the use of the data further reduced the risk of response bias. Respondents could choose the language of communication (French or Arabic); only 9% chose to respond in Arabic.[43] The data were analysed by application of multiple regression analyses that regressed the attitudes of individual state officials toward democratic governance on participation in the twinning project, controlling for alternative transnational influences (specifically, international education and foreign media usage) and the socio-demographic factors of age and gender. The analyses were performed with a maximum likelihood parameter estimator (MLMV) that provided estimates with standard errors and mean- and variance-adjusted χ-square test statistics because of its robustness to non-normality of continuous data.[44]

EU–Morocco cooperation on water management: empirical case study

Water governance is a suitable policy field for investigation of the impact that EU functional cooperation might have on the legitimacy of policy-making at various levels in Morocco. Water is a 'hot issue', not only in connection with the pollution of the Mediterranean Sea, the water basin the North African countries share with their European partners, but more significantly because of its scarcity.[45] Morocco is among the countries that have recently been entered on the water-deficit list, meaning that its population experiences water scarcity in a physical sense, negatively affecting food production and productive water use.[46]

Considering the direct implications for human health, ecosystems, and the socio-economic development of both water quality and supply,[47] water resource management is crucial for the maintenance of governmental regimes. There was a reason why former World Bank Vice President Ismail Serageldin famously prophesized that whereas many of the wars in the twentieth century were fought over oil, 'wars of the next generation will be over water'.[48] However, while water scarcity is rather unlikely to trigger global and regional conflicts,[49] it is central for state–society relations. Water is generally expected to be provided by the state, and as such it is the subject of local conflicts worldwide. The Moroccan political elite are aware of the need for a change in policy that will prioritize efficient and sustainable water management. For example, in his 2001 speech to the Higher Council of Water and Climate, Morocco's King Mohamed VI declared that 'the time has come for us to radically change our perceptions and our attitudes towards water through managing the demand for this resource and the rationalisation of its consumption'.[50] To this end, the Moroccan government has requested functional cooperation with external experts on water management.[51]

Cooperation between the EU and its southern neighbours in the field of environmental concerns and water management in particular has 'both intensified and encompassed a structured political process engaging all countries as key factors in tackling the increasing economic, environmental, and security challenges as well as the implementation of concrete projects'.[52] In comparison to other environmental issues, the EU has been especially involved in cooperation concerning water management. In recognition of the political and economic importance of water, in March 2011, the European Commission launched the new regional programme 'Sustainable Water Integrated Management' (SWIM), to be implemented under the European Neighbourhood and Partnership Instrument (ENPI). This project aims to actively promote the extensive dissemination of sustainable water management policies and practices. It complements or replaces existing regional programmes, including the Short and Medium-term Priority Environmental Action Programme (SMAP) in the framework of the Euro-Mediterranean Partnership, the transnational 'LIFE'-third countries programme established by the Sixth Environmental Action Programme,[53] and multilateral platforms such as the Mediterranean component of the EU Water Initiative (EUWI), among others. In addition, the ENPI has introduced new instruments of bilateral administrative interchange, notably the short-term Technical Assistance and Information Exchange Programme (TAIEX), by providing targeted expert assistance, and long-term twinning programmes for cooperation on specific policy issues between sub-units of public administration. In the following section I empirically illustrate the impact that functional cooperation on water management has had on the legitimacy of policy-making in Morocco at three levels: the macro-level of the regime, the meso-level of state administration, and the micro-level of individual state officials. As will be demonstrated, the conflict of objectives between political stability and democratic change inherent in functional cooperation with authoritarian regimes is multifaceted and allows no simple or unambiguous answers.

The macro-level of the regime

Mass (youth) unemployment, lack of prospects for the future, poverty, repression, and injustice are widely given as explanations for the recent political upheavals in the Arab world. A less commonly recognized reason for the revolts is the increase in food prices that can be traced back to water scarcity.[54] Structural problems, including the regional water crisis together with demographic pressures and climate change, are 'political dynamite' and, as such, are politically destabilizing.[55] 'Water is a fundamental part of the social contract' in the authoritarian Arab regimes, where 'along with subsidized food and fuel, governments provide cheap or even free water in order to ensure the consent of the governed.'[56] If delivery of these subsidized commodities is no longer maintained, political instability can follow. However, some countries perform better in water management than others, and Morocco is a 'champion' in the Middle East and North African region in this regard.[57] Although Morocco is one of the poorer countries in the region – its per capita gross national income is less than half that of Tunisia[58] – in terms of political upheaval, Morocco appears to be among the region's most stable countries.[59]

According to the World Bank, Morocco is 'on track to exceed the targets for water and sanitation services contained in the Millennium Development Goals'.[60] The country has increased urban and rural water supply and sanitation infrastructure programmes, allocating up to 25% of its public expenditures for water services in 2009. As a result, access to potable water increased from 50% of the Moroccan population in 2004 to 87% in 2009. While earlier policy reforms can be explained by religious and historical influences (for example, colonial requirements), recent reforms have predominantly been driven by social, economic, and political factors.[61] Foreign aid ranks high among these political considerations, as it allows the incumbent government to efficiently and effectively address pressures for reform from below. Almost all of Morocco's development partners undertake programmes in the sector of water management, and the European Union is particularly active in this field. In December 2001, for instance, the European Commission approved a €120 million aid package targeted at improving the efficiency of water use, in particular for agriculture.[62] With the help of foreign actors, the Moroccan government has managed to establish a water strategy that seems to be effectively dealing with the problem of water scarcity. It would be an exaggeration to claim that environmental cooperation was the only reason underlying Morocco's stability. The point here is that at the macro-level, functional cooperation can *contribute* to the generation of output legitimacy and thus to the stabilization of the regime.

The meso-level of state administration

At the meso-level of sectoral policy-making, functional cooperation influences domestic law codes and administrative practices by implanting the provisions of participatory governance in national legislation and supporting their implementation. In the EU–Morocco cooperation on water management, administrative structures and procedures were a major part of the discussions in the sub-committee that was charged with the implementation of the ENP Action Plan.[63] The agenda of sub-committee meetings included topics such as the involvement of civil societal actors and local authorities, and the modification and implementation of sectoral legislation, in particular the Law on Water 10-95. The Italian/Austrian–Moroccan twinning project is said to have decisively shaped the current state of the water management in Morocco.[64] The 1995 water law has been complemented by horizontal framework legislation, such as the three adopted or drafted laws, that is, the Law on Environmental Impact Studies 12-03, the Environmental Protection Act of 2003, and the draft Law on Access to Environmental Legislation following the Aarhus Convention. All four legislative texts incorporate provisions of democratic environmental governance. The law on environmental protection, for instance, explicitly lists 'good environmental governance' among its objectives: it requires 'participation, information, and determination of responsibilities'.[65] The 1995 water law established the Supreme Council on Water and Climate, a non-permanent consultative institution consisting of scientific experts and association representatives, designed to serve as a platform for the exchange of ideas.[66] Over the last five years, with the establishment of this Council, the creation of water basin agencies – local *'petits parlements de l'eau'*[67] – and the development of contractualization (that is, the notion of a contract as a legal tool to formalize reciprocal commitments, firmly embedded in society), Morocco has developed a participatory approach to water management.[68]

Although the EU has been quite successful in inserting participatory provisions of administrative governance in Moroccan environmental legislation, these provisions are hardly applied in administrative practice. The legally created administrative structures are 'empty', and Moroccan environmental legislation is rarely addressed by appropriate implementing decrees. Typically, the Water Council presided over by the Prime Minister does not function properly.[69] For the most part, the participation of non-state actors in environmental decision-making is currently *protocolaire*; that is, representatives are consulted after decisions have been taken.[70] Nevertheless, the codification of these legal structures is crucial in order to prepare 'a solid institutional foundation for promoting an economically responsive, user-oriented and allocation-based water sector'.[71] The fact that participatory governance is guaranteed by Moroccan law not only fosters the activities of international actors (who can refer to the domestically legitimized legal provisions) but also strengthens the standing of domestic non-governmental agents demanding true access to decision-making forums.[72] At the meso-level of state administration, functional cooperation can, thus, lay the legal foundations for democratic administrative decision-making and support *demand* for *its realization*.

The micro-level of attitudes of individual state officials

At the micro-level, participation in activities implementing functional cooperation can shape the attitudes of state officials towards democratic governance. Moroccan state officials involved in the EU's twinning project on the harmonization of national environmental legislation show a significantly more positive attitude toward public participation in decision-making processes than their non-participating colleagues.[73] The twinning project was centred on intensive working partnerships between European and Moroccan bureaucrats on a day-to-day basis for a significant period of time; the project attached particular importance to the establishment of 'procedures concerning access to information and public participation'.[74]

Table 2 presents the descriptive statistics of the responses of Moroccan state officials to four statement items on participatory governance. The items address the involvement of non-state actors in administrative decision-making to different degrees. Item 1 asks whether citizens' interests and concerns should be taken into account before decisions are made, implying that citizens should have the opportunity to express their interests and concerns in the first place. Item 3 goes one step further, postulating that citizens' views should actually shape the decisions made, whereas Item 2 addresses the pre-requisite for any meaningful participation, that is, access to updated information. The questionnaire also includes an item with a negative orientation toward public participation, which expresses an idea that distorts the meaning of democratic governance. For state officials employed in an authoritarian regime that presents itself as 'modern' and 'advanced', agreeing with positively framed democratic items is assumed to be 'easier' and more justifiable than explicitly rejecting their logical opposites (as would be consistent with the prevailing authoritarian culture). The negatively oriented Item 4 reverses the direction of influence – that is, citizens' views should be brought in line with governmental policies rather than shape them – thus reflecting the typically authoritarian assumption of unlimited approval.

Table 2. Descriptive statistics of responses to individual items.

		N	Min.	Max.	Mean	SD
A state official should…						
• take into account the views and concerns of affected citizens before making decisions (item 1).	P	31	4	5	4.81	0.402
	NP	24	1	5	4.21	1.141
• offer updated information on governmental policy (item 2)	P	28	4	5	4.71	0.460
	NP	24	2	5	4.17	1.007
• ensure that citizens' views and concerns have an influence on shaping policies (item 3)	P	29	4	5	4.79	0.412
	NP	25	3	5	4.12	0.833
• always seek to bring the public into accordance with governmental policy (item 4; negative-oriented item)	P	28	1	5	4.29	1.084
	NP	23	1	5	3.57	1.199

Notes: Values range from 1 (non-democratic) to 5 (democratic); answer categories range from 1 (disagree strongly) to 5 (agree strongly), with reversed values for the negatively-oriented item. Min. = Minimum value, Max. = Maximum value, SD = Standard deviation, P = participants in a twinning project, NP = non-participants.

It appears that Moroccan state officials involved with environmental matters generally dislike the idea of their bureaucracy being reduced to a 'service tool' of the political leaders in which 'compliance with orders of the central authority is the mode of operation'. When asked what it takes to be a 'good' civil servant,[75] (almost) 80% of those involved in the twinning projects ('P') strongly agreed that a civil servant should 'take into account the views and concerns of affected citizens before making decisions', 'offer updated information on governmental policy', and 'ensure that the citizens' views and concerns have an influence on shaping policies'. None of the twinning participants disagreed with regard to whether officials should have these qualities; they all claimed to at least 'agree' with the statement items, as indicated by a minimum value of '4'. Their non-participating colleagues ('NP') expressed more diverse attitudes toward public participation in administrative decision-making; the standard deviation in their responses to the individual items ranged from 0.833 to 1.199. Overall, they seemed to agree to a lesser extent that citizens should be involved in administrative decision-making. Moreover, whereas more than 60% of the twinning participants opposed the negatively oriented item, only about 20% of their non-participating colleagues did so. To what extent is this difference in attitude between state officials involved in functional cooperation and their non-participating colleagues statistically significant? A series of t-tests reveals statistically reliable differences between the mean attitudes of twinning participants and non-participants ($\alpha = 0.05$, two-tailed; item 1 $t(27.4) = 2.453$, $p = 0.021$; item 2 $t(31.1) = 2.453$, $p = 0.021$; item 3 $t(34) = 3.672$, $p = 0.001$; item 4 $t(49) = 2.251$, $p = 0.029$).

Can this difference be traced back to participation in twinning activities rather than alternative transnational influences or the individual characteristics of the state officials? I use multiple regression analyses to examine the association of explanatory variables related to characteristics of the state officials and their attitudes toward democratic governance. The analyses were first conducted entering the key variable – participation in a twinning project ('cooperation') – as a dichotomous variable measuring whether the individual state official had been involved in a project or not. Drawing on the literature on transnational influences, I subsequently controlled for the effect of transnational influences other than cooperation, specifically the use of foreign media for political information and time spent abroad in established democracies,[76] and for the effects of the socio-demographic features of age and gender.[77]

The regression results reported in Table 3 support the democratizing potential of functional cooperation. Participation in a twinning project significantly predicts a positive democratic attitude; the coefficient is positive and significant ($\beta = 0.823$, $t(35) = 4.98$, $p \leq 0.001$). Participation in a twinning project alone also explains about one-third of the variance in the attitudes of individual state officials toward democratic governance ($R^2 = 0.314$). At the micro-level, functional cooperation can positively shape the attitudes of state officials toward democratic governance. Hence, principles of democratic governance appear to provide concrete guidelines that local administrations can learn from foreign experts.

Table 3: Estimation results of multiple regression analyses.

	(1)	(2)	(3)	(4)
Cooperation	0.560 (0.100)***	0.823 (0.167)***		
Stay abroad		−0.347 (0.169)*	−0.322 (0.142)*	
Foreign media		−0.242 (0.192)	−0.086 (0.130)	
Gender (1= female)		0.358 (0.210)		0.235 (0.195)
Age		−0.002 (0.018)		−0.013 (0.014)
R^2	.314	0.484	0.100	0.061
AIC	155.044	531.976	190.318	471.438
Log Likelihood	−74.522	−258.988	−91.159	−231.719
N	49	41	42	48

Notes: Multiple regression analyses (MLMV). Regression coefficients are unstandardized; standard errors in parentheses; cases with missing cases deleted listwise; $^*p \leq .05$, $^{**}p \leq .01$, $^{***}p \leq .001$.

Conclusion

In view of the recent political upheavals in the Arab world, Western democracies have been criticized for their support of authoritarian regimes as protection against the potential instability if Islamic extremist gained power. In particular, the EU and its member states have been accused of inappropriate engagement, of having invested billions of euros in the region but only rarely challenged the established authoritarian regimes. In other words, 'Europe' has been criticized for having valued short-term political stability over long-term democratization in an attempt to safeguard security in 'Wider Europe'.[78] The European Neighbourhood Policy (ENP) represents a prominent example of the EU's interest in creating a ring of security and prosperity through functional cooperation with its neighbours. The ENP was launched by the European Commission in order to jointly 'tackle trans-boundary threats – from terrorism to air-borne pollution'.[79] This way, the EU's neighbourhood policy exemplifies the conflict of foreign policy objectives between short-term political stability and long-term democratic change that international actors face in their relations with authoritarian regimes.

This article takes as its starting point the conventional wisdom that functional cooperation with authoritarian regimes helps such regimes to remain in power by contributing to the effective handling of social and economic grievances, and that cooperation consequently helps the stability in the country rather than leading to democratization. This article investigates both the impact of functional cooperation at the macro-level of the overall polity and lower-level dynamics within the state administration. Examining the case of EU–Morocco cooperation on water issues, the multi-level analysis reveals that while external activities contribute to stabilization at the regime level, they also create processes of governance-driven democratization, creating 'democratic enclaves' within the state administration.[80]

To provide a more comprehensive assessment of the importance that functional cooperation can have on the promotion of democracy, it is necessary to carry out systematic comparative analyses that explore the impact of functional cooperation in various policy fields and trace the resultant dynamics over time. On the basis of the above study, the long-term effect of functional cooperation is difficult to predict, because democratic administrative governance may be causally linked to both the deterioration and the persistence of an authoritarian regime. A pessimistic scenario would suggest that democratic practices within state administrations could strengthen authoritarian regimes, as they might give citizens a sense of participation. An optimistic reading, in turn, would predict that a reform-minded bureaucracy might not only signify a problem for the maintenance of an autocratic regime, but could be of primary importance for the establishment of sustainable democratic transformation. In the end, in any political system, it is the administrative staff that is of particular importance in policy-making and policy implementation. Successful democratic reforms ultimately require state officials familiar with democratic modes of governance.

Against the backdrop of this ambiguous phenomenological picture of the potential effects of functional cooperation for political regime development in authoritarian contexts, this article endeavours to encourage future research on the conflict of objectives inherent in development cooperation, which will consider the effects that cooperation with authoritarian regimes may have at different levels and how these effects interact. Finally, this study prepares the foundation for research on the conditions under which governance-driven democratization may contribute to attitude change and ultimately to the dynamics leading to democratic regime change.

Acknowledgements

This article complements research undertaken in the framework of the project entitled 'Promoting Democracy in the EU's Neighbourhood' led by Sandra Lavenex and Frank Schimmelfennig at the Swiss National Centre for Competence in Research (NCCR) 'Challenges to Democracy in the 21st Century'. Financial support from the Swiss National Science Foundation (SNSF) is gratefully acknowledged. I cordially thank Frank Schimmelfennig, Vera van Hüllen, Britta Weiffen, Rebecca Welge, the participants at the author workshop in Zurich (in particular Jörg Faust, Sandra Pogodda, Solveig Richter, Jonas Wolff), my co-editors of this special issue, Julia Leininger and Sonja Grimm, and the *Democratization* editorial team for their valuable suggestions. Moreover, I would like to express my gratitude to the EU officials, representatives of international organizations, and Moroccan officials and civil society activists who provided invaluable information for the empirical study.

Notes

1. Freyburg et al., 'EU Promotion of Democratic Governance'; Lavenex and Schimmelfennig, 'EU Rules'.
2. Youngs, 'Democracy Promotion as External Governance', 900.
3. Spanger and Wolff, 'Universales Ziel'; Grimm and Leininger, 'Not All Good Things'.
4. Russett, *Grasping the Democratic Peace*; Chan, 'In Search of Democratic Peace'; Mansfield, Milner, and Rosendorff, 'Why Democracies Cooperate More'.
5. Knack, 'Foreign Aid'; Lipset, 'Social Prerequisites'.

6. Olsen, 'Promotion of Democracy'; Schlumberger, 'Dancing with Wolves', 39; Faust and Leiderer, 'Zur Effektivität'.
7. Mansfield and Snyder, 'Democratization and the Danger of War'; Cederman, Hug, and Wenger, 'Democratization and War', 510; Cederman Hug, and Krebs, 'Democratization and Civil War', 377.
8. Bueno de Mesquita and Downs, 'Development', 85; Youngs, 'Democracy Promotion as External Governance'.
9. Harders, 'Analyzing Regional Cooperation'; Albrecht and Schlumberger, 'Waiting for Godot'; Schlumberger, 'Dancing with Wolves'.
10. Knack, 'Foreign Aid'; Freyburg et al., 'EU Promotion of Democratic Governance'; Freyburg et al., 'Democracy Promotion through Functional Cooperation?'; Freyburg, 'Transgovernmental Policy Networks'; Casier, 'The EU's Two-track Approach'; but see Youngs, 'Democracy Promotion as External Governance?', for a critical note.
11. Brumberg, 'Democratization in the Arab World?'.
12. Diamond, 'Thinking about Hybrid Regimes'; Levitsky and Way, 'Rise of Competitive Authoritarianism'.
13. Conca, 'New Face of Water Conflict', 1.
14. Sgobbi and Fraviga, 'Governance and Water Management'; Lesser, 'Greening the Mediterranean'.
15. In order to guarantee the anonymity of my interview partners, I refer to information obtained from the interviews by interview codes. EU refers to actors from the European Union, MA to those from Morocco, and IO to representatives of international organizations located in Rabat; see Appendix Table 1.
16. Cf. definition of a political system as characterized by 'interactions through which values are authoritatively allocated for a society', in Easton, 'Analysis of Political Systems', 21.
17. Janoski, *Handbook*.
18. Weber, *Wirtschaft und Gesellschaft*, as translated (and interpreted) by Habermas, 'Hannah Arendt', 74.
19. Weber, *Wirtschaft und Gesellschaft*.
20. Scharpf, *Regieren in Europa*, 16.
21. See, for instance, Beetham and Lord, *Legitimacy*.
22. Friedrich, 'Old Wine in New Bottles', 5; Schmitter, 'Participation in Governance', 56.
23. Verba, 'Democratic Participation', 55–6; Verba, *Small Groups*, 220–1.
24. Göbel and Lambach, 'Accounting for the (In-)Stability', 3; cf. Brumberg, 'Democratization in the Arab World'.
25. Lipset, 'Social Prerequisites'; Gandhi and Przeworski, 'Authoritarian Institutions'; Göbel and Lambach, 'Accounting for the (In-)Stability'; Gilley, 'Democratic Enclaves'; Remmer, 'Sustainability of Political Democracy'; Przeworski et al., 'Democracy and Development'.
26. Morrison, 'Natural Resources', 366; Dutta, Leeson, and Williamson, 'Amplification Effect'.
27. See, for instance, the studies on the micro-macro-paradox in impact research reviewed by Faust and Leiderer, 'Zur Effektivität', 132–3.
28. Easton, 'Analysis of Political Systems', 385.
29. Baker, 'Introduction', 5; Jreisat, 'Arab World'.
30. Greenhill, Mosley, and Prakash, 'Trade-based Diffusion'; Goldstein et al., *Legalization*.
31. Brownlee, 'Explaining Survival'; Gandhi and Przeworski, 'Authoritarian Institutions'; Göbel and Lambach, 'Accounting for the (In-)Stability'; Burnell and Schlumberger, 'Promoting Democracy'.
32. Faust and Leiderer, 'Zur Effektivität', 138; Morrison, 'Natural Resources', 366.

33. Albrecht and Schlumberger, 'Waiting for Godot'; Schlumberger, 'Dancing with Wolves'; Harders, 'Analyzing Regional Cooperation'.
34. Lavenex and Schimmelfennig, 'EU Rules'; Freyburg et al., 'EU Promotion of Democratic Governance'; Freyburg et al., 'Democracy Promotion through Functional Cooperation'.
35. Freyburg et al., 'EU Promotion of Democratic Governance'; Freyburg et al., 'Democracy Promotion through Functional Cooperation'.
36. Freyburg, Skripka, and Wetzel, 'Democracy between the Lines'.
37. Friedrich, 'Old Wine in New Bottles', 5; Schmitter, 'Participation in Governance', 56.
38. Johnston, 'Treating International Institutions'; Checkel, 'International Institutions'.
39. Freyburg, 'Transgovernmental Policy Networks'; Freyburg, 'Demokratisierung durch Zusammenarbeit?'.
40. See, for instance, Braga, 'The Management of Urban Water Conflicts'; Hsu, 'Democratization and Water Management in Taiwan'; Luzi, 'Driving Forces and Patterns of Water Policy Making in Egypt'; Wolf, 'Conflict and Cooperation along International Waterways'.
41. European Commission, 'Wider Europe – Neighbourhood'.
42. European Council, 'Public Access to Environmental Information'; European Council, 'Public Participation'; European Council, 'Aarhus Convention'; European Council, 'Water Policy'.
43. For further details on data collection, see Freyburg, 'Demokratisierung durch Zusammenarbeit?'; Freyburg, 'Transgovernmental Policy Networks'.
44. Brown, *Confirmatory Factor Analysis*, 379; Muthén and Muthén, 'Mplus User's Guide', 426. The MLMV estimation is based on a MLM estimation that corresponds to Satorra-Bentler χ-square statistics.
45. Taleb, 'Water Management', 179.
46. Wallace, 'Agricultural Water Use'; Yang et al., 'Water Resources'.
47. Gleick et al., *The World's Water*.
48. *Financial Times*, August 7, 1995, as quoted in Selby, 'Oil and Water', 201, although the author considers the oil–water analogy to be mistaken and misleading.
49. For the link between water-related cooperation and conflict in the international realm, see, for example, Bernauer and Kalbhenn, 'International Freshwater Resources'; Dinar, *International Water Treaties*.
50. Quote taken from the World Bank's website on Morocco, http://web.worldbank.org/WBSITE/EXTERNAL/COUNTRIES/MENAEXT/MOROCCOEXTN/0,contentMDK:21722173~menuPK:50003484~pagePK:2865066~piPK:2865079~theSitePK:294540,00.html (accessed May 31, 2011).
51. See, for instance, the Twinning Project Fiche, 'Fiche de jumelage institutionnel dans le domaine de l'Environnement dans le cadre du Programme d'Appui à l'Accord d'Association entre l'U.E. et le Maroc', MA04/AA/EE03.
52. European Commission, 'Sustainable Water Integrated Management'. For a more detailed overview of Euro–Mediterranean cooperation in the field of environmental protection, see, for example, Costa, 'Convergence on the Fringe', 150–4.
53. The 'LIFE'-programme is the EU's funding instrument for the environment, for more information please refer to the programme website, http://ec.europa.eu/environment/life/about/index.htm.
54. Vidal, 'Costs of Water Shortage'. See also research on the 'water-food-environment nexus' published by the International Water Management Institute (IWMI), http://www.iwmi.cgiar.org.
55. Vidal, 'What Does the Arab World Do When Its Water Runs Out?'. See also, for example, the Swiss and Swedish government-funded report 'The Blue Peace: Rethinking Middle East Water', http://www.deza.admin.ch/en/Home/News/Close_up?itemID=198455 (accessed May 30, 2011).

56. Alterman and Dziuban, 'Clear Gold', v.
57. Information on Morocco's performance in water management is available at the World Bank's website 'Accountability for Better Water Management Results', http://web.worldbank.org/WBSITE/EXTERNAL/COUNTRIES/MENAEXT/MOROCCOEXTN/0,contentMDK:21722173~menuPK:50003484~pagePK:2865066~piPK:2865079~theSitePK:294540,00.html (accessed May 30, 2011).
58. According to World Bank data, Morocco's gross national income (GNI) per capita in 2008 and 2009 was $2520 and $2770, respectively. It was thus higher than the GNI per capita in Egypt ($1800 and $2070) and Syria ($2150 and $2410) but lower than in Tunisia ($3540 and $3720). Data are given in current US dollars, http://data.worldbank.org/indicator/NY.GNP.PCAP.CD/countries/1W?display=default (accessed May 30, 2011).
59. See, for instance, 'Mapping the Arab World', *The Economist*, February 17, 2011; Stuart Schaar, 'Morocco: Can Dinosaurs Become Butterflies?', *The Independent*, April 6, 2011; 'Morocco – Cosmetic Reform or New Social Contract?', *Democracy Digest*, March 23, 2011.
60. Information is provided at the World Bank's website, 'Morocco: Water Sector Projects', http://web.worldbank.org/WBSITE/EXTERNAL/COUNTRIES/MENAEXT/0,contentMDK:22716336~menuPK:3949143~pagePK:146736~piPK:226340~theSitePK:256299,00.html (accessed May 30, 2011).
61. Doukkali, 'Water Institutional Reforms'.
62. 'EU/Morocco: EURO 120 Million for Integrated Water Management Project', Brussels: European Report, January 9, 2002.
63. Information obtained in interview EU3.
64. Information obtained in interview MA8.
65. Dahir no. 1-03-59 du 10 rabii I 1424 portant promulgation de la loi no. 11-03 relative à la protection et à la mise en valeur de l'environnement, May 12, 2003.
66. Decree on the Composition and Functioning of the Water and Climate Council, 2-96-158, November 20, 1996.
67. Hatimy, 'Loi Sur l'Eau', 107.
68. Agoumi and Debbarh, 'Ressources en Eau', 51; Saleth and Dinar, 'Institutional Changes', 184; Doukkali, 'Water Institutional Reforms', 73.
69. Information obtained in interview MA7; cf. Chaouni, *La Loi sur l'Eau*; Sadeq, *Du Droit de l'Eau*, 138–40.
70. Information obtained in interview MA7.
71. Doukkali, 'Water Institutional Reforms', 87.
72. Information obtained in interviews MA3 and IO1; cf. Freyburg et al., 'Democracy Promotion through Functional Cooperation'.
73. For a more detailed analysis of the attitudes of state officials in Morocco toward democratic governance, see Freyburg, 'Demokratisierung durch Zusammenarbeit?'.
74. European Commission, 'EU/Morocco Action Plan', 36.
75. The original wording of the question states, 'There are different opinions as to what it takes to be a "good" civil servant. To what extent do you personally agree or disagree that a civil servant should have the following qualities?'.
76. Whitehead, 'Three International Dimensions', 6–8; Wejnert, 'Diffusion, Development', 56; Kern and Hainmueller, 'Opium for the Masses'; Atkinson, 'Soft Power'. Officials who spent a considerable time in 'the West' did not report substantially more frequent use of Western media. The two variables are not significantly interrelated (see correlation matrix in Appendix Table 2).
77. For operationalization and summary statistics, see Appendix Table 2 and Appendix Table 3.

78. This criticism is reflected in the scholarly literature, for example, Schmid, 'Use of Conditionality'; Biscop, 'ENP, Security and Democracy'; Youngs, 'Democracy and Security'; Cavatorta et al., 'EU External Policy-making'.
79. European Commission, 'Wider Europe – Neighbourhood', 3.
80. Gilley, 'Democratic Enclaves'.

Notes on contributor

Tina Freyburg is a post-doctoral researcher in European Politics at the Centre of Comparative and International Studies (CIS), ETH Zurich in Switzerland; she is currently at the European University Institute (EUI) Florence in Italy as Max Weber Fellow. Her main research interest is in International and EU Studies. Current research projects focus on the democratizing effect of transgovernmental networks that are created in order to implement international cooperation on transnational policy challenges.

Bibliography

Agoumi, Ali, and Abdelhafid Debbarh. 'Ressources en Eau et Bassins versants du Maroc: 50 Ans de Développement (1955–2005)'. *50 Ans de Développement Humains Perspectives 2025*. 2006. http://www.rdh50.ma/fr/pdf/contributions/GT8-1.pdf(accessed March 10, 2011)

Albrecht, Holger, and Oliver Schlumberger. '"Waiting for Godot": Regime Change Without Democratization in the Middle East'. *International Political Science Review* 25, no. 4 (2004): 371–92.

Alterman, Jon B., and Michael Dziuban. 'Clear Gold: Water as a Strategic Resource in the Middle East'. *Report of the Center for Strategic & International Studies (CSIS) Middle East Program*. Washington, DC, 2010.

Atkinson, Carol. 'Does Soft Power Matter? A Comparative Analysis of Student Exchange Programs 1980–2006'. *Foreign Policy Analysis* 6, no. 1 (2010): 1–22.

Baker, Randall. 'Introduction: Transition and Reform in Post-authoritarian States'. In *Transitions from Authoritarianism: The Role of the Bureaucracy*, ed. Randall Baker, 1–13. London: Praeger, 2002.

Beetham, David, and Christopher Lord. *Legitimacy and the European Union*. London: Longman, 1998.

Bernauer, Thomas, and Anna Kalbhenn. 'The Politics of International Freshwater Resources'. In *The International Studies Encyclopedia*, ed. Robert A. Denemark. Oxford: Blackwell Reference Online, 2009, http://www.isacompendium.com/subscriber/tocnode?id=g9781444336597_chunk_g978144433659716_ss1-13 (accessed March 10, 2011).

Biscop, Sven. 'The ENP, Security and Democracy in the Context of the European Security Strategy'. In *The European Neighbourhood Policy in Perspective: Context, Implementation and Impact*, ed. Richard G. Whitman and Stefan Wolff, 73–88. Houndmills: Palgrave, 2010.

Braga, Benedito P.F. 'The Management of Urban Water Conflicts in the Metropolitican Region of São Paulo'. *Water International* 25, no. 2 (2000): 208–13.

Brown, Timothy A. *Confirmatory Factor Analysis for Applied Research*. New York: Guilford, 2006.

Brownlee, Jason. '... And Yet They Persist: Explaining Survival and Transition in Neopatrimonial Regimes'. *Studies in Comparative International Development* 37, no. 3 (2002): 35–63.

Brumberg, Daniel. 'Democratization in the Arab World? The Trap of Liberalized Autocracy'. *Journal of Democracy* 13, no. 4 (2002): 56–68.

Bueno de Mesquita, Bruce, and George W. Downs. 'Development and Democracy'. *Foreign Affairs* 84, no. 5 (2005): 77–86.

Burnell, Peter, and Oliver Schlumberger. 'Promoting Democracy – Promoting Autocracy?' International Politics and National Political Regimes. *Contemporary Politics* 16, no. 1 (2010): 1–15.

Casier, Tom. 'The EU's Two-track Approach to Democracy Promotion: The Case of Ukraine'. *Democratization* 18, no. 3 (2011): 956–77.

Cavatorta, Francesco, Raj Chari, Sylvia Kritzinger, and Arantza Gomez Arana. 'EU External Policy-making and the Case of Morocco: "Realistically" Dealing with Authoritarianism?'. *European Foreign Affairs Review* 13, no. 3 (2008): 357–76.

Cederman, Lars-Eric, Simon Hug, and Lutz Krebs. 'Democratization and Civil War: Empirical Evidence'. *Journal of Peace Research* 47, no. 4 (2010): 377–94.

Cederman, Lars-Eric, Simon Hug, and Andreas Wenger. 'Democratization and War in Political Science'. *Democratization* 15, no. 3 (2008): 509–24.

Chan, Steve. 'In Search of Democratic Peace: Problems and Promise'. *Mershon International Studies Review* 41, no. 1 (1997): 59–91.

Chaouni, Mohamed. *La Loi sur l'Eau et le Droit à l'Eau. Une Intéerpretation de la Réglementation de l'Eau. A l'Usage des Utilisateurs et des Gestionnaires des Ressources en Eau*. Rabat: El Maârif, 2005.

Checkel, Jeffrey T. 'International Institutions and Socialization in Europe: Introduction and Framework'. *International Organization* 59, no. 4 (2005): 801–26.

Conca, Ken. 'The New Face of Water Conflict'. *Navigating Peace* no. 3, http://www.wilsoncenter.org/topics/pubs/NavigatingPeaceIssue3.pdf (accessed March 10, 2011).

Costa, Oriol. 'Convergence on the Fringe: The Environmental Dimension of Euro-Mediterranean Cooperation'. *Mediterranean Politics* 15, no. 2 (2010): 149–68.

Diamond, Larry. 'Thinking about Hybrid Regimes'. *Journal of Democracy* 13, no. 2 (2002): 21–35.

Dinar, Shlomi. *International Water Treaties: Negotiation and Cooperation along Transboundary Rivers*. New York: Routledge, 2008.

Doukkali, Mohammed Rachid. 'Water Institutional Reforms in Morocco'. *Water Policy* 7, no. 1 (2005): 71–88.

Dutta, Nabamita, Peter T. Leeson, and Claudia R. Williamson. 'The Amplification Effect: Foreign Aid's Impact on Political Institutions'. Mimeo, 2011.

Easton, David. 'An Approach to the Analysis of Political Systems'. *World Politics* 9, no. 3 (1957): 383–400.

European Commission. 'Communication from the Commission to the Council and the European Parliament: Wider Europe – Neighbourhood: A New Framework for Relations with our Eastern and Southern Neighbours'. COM(2003)104 final, March 11, 2003.

European Commission. 'Sustainable Water Integrated Management (SWIM) – Demonstration Projects. Call for Proposals. EuropeAid/131046/C//ACT/Multi'. http://eeas.europa.eu/delegations/morocco/funding_opportunities/grants/index_fr.htm (accessed May 24, 2011).

European Commission. 'EU/Morocco Action Plan, Annex to Proposal for a Council Decision on the Position to be Adopted by the European Community and its Member States [...] on the Implementation of the EU–Morocco Action Plan'. COM(2004) 788 final, December 9, 2004.

European Council. 'Directive 2000/60/EC of the European Parliament and of the Council of 23 October 2000 Establishing a Framework for Community Action in the Field of Water Policy'. *Official Journal of the European Communities* L327: 1–72.

European Council. 'Directive 2003/4/EC of the European Parliament and of the Council of 28 January 2003 on Public Access to Environmental Information and Repealing Council Directive 90/313/EEC'. *Official Journal of the European Communities* L41: 26–32.

European Council. 'Directive 2003/35/EC of the European Parliament and of the Council of 26 May 2003 Providing for Public Participation in Respect of the Drawing up of Certain Plans and Programmes Relating to the Environment and Amending with Regard to Public Participation and Access to Justice Council Directives 85/337/EEC and 96/61/EC'. *Official Journal of the European Communities* L156: 17–24.

European Council. 'Regulation (EC) No 1367/2006 of the European Parliament and of the Council of 6 September 2006 on the Application of the Provisions of the Aarhus Convention on Access to Information, Public Participation in Decision-making and Access to Justice in Environmental Matters to Community Institutions and Bodies'. *Official Journal of the European Communities* L264: 13–19.

Faust, Jörg, and Stefan Leiderer. 'Zur Effektivität und politischen Ökonomie der Entwicklungszusammenarbeit'. *PVS Politische Vierteljahresschrift* 49, no. 1(2008): 129–52.

Freyburg, Tina. 'Demokratisierung durch Zusammenarbeit? Funktionale Kooperation mit autoritären Regimen und Sozialisation in demokratischem Regieren'. *Zeitschrift für Internationale Beziehungen* 18, no. 1 (2011): 5–46.

Freyburg, Tina. 'Transgovernmental Policy Networks as Catalysts for Democratic Change? EU Functional Cooperation and Socialization into Democratic Governance'. *Democratization* 18, no. 4 (2011): 1001–25.

Freyburg, Tina, Sandra Lavenex, Frank Schimmelfennig, Tatiana Skripka, and Anne Wetzel. 'EU Promotion of Democratic Governance in the Neighbourhood'. *Journal of European Public Policy* 16, no. 6 (2009): 916–34.

Freyburg, Tina, Sandra Lavenex, Frank Schimmelfennig, and Anne Wetzel. 'Democracy Promotion through Functional Cooperation? The Case of the European Neighbourhood Policy'. *Democratization* 18, no. 4 (2011): 1026–54.

Freyburg, Tina, Tatiana Skripka, and Anne Wetzel. 'Democracy between the Lines? EU Promotion of Democratic Governance via Sector-specific Co-operation'. NCCR Democracy Working Paper 5. National Centre of Competence in Research (NCCR) Challenges to Democracy in the 21st Century, University of Zurich, 2007. Available from: http://www.nccr-democracy.uzh.ch/publications/workingpaper/pdf/WP5.pdf (accessed April 10).

Friedrich, Dawid. 'Old Wine in New Bottles? The Actual and Potential Contribution of Civil Society Organisations to Democratic Governance in Europe'. RECON Online Working Paper 8. University of Oslo 2007. Centre for European Studies, University of Oslo. Available from: http://www.reconproject.eu/main.php/RECON_wp_0708.pdf?fileitem=5456965 (accessed April 10).

Gandhi, Jennifer, and Adam Przeworski. 'Authoritarian Institutions and the Survival of Autocrats'. *Comparative Political Studies* 40, no. 11 (2007): 1279–301.

Gilley, Bruce. 'Democratic Enclaves in Authoritarian Regimes'. *Democratization* 17, no. 3 (2010): 389–415.

Gleick, Peter H., Heather Cooley, David Katz, Emily Lee, Jason Morrison, Meena Palaniappan, Andrea Samulon, and Gary H. Wolff, eds. *The World's Water, 2006–2007: The Biennial Report on Freshwater Resources*. Washington, DC: Island Press, 2006.

Göbel, Christian, and Daniel Lambach. 'Accounting for the (In-)Stability of Authoritarian Regimes: Evidence from East Asia and Sub-saharan Africa'. Mimeo, 2011.

Goldstein, Judith, Miles Kahler, Robert O. Keohane, and Anne-Marie Slaughter, eds. *Legalization and World Politics*. Cambridge: MIT Press, 2001.

Greenhill, Brian, Layna Mosley, and Aseem Prakash. 'Trade-based Diffusion of Labor Rights: A Panel Study, 1986–2002'. *American Political Science Review* 102, no. 4 (2009): 669–89.

Grimm, Sonja, and Julia Leininger. 'Not All Good Things Go Together: Conflicting Objectives in Democracy Promotion'. Democratization 19, no. 3 (2012): 391–414.
Habermas, Jürgen. 'Hannah Arendt's Communications Concept of Power'. In *Power*, ed. Steven Lukes, 75–89. New York: New York University Press, 1986.
Harders, Cilja. 'Analyzing Regional Cooperation after September 11, 2001: The Emergence of a New Regional Order in the Arab World'. In *Beyond Regionalism? Regional Cooperation, Regionalism and Regionalization in the Middle East*, ed. Cilja Harders and Matteo Legrenzi, 33–50. Aldershot: Ashgate, 2008.
Hatimy, Farid. 'Loi Sur l'Eau: Aspects Innovants et Acteurs Intervenants'. *Revue Marocaine d'Administration Locale et de Développement* no. 37 (2001): 69–112.
Hsu, Shu-Hsiang. 'Democratization and Water Management in Taiwan'. *Water International* 29, no. 1 (2004): 61–9.
Janoski, Thomas. *Handbook of Political Sociology: States, Civil Societies, and Globalization*. Cambridge: Cambridge University Press, 2005.
Johnston, Alaistair Iain. 'Treating International Institutions as Social Environments'. *International Studies Quarterly* 45, no. 4 (2001): 487–515.
Jreisat, Jamil E. 'The Arab World. Reform or Stalemate'. *Journal of Asian and African Studies* 41, nos 5–6 (2006): 411–37.
Kern, Holger Lutz, and Jens Hainmueller. 'Opium for the Masses: How Foreign Media Can Stabilize Authoritarian Regimes'. *Political Analysis* 17, no. 4 (2009): 377–99.
Knack, Stephen. 'Does Foreign Aid Promote Democracy?'. *International Studies Quarterly* 48, no.1 (2004): 251–66.
Lavenex, Sandra, and Frank Schimmelfennig. 'EU Rules beyond EU Borders: Theorizing External Governance in European Politics'. *Journal of European Public Policy* 16, no. 6 (2009): 791–812.
Lesser, Pamela. 'Greening the Mediterranean: Europe's Environmental Policy toward Mediterranean Neighbors'. *Mediterranean Quarterly* 20, no. 2 (2009): 26–39.
Levitsky, Stephen, and Lucan A. Way. 'The Rise of Competitive Authoritarianism'. *Journal of Democracy* 13, no. 2 (2002): 51–65.
Lipset, Seymour Martin. 'The Social Prerequisites of Democracy Revisited'. *American Sociological Review* 59, no. 1 (2004): 1–22.
Luzi, Samuel. 'Driving Forces and Patterns of Water Policy Making in Egypt'. *Water Policy* 12, no. 1 (2010): 92–113.
Mansfield, Edward D., Helen V. Milner, and B. Peter Rosendorff. 'Why Democracies Cooperate More: Electoral Control and International Trade Agreements'. *International Organization* 56, no. 3 (2002): 477–513.
Mansfield, Edward D., and Jack Snyder. 'Democratization and the Danger of War'. *International Security* 20, no. 1 (1995): 5–38.
Morrison, Kevin M. 'Natural Resources, Aid, and Democratization: A Best-case Scenario'. *Public Choice* 131, no. 3 (2007): 365–86.
Muthén, Linda K. and Bengt O. Muthén. *Mplus User's Guide*, 4th ed. Los Angeles, CA: Muthén and Muthén, 2006.
Olsen, Gorm R. 'Promotion of Democracy as Foreign Policy Instrument of "Europe": Limits to International Idealism'. *Democratization* 7, no. 2 (2002): 142–67.
Przeworski, Adam, Michael E. Alvarez, José A. Cheibub, and Fernando Limongi. *Democracy and Development: Political Institutions and Material Well-being in the World, 1950–1990*. Cambridge: Cambridge University Press, 2000.
Remmer, Karen L. 'The Sustainability of Political Democracy'. *Comparative Political Studies* 29, no. 6 (1996): 611–34.
Russett, Bruce. *Grasping the Democratic Peace: Principles for a Post-Cold War World*. Princeton, NJ: Princeton University Press, 1993.

Sadeq, Houria Tazi. *Du Droit de l'Eau au Droit à l'Eau au Maroc et Ailleurs*. Casablanca: EDDIF, 2006.
Saleth, R. Maria, and Ariel Dinar. 'Institutional Changes in Global Water Sector: Trends, Patterns, and Implications'. *Water Policy* 2, no. 3 (2000): 175–99.
Scharpf, Fritz W. *Regieren in Europa. Effektiv und Demokratisch?* Frankfurt/Main: Campus, 1999.
Schlumberger, Oliver. 'Dancing with Wolves: Dilemmas of Democracy Promotion in Authoritarian Contexts'. In *Democratization and Development: New Political Strategies for the Middle East*, ed. Dieter Jung, 33–60. New York: Palgrave Macmillan, 2006.
Schmid, Dorothée. 'The Use of Conditionality in Support of Political, Economic and Social Rights: Unveiling the Euro–Mediterranean Partnership's True Hierarchy of Objectives'. *Mediterranean Politics* 9, no. 3 (2004): 369–421.
Schmitter, Philippe C. 'Participation in Governance Arrangements: Is There a Reason to Expect it Will Achieve "Sustainable and Innovative Policies in a Multi-level Context"?'. In *Participatory Governance: Political and Societal Implications*, ed. Jürgen R. Grote and Bernard Gbikpi, 51–69. Opladen: Leske+Budrich, 2002.
Selby, Jan. 'Oil and Water: The Contrasting Anatomies of Resource Conflicts'. *Government and Opposition* 40, no. 2 (2005): 200–24.
Sgobbi, Alessandra, and Gregorio Fraviga. 'Governance and Water Management: Progress and Tools in Mediterranean Countries'. Fondazione Eni Enrico Mattei Working Papers no. 101. Fondazione Eni Enrico Mattei, Milan, 2006.
Spanger, Hans-Joachim, and Jonas Wolff. 'Universales Ziel – partikulare Wege? Externe Demokratieförderung zwischen einheitlicher Rhetorik und vielfältiger Praxis'. In *Schattenseiten des Demokratischen Friedens. Zur Kritik einer Theorie liberaler Aussen- und Sicherheitspolitik*, ed. Anna Geis, Harald Müller, and Wolfgang Wagner, 261–84. Frankfurt: Campus, 2007.
Taleb, Hamid. 'Water Management in Morocco'. In *Management of Intentional and Accidental Water Pollution*, ed. Gyula Dura, Veska Kambourova, and Fina Simeonova, 177–80. The Netherlands: Springer, 2006.
Verba, Sidney. 'Democratic Participation'. *Annals of the American Academy of Political and Social Science* 373, no. 2 (1967): 53–78.
Verba, Sidney. *Small Groups and Political Behavior*. Princeton, NJ: Princeton University Press, 1961.
Vidal, John. 'Costs of Water Shortage: Civil Unrest, Mass Migration and Economic Collapse'. *The Guardian*, August 17, 2006, http://www.guardian.co.uk (accessed September 27, 2011).
Vidal, John. 'What Does the Arab World Do When Its Water Runs Out?'. *The Observer*, February 20, 2011, http://www.guardian.co.uk (accessed May 30, 2011).
Wallace, J. 'Increasing Agricultural Water Use Efficiency to Meet Future Food Production'. *Agriculture, Ecosystems & Environment* 82, nos 1–3 (2000): 105–19.
Weber, Max. *Wirtschaft und Gesellschaft. Grundriß der verstehenden Soziologie*. Tübingen: J.C B. Mohr, 1976.
Wejnert, Barbara. 'Diffusion, Development, and Democracy, 1800–1999'. *American Sociological Review* 70, no. 1 (2005): 53–81.
Whitehead, Laurence. 'Three International Dimensions of Democratization'. In *The International Dimensions of Democratization: Europe and the Americas*, ed. Laurence Whitehead, 1–25. Oxford: Oxford University Press, 1996.
Wolf, Aaron T. 'Conflict and Cooperation along International Waterways'. *Water Policy* 1, no. 2 (1998): 251–65.
Yang, Hong, Peter Reichert, Karim C. Abbaspour, and Alexander J.B. Zehnder. 'A Water Resources Threshold and its Implications for Food Security'. *Environmental Science & Technology* 37, no. 14 (2003): 3048–54.

Youngs, Richard. 'Democracy and Security in the Middle East'. FRIDE Working Paper no. 21. 2006. Madrid: Fundacián para las Relaciones Internacionales y el Diálogo Exterior (FRIDE). Available from: http://www.fride.org/publication/58/democracy-and-security-in-the-middle-east (accessed April 10).

Youngs, Richard. 'Democracy Promotion as External Governance?'. *Journal of European Public Policy* 16, no. 6 (2009): 895–915.

Appendix

Appendix Table 1. Interview codes.

Interview partner	Interview date	Interview code(s)
European Commission		
DG AIDCO Brussels	12.2007	EU1
DG RELEX Brussels	12.2007	EU2-5
DG RELEX Rabat	05–08.2008	EU6-9
Morocco		
Government representatives	05–08.2008	MA1-10
Non-governmental representatives	05–08.2008	MA11
Representatives of alternative international actors (GTZ)	05–08.2008	IO1-2

Appendix Table 2. Summary statistics of variables.

	Democratic governance	Cooperation	Stay abroad	Foreign media	Gender	Age
Mean	0.55	0.55	0.47	0.81	0.31	41.29
Median	1	1	0	1	0	41.00
Frequencies '0'		44.8	52.7	18.9	69.0	
'1'		55.2	47.3	81.1	31.0	
Min	2.5					25
Max	5					57
Standard deviation	0.657	0.502	0.504	0.395	0.467	7.04
N	49	49	55	53	58	56
(1) Cooperation		1.00				
(2) Stay abroad		−0.125	1.00			
(3) Foreign media		0.259*	−0.140	1.00		
(4) Gender		−0.220*	−0.082	−0.289*	1.00	
(5) Age		0.058	0.214	0.300*	−0.428**	1.00

Notes: Frequencies in percentage; $N = 58$, cases with missing values excluded listwise. One-tailed p-value of non-parametric Spearman-rho coefficients; $^*p \leq .05$, $^{**}p \leq .01$.

Appendix Table 3. Variables and operationalization.

Variable	Operationalization
Dependent variable	
Democratic attitude	Aggregated responses to four statement items on democratic governance, measured on 5-point Likert agreement scale
Independent variables	
Cooperation	Binary variable with 1 = participation in twinning project
Alternative transnational influences	
Foreign media	Binary variable with 1 = regular usage of European newspaper/magazines and television channels for political information (rather than as a source of entertainment)
Stay abroad	Binary variable with 1 = residence in the EU 'old' member states and/or in the United States/Canada for at least six months for educational or professional reasons
Socio-demographic factors	
Gender	Binary variable with 1 = female
Age	Age in years at the time of survey

Index

Note: Page numbers in **bold** type refer to **figures**
Page numbers in *italic* type refer to *tables*
Page number followed by 'n' refer to notes

Abbas, M. 154, 155
Accra Declaration (2008) 53
acquis communautaire 125, 193
Afghanistan 10, 13; Bonn Agreement (2001) 166, 171, 173, 182; Community Development Councils (CDCs) 172; High Peace Council (HPC) 172; Independent Human Rights Commission (AIHRC) 177; International Security Assistance Force (ISAF) 170, 171, 175, 176, 179; National Community Recovery 182; Provincial Reconstruction Teams (PRT) 176; Public Protection Force (APPF) 172; regime change 28
Afghanistan Peace and Reintegration Programme (APRP) 165-82; democracy meaning and/or acceptance 177-8, 181; democracy promotion definition 168-9; extrinsic contradictions 179-80; good things go together? 182-3; inclusion/exclusion contradictions 170, 173-9; internal and external actors disparities 175-6, 180-1; *Jirga* 171; methodology and data collection 170-1; peace-building agreement and reconciliation 182; peace-building and democracy 169-70, 171-3; politically relevant factions and exclusion of others 180
African Development Bank (AfDB) 57, 63, 68
African National Congress (ANC) 112

An Agenda for Democratization (Boutros-Ghali) 87
An Agenda for Peace (Boutros-Ghali) 79
Ahtisaari, M. 85
aid: dependency 52, 57-8; effectiveness 52-4; foreign 193; fragmentation 53; German aid peace and conflict resolution 41; reform strategy 53-4
Anan, K. 88
Andean Trade Promotion and Drug Eradication Act (ATPDEA: 2002) 35
Arafat, Y. 151, 152, 154, 157
Ashdown, P. 109
At War's End (Paris) 80
Austria 196
authoritarian regimes 187-203; cooperation and legitimacy 190-2; estimation results of multiple regression analyses *202*; EU-Morocco cooperation on water management 196-202; external governance, legal approximation and democratic governance 193-4; foreign aid, problem-solution and regime stabilization 193; functional cooperation - methodology 194-5; functional cooperation and administrative governance 195; functional cooperation and state officials' attitudes 195-6; international socialization, trans-governmental networks and democratic attitudes 194; statistics of responses to items *200*; theoretical approaches *191*, 192-3
authoritarianism 28, 166, 193

Balkans, Western *130*; democracy (2011) *130*; democracy and security 119-23

INDEX

Ban Ki-Moon 89
Banda, R. 58
Bashardost, R. 178, 179
Bin Laden, O. 173
Bolivia 10, 12, 27–45; coca 33, 35, 39; Constitution 32; empowerment vs protection of democracy 43–4; FIDEM 36, 38; and Germany 38–9, 39–42; indigenous law 32; intercultural legal system 41; oil and gas 39; political empowerment vs intrastate peace 44; self-determination and empowerment challenges 29–31; self-determination vs donor interests 42–3; self-determination vs universalist donor interests 43; transformation of democracy 31–4; and US 34–6, 36–8
Bonn Peace Implementation Council Summit (1997) 109
Bosnia and Herzegovina 13, 99–100, 103–5, *110*; Alliance for Change 109, 111; elections 109; institution-building 111; institutional confidence *111*; institutions 105–8; peace-building 10; peace-making 105; socio-economics 104
Bosnian Civil War (1992–5) 104
Boutros-Ghali, B.: *An Agenda for Change* 79, 87; *An Agenda for Democratization* 87
Brahimi Report (2000) 79, 90
Busan Summit (2011) 53
Bush, G.W. 35, 153

Cady, J-C. 86
Call, C. 87
capacity-building 150
Caplan, R. 90
Carothers, T. 87
Chandler, D. 88
Chesterman, S. 89
Chiluba, F. 58
Chopra, J. 87, 88
civil liberties: Zambia 58
civil society 37, 56; UK 68
civil war: Bosnia (1992–5) 104; Mozambique (1977–92) 113; negotiated settlements after Cold War *100*; peace trap in negotiated settlement 101–3; power-sharing 101; recurring 98; short and long-term objectives 102

Cold War (1945–91): negotiated settlements *100*
conflict: ethnic 122; management 6; resolution 41
conflicting objectives 3–21, *30*; compromise 18, 19; concepts and realities 8–12; consequences 19–20; definition 9, 81; emergence in policy process **14**; extrinsic 9, *10*, 11; facing 17–18; impact on effectiveness of democracy promotion **17**; intrinsic 9, **10**; no action 17, 21; normative phase 12–13; operative phase 13; phases and causes 12–17; prioritization 17, 19; research gaps 5–8; sequencing 17, 18; strategic phase 13
Congressional Budget Justification (CBJ) 38
consequences: intended 127–9
Cook, S. 87
Coordinated Management for the Environment and Harmonization of National Environmental Legislation 196
Copenhagen Criteria 120–1, 133
Copenhagen-Plus Criteria 121–2, 125–33
corruption 54; Zambia 58–9, 64–5
Counter-Insurgency Campaign (COIN) 168, 169
Covey, J. 83
Cyprus 102

Dahlan, M. 155
Danish International Co-operation Agency 63
Dayton Constitution (1995) 107
Dayton Peace Accords (1995) 13, 104, 105, 106, 107
debt relief 54
defects: democratic 28
democracy: definitions 140n
democracy promotion: definition 8–9; effectiveness **17**
democratization: Palestine 149–51, 156–9; post-civil war 103; state-building 87
developing countries 29
discrimination: racial 149
donors: harmonization 53, 54, 64–8, 70n; interests and self-determination 42–3
Drug Enforcement Administration (US) 35

INDEX

Easton, D. 123
Egypt 147–8
Eide, K. 85
El Salvador 103
empowerment 29–31; democracy protection 43–4; local 77–92; political 30, 44
enforcement: democracy 121
ethnic cleansing 149
ethnic conflict 122
ethnic-based federalism 106
Euro-Mediterranean Partnership (EUROMED or Barcelona Process) 197
European Commission (EC) 54, 57, 66; Sustainable Water Integrated Management (SWIM) 197
European Neighbourhood and Partnership Instrument (enpi) 197
European Partnership (2006/2008) 132
European Union (EU) 136–7; Common Foreign and Security Policy (CFSP) 120; Coordinating Office for Palestinian Police Support (EUPOL COPPS) 155; democracy promotion instruments 122–3; donor priorities 56; enlargement 122; environment project (2005–7) 196; European Council (Copenhagen; 1993) 120–33; European Neighbourhood Policy (ENP) 199, 202; integration 132; security 121; Security Strategy (2003) 153; Stabilization and Association Process (SAP) 120; water directives 195; Water Initiative (EUWI) 197, *see also* political conditionality
European Union Force (EUFOR) 108

Fatah 147, 150, 154–6, 158
Fayyad, S. 147, 148, 155, 156
federalism: ethnic-based 106
Finland 57
foreign aid 193
Forward Strategy to Freedom (Bush 2002) 153
Franco, A. 35
Freedom House 58, 140n
Freyburg, T. 15, 21, 126

Galbraith, P. 84
Germany: aid for peace and conflict resolution 41; Decentralized Governance and Poverty Reduction Support 40; democracy assistance 41; donor priorities 56; Official Development Assistance (ODA) 40
Goldberg, P. 35
governance 9, 190; participatory 88; for the people (*output legitimacy*) 190
Greece: Macedonia 131
Grimm, S. 80–1, 148, 156, 168–9, 175–6, 180
Gruveski, N. 131, 132, 133, 134
Guatemala 99
Gusmao, X. 78: 81; 84; 86 !

Hamas 147, 148, 154, 155, 156, 158
Haniyeh, I. 147, 148, 155, 158
Haqqani network 174, 180
Heavily Indebted Poor Countries (HIPC) 54
Hizb-e Islami 173, 174
Hohe, T. 87, 88
Holbrooke, R. 107
Hotak, M. 178
hudna 158
human rights 6, 56, 125, 152, 178
Huntington, S.: *Political Order in Changing Societies* 1

incentive model 125
indigenous law: Bolivia 32
Inglis, S. 83
input legitimacy 190
institution-building 101; Bosnia and Herzegovina 111; definition 79; Timor-Leste and Kosovo 77–90
institutionalization before liberalization strategy 79, 80, 86
institutions: rigidity 102
International Criminal Tribunal for former Yugoslavia (ICTY) 121
International Crisis Group (ICG) 85
International Monetary Fund (IMF) 54, 57
International Peace Academy (IPA) 90
International Republican Institute (IRI) 37
Iraq: regime change 28
Islamist dilemma 180
Israel 149–50
Israeli Defence Forces (IDF) 150, 153
Israeli-Palestinian Interim Agreement (1995) 151
Italy 196

Jung, J.K. 10, 11

INDEX

Karzai, H. 176
Kaunda, K. 58
King, I. 85
Kosovo 10; international architecture 80–2; Joint Interim Administrative Structure (JIAS; 2000) 82; Liberation Army (KLA) 78; Provisional Institutions of Self-Government (PISG) 83; Standards before Status policy (2003) 83; and Timor-Leste 77–90; Transitional Council (KTC) 82; UN Interim Administrative Council Mission (UNMIK) 82
Kouchner, B. 82
Krasner, S.D. 166
Kreilkamp, J. 90

law: Bolivia 32
learning: by doing 20
Lebanon 102
legal system: Bolivia 41
legitimacy 86, 87, 190
Leininger, J. 80–1, 148, 156, 168–9, 175–6, 180
leverage model 125
LIFE programme 197
Lijphart, A. 101
Lipset, S.M. 6
local empowerment 77–90; conflicting objectives 84–6; increasing 86–8; institutions first 82–4; Kosovo and Timor-Leste 80–92
Lozada, S. de 31, 33, 34, 36

McDonald, S. 169
Macedonia: euphoria to disillusion 129–31; and Greece 131; incomplete inter-ethnic integration and stagnating democratization process 134–6; Ohrid Framework Agreement (2001) 123, 130–7; political conditionality 129–36; rational and appropriate behaviour 133–4; SDSM 133–6; Stabilization and Association Agreement (SAA) 130
market economy 6
Marshall, D. 92
Mason, W. 85
meaning: conceptions and acceptance 177–8
Mello, S.V. de 78, 81, 83, 85, 86, 89
Merkel, A. 39
Millennium Challenge Account (MCA) 35

Millennium Challenge Corporation (MCC) 36
Millennium Development Goals (MDGs) 54, 198
Milosevic, S. 78
minority politics 32
modernization 6
Mohamed VI, King of Morocco 197
Morales, E. 31–6, 38–44
Morocco 15, 19; water management cooperation with EU 196–202; World Bank 198
Mozambique 99, 103, 112; Civil War (1977–92) 113
mujahidin 174
multi-donor budget support (MDBS): Performance Assessment Framework 55, 56; Zambia 51, 54–5, 61–2
Mwanawasa, L. 58

Namibia 99
nation-building 126
National Council of Timorese Resistance (CNRT) 83
National Democratic Institute (NDI) 37
National Endowment for Democracy (NED) 37
National Liberation Army (NLA) 130
NATO (North Atlantic Treaty Organization): Implementation Force (IFOR) 105, 108
Nazimi, M. 177, 178
Negroponte, J. 35
Netherlands 57
Nicaragua 99
Nixon, R. 83
Norway 57
Noutcheva, G. 126

Obama, B. 36
Ohrid Framework Agreement (2001) 123, 130–7
oil and gas: Bolivia 39
Omar, M.M. 174
O'Neill, W. 89
Operation Defensive Shield (2002) 153
Organization for Co-operation and Security in Europe (OSCE) 120
Organization for Economic Co-operation and Development (OECD) 6, 60
Orr, R. 88
Oslo Accords (1993): land for peace 152
Ottaway, M. 88, 99

INDEX

output legitimacy (governance for the people) 190

Palestine 147–59; democratization, security, state-building 149–51, 156–9; elections (2006) 158; inner-Palestinian division phase (2006) 154–6; objectives' implementation *157*; Oslo era (1993–2002) 151–3; Roadmap phase (2002–6) 153–4; unemployment rate 152
Palestinian Legislative Council 151
Palestinian Liberation Organization (PLO) 149
Palestinian (National) Authority (PA): Declaration of Principles (1993) 148, 151
Paris Declaration on Aid Effectiveness (2005) 11, 53, 69n
Paris, R. 80, 86; *At War's End* 80
participatory governance 88
peace 41, 44
peace-building 107, 121, 169–70; Bosnia and Herzegovina 10; definition 79, 99; long-term 108–12
Peace-building Commission (2007) 89
peace-making: definition 99; short-term institutional design 105–8
peacekeeping operations (PKOs): UN 103–4
Philippines 103
political conditionality: compliance patterns in democracy promotion and security issues 125–7; credibility and consistency 124–5; Macedonia 129–36; success and effectiveness 123–4; unintended consequences 127–9; variables and emergence of conflict of objectives *124*
political empowerment 30; peace 44
Political Order in Changing Societies (Huntington) 1
poverty: alleviation 54
Poverty Reduction Budget Support (PRBS) 57
Power, S. 84
power-sharing 101, 102, 122
protection: empowerment 43–4
public financial management (PFM) 54, 56, 61

Qassam Brigade 155
Quie, M. 12, 16

Rabbani, B. 174
racial discrimination 149
Rafiee, A. 178
Ramos-Horta, J. 84
reconstruction model 99
Redman, C. 105
regime change 28
rights: human 6, 56, 125, 152, 178
Roadmap (Palestine) 153–4
Rocha, M. 35
Roeder, P. 78
Rome Declaration (2003) 53
Rothchild, D. 78
Rugova, I. 78

Saleh, A. 174
Sata, M.C. 59
Scharpf, F. 190
Scheiner, C. 86
security 6, 119–23; EU 121, 153; Palestine 149–51, 156–9
self-determination 29–31, 30; donors' interests 42–3
Sharon, A. 153
socialization 126, 194
socio-economic development 6
South Africa 99, 112
Spanger, H-J. 9, 31
Stanekzai, M. 169
state-building: democratization 87; Palestine 149–51, 156–9
state-capacity 107
Steinmeier, F-W. 39
support: harmonization and conflicting objectives 56–7; multi-donor budget (MDBS) 51, 54–5, 61–2
Sweden 57, 64, 66

Taliban 165–83
Technical Assistance and Information Exchange Programme (TAIEX) 197
terrorism 153
Thaci, H. 78
Timor-Leste 77–90; coerced transitions 77–80; conflicting objectives 84–6; increasing local empowerment 86–8; institutions first 82–4; international architecture 80–2; and Kosovo institution-building 77–90; second Timorization 86; Second Transitional Government 86; UN Division of Health Service 90
Twinning Projects 196

INDEX

United Kingdom (UK) 54, 57; civil society 68; donor priorities 56
United Nations Development Programme (UNDP) 170
United Nations Interim Administration Mission in Kosovo (UNMIK) 81, 83, 89
United Nations Interim Administrational Administration (UNTAET) 81, 84–6
United Nations (UN): Charter Chapter VII 104; civil war transition 99; peace-building 77; peacekeeping operations (PKOs) 103–4; power-sharing 101
United States of America (USA): war on terror 166
universalist donor conceptions: self-determination 43
US Agency for International Development (USAID): Bolivia 35–8, 43; Office of Transition Initiatives 36

Venezuela 35

Walter, B. 101
War on Drugs 29, 33, 35, 42
water management: Morocco-EU cooperation 196–202
Weber, M. 190
Wolff, J. 9–12, 15, 18, 31
Wolpe, H. 169
World Bank 68, 154, 197; Morocco 198; Zambia 54, 57, 63
World Values Surveys (2001): BiH 110, 111

Zambia 11, 16, 50–68; civil liberties 58; corruption 58–9, 64–5; Decentralization Implementation Plan (DIP; 2009–13) 65; Memorandum of Understanding (MOU) 57, 60; multi-donor budget support 54–5, 59–62